D1373142

THE GREATEST TIME TO FLY

By Captain Douglas H. Parrott

Second Edition
2016, October
Author: Captain Douglas H. Parrott
Edited by Matthew Pruitt
Forward by Donald Parrott

DEDICATION

This book is dedicated to my beautiful wife Shirley.
Her endless support and love has enabled me to pursue my
passion for aviation over a lifetime.

TABLE OF CONTENTS

****

Forward

A cloth covered, open cockpit bi-plane was the first aircraft Doug Parrott flew after enlisting in the Navy in 1944. This sturdy airplane, commonly known as the Stearman, was the state of the art primary trainer for both the U.S. Navy and Army Air Corps. The Stearman (named for its designer) carried a pilot and one passenger, cruised at 100 miles per hour, and had a range of about 250 miles. By contrast, the aircraft Doug flew at the time of his retirement as a Captain for Northwest Airlines was the Boeing 747. This four engine behemoth carried 380 passengers, flew at 555 miles per hour, lifted off at 833,000 pounds when fully loaded, could fly 7,880 miles without stopping, and held 52,410 gallons of fuel! This remarkable aircraft was introduced by Boeing in 1968, just twenty-four years after Doug's military training in the little bi-plane.

The rapid advance of aviation in the forty-year span from 1940 to 1980 can be rivaled by no other industry. Even the spectacular advancements in digital technology have been slow by comparison. After all, the first commercially available general purpose computer, the Ferranti Mark I, was introduced in 1951. Yet, it would be thirty years before personal computers were available and another fifteen years before they were truly user friendly and widely adopted. As you will see in the story that follows, the rapid improvements in aircraft size, speed, productivity, and safety during this four-decade period are, even today, hard to fully comprehend.

In 1953, when Doug started his airline career, he flew the venerable Douglas DC-3, which carried 21 passengers at the exciting speed of two hundred miles per hour. It could cross the continental U.S. in fifteen hours with three fuel stops. Later in his career he would regularly fly the 747 non-stop from Chicago to Tokyo, Japan in less time. When his airline career began, air travel was an elite form of transportation which very few people experienced; today it more closely resembles mass transit. In 2013, according to the International Air Transport Association (IATA), 3.1 billion people flew the airlines – the equivalent of 44% of the world's population. In addition, 50 million tons of cargo valued at $6.4 trillion was transported by air – approximately 35% of the value of all goods traded internationally.

This book is not intended to be a history of aviation during this period, nor is it an autobiography of Captain Parrott. Rather, it is a firsthand account of this amazing time in aviation as told by one of its most passionate participants. So great is his love of aviation that Doug likes to say that "I was employed by Northwest Airlines for 32 years but never worked a day". In the pages to come, you will be treated to an enthusiastic description of each marvelous advancement in aircraft performance, navigation, weather forecasting, and route pioneering. You will meet some of the men who helped build the airline industry and many of those who are important to the advancement of general aviation.

So, fasten your seat belt and enjoy a view from the cockpit of the most transformative period of the most innovative industry. An industry that advanced so rapidly that one man's career began in an open cockpit bi-plane and ended as an international 747 Captain flying to Europe and the Orient. Ride along in a DC-3 on the milk run through the Rocky Mountains, experience the challenge of radio navigation, experience the advent of the jet age, ride along on one of the first civilian flights into China, see firsthand the challenge of Military Airlift Command flights in Vietnam, and enjoy the comradery of the brotherhood of pilots.

Chapter 1: The Golden Age of Flight

The life of an aviator seemed to me ideal. It involved skill. It brought adventure. It made use of the latest developments of science. Mechanical engineers were fettered to factories and drafting boards while pilots have the freedom of wind with the expanse of sky. There were times in an aero plane when it seemed I had escaped mortality to look down on earth like a God.
– Charles A. Lindbergh, 1927

The nation's eyes were directed to the heavens. We had seen one man dare to push the limits of aviation, and the Spirit of St. Louis was a title that all of America was familiar with.

In 1919, a New York City hotel owner named Raymond Orteig offered $25,000 to the first aviator to fly nonstop from New York to Paris. Several pilots were killed or injured trying to earn the prize, and in 1927 it remained unclaimed.

However, a young pilot by the name of Charles Lindbergh believed that, with the right airplane, he could meet Orteig's challenge. He persuaded nine St. Louis businessmen to help him finance the cost of a plane, which he later named The Spirit of St. Louis. On May 10-11, 1927, Lindbergh tested the plane by flying from San Diego to New York City, with an overnight stop in St. Louis. The flight took 20 hours and 21 minutes, a transcontinental record.

On May 20, Lindbergh took off in the Spirit of St. Louis from Roosevelt Field, near New York City, at 7:52 A.M. He landed at Le Bourget Field, near Paris, on May 21 at 10:21 P.M. Paris time (5:21 P.M. New York time). Thousands of cheering people had gathered to meet him. He had flown more than 3,600 miles in 33 ½ hours.

Following the successful flight, Lindbergh went on tour with his renowned airplane, bringing further attention to the possibilities of aviation.

In 1930, a pilot by the name of Wiley Post took Lindbergh's feat a step further, in the first circumnavigation of the earth by a fixed-wing aircraft. The task took Post and his navigator 8 days, 15 hours, and 51 minutes. Post was later killed in a plane wreck in the Alaskan Territory, but his accomplishment continued to feed the imaginations of all those who dared to see possible in the impossible.

With these first steps into the Golden Age of Aviation, the wheels were just beginning to spin (or perhaps I should say the propeller was just beginning to turn), and little did I know that my home town of Spokane, Washington would have a part to play in the beginning of this exciting new era.

In August 1929, only one year before Wiley Post's flight, a Washington pilot by the name of Nick Mamer, along with his co-pilot Art Walker, flew the Spokane Sun God on the first non-stop, transcontinental flight. They accomplished this using aerial refueling, a tactic which required much more courage and ingenuity than it does today. At one point, Mamer and Walker were supplied fuel in five-gallon milk cans which were lowered down to them on ropes by a man hanging from the cockpit of another aircraft.

Mamer later pioneered some of the routes for Northwest Airlines, and became a pilot for Northwest. He was killed in a plane wreck in 1938 when a Northwest Lockheed 14H Zephyr lost its tail while flying east out of Bozeman, Montana.

In addition to these accomplishments, Nick Mamer worked with a man named Roy Shreck, flying out of Felts Field in Spokane. Together they trained pilots, flew charters, and did weather observations. During this time, Roy Shreck was on a weather observation flight and crashed on Mount Spokane due to bad weather. It took him several days, but Shreck eventually walked to a location where he could be rescued. He was then hospitalized for a short time in order to recover from his injuries. It was at this time that I was able to meet Mr. Shreck.

A paper boy for the Spokane Press, I never expected to actually meet some of the men that adorned the front pages of those papers I was delivering each day. But, on one particular day, my supervisor gave me an extra copy of the paper that headlined Shreck's flight and his rescue, and directed me to deliver it to Roy at the hospital.

I was in awe. We were in the midst of the Golden Days of Aviation, and Spokane was a focal point of aviation news. Carrying the paper to the hospital on that day, I felt that I was a part of something special.

My first real experience with flying came when I was five years old. My dad took me out to Felts Field to watch the airplanes. He had always had a curiosity about aviation, and that day he hired an airplane to take us for a ride over Spokane. I will never forget the experience.

After our short taxi to the runway, the airplane began to speed up. It amazed me how quickly we seemed to gain speed. The ground was rushing past us and I could feel my stomach clench. The engine revved and the cockpit was filled with its buzz. But then, suddenly, everything stopped. The earth dropped away below us and everything became small. The knots in my stomach dissipated, and it occurred to me that we were *flying.*

Throughout the flight, dad pointed out landmarks beneath us, all of them small but recognizable. I gazed out the windows at them, in awe of this new, exhilarating perspective. The flight seemed to pass in a heartbeat, and soon the ground was rushing toward us. The slowed, detached feeling of flying was replaced once again by the ground along the runway, rushing past the windows. This was my first experience with flight, and I was captivated.

When I was twelve, the radio was a source of at-home entertainment. Dad would listen to the evening news, mom her daily soap operas, and most kids that I knew would listen to Jack Armstrong the All American Boy in the evenings after school, but my favorite program was The Adventures of Jimmie Allen.

The Adventures of Jimmie Allen was a serial adventure broadcast centered on aviation. It was sponsored by Richfield Oil Co. (who always carried printed material from the show, so guess where dad often had to buy his gasoline?) and featured stories about Speed Robertson, the program's hero, working with Jimmie to compete in air races, thwart hijackings, and take part in death-defying aerial stunts.

At the end of each show they would mention the fact that they stored their airplanes back in hangars. At the time, I imagined their airplanes hanging from the ceiling on some type of wire system, and I never could visualize the concept.

Still, I was enamored with the idea of flight, and my dreams of one day being a pilot continued to grow. In the summer of 1940, my cousin Hank Troh flew his Bird Bi-Plane to Spokane. He stayed overnight with us and departed the next day, at which point I got to watch him take off, a real thrill for a young boy such as myself.

Prior to WWII, I had watched the airliners going into Spokane's Felts Field. United Airlines was flying the Boeing 247, a large twin engine transport. At the time, Northwest Airlines was flying the Twin-Tailed Lockheed Zephyr. It was the sleekest looking, with its lower twin

4

rudders, so it seemed to be the fastest (Lockheed continued their twin tail concept through the WWII P-38 Lightning, their Lockheed Ventura Transports, and finally the triple tailed, four-engine Constellation, transports). The airlines were expanding, adding more and more routes, many flying in and out of Spokane, which left me with plenty of aircraft to watch and admire.

When World War II began, the Army Air Corp constructed Geiger Field west of Spokane. It was used as a training base for Boeing B-17s, and I remember watching them in formation, leaving contrails across the sky. These were the first contrails I had ever seen, and I was amazed at the way in which they cut across the heavens, almost as if they were beckoning those of us watching from the ground. Years later the sentiments I held were summed up poetically by an anonymous fifth grader in a now famous paper:

I Want To Be a Pilot

I want to be a pilot when I grow up because it's a fun job and easy to do. That's why there are so many pilots flying today. Pilots don't need much school, they just have to learn numbers so they can read instruments.

I guess they should be able to read road maps so they can find their way if they are lost. Pilots should be brave so they won't be scared if it's foggy and they can't see, or if a wing or motor falls off they should stay calm so they'll know what to do.

Pilots have to have good eyes to see through clouds and they can't be afraid of lightning or thunder because they're closer to them than we are.

The salary pilots make is another thing I like; they make more than they can spend. This is because most people think flying is dangerous except pilots don't because they know how easy it is.

There isn't much I don't like, except girls like pilots and all the stewardesses want to marry pilots so they always have to chase them away so they don't bother them.

I hope I don't get air sick because I get car sick and if I get air sick I couldn't be a pilot and then I'd have to go to work.

Written by a Fifth Grader

Between my junior and senior years of high school, the

airwaves were filled with reports about the war in Europe and the Pacific. That summer I got a job as an apprentice carpenter at Ephrata, Washington, building barracks and warehousing for the Army Air Base there. We worked seven ten-hour days per week to keep up with the demands of the war, but it was a good paying job for a seventeen-year-old at the time. The best part of the job, however, was the fact that I got to spend my days watching the B-17 crews landing and taking off from the nearby runways, their contrails always holding my attention until the planes slipped away over the horizon.

Chapter 2: Enlistment and Training

      It was during World War II that aviation became a key component of warfare. From the Battle of Britain, to the aircraft carrier battles in the Pacific, it was clear that aviation technology was going to play a key role in our world's future. Charles Lindbergh's groundbreaking flight had captured the world's attention, and now the nations were fighting for dominance of the skies. With all of this news circulating about the war taking to the air, I was becoming more and more determined to become a pilot. While attending Lindberg High School in Valleyford, Washington, I applied to the V-5 Naval Aviation Cadet Program, or NavCad, of the U.S. Navy. I was accepted in February of 1944.

      The NavCad program was established in 1935 as a means of sending civilian and enlisted candidates to train as aviation cadets. Candidates had to be between the ages of 19 and 25, have an associate's degree or at least two years of college, and had to complete a bachelor's degree within six years after graduation to keep their commission. Training was for 18 months and candidates had to agree to not marry during training and to serve for at least three more years of active duty service.

Candidates who were selected went on to Naval Flight Preparatory School. This was a course in physical training (to get the cadets in shape and weed out the unfit), military skills (marching, standing in formation, and performing the manual of arms), and naval customs and etiquette (as a naval officer was considered a gentleman). Pre-flight school was a refresher course in mathematics and physics with practical applications of these skills in flight. This was followed by a short preliminary flight training module in which the cadets did 10 hours in a simulator followed by a one-hour test flight with an instructor. Those that passed received V-5 flight badges (gold-metal aviator's wings with the V-5 badge set in the center). They were then sent on to primary and basic flight training at NAS Pensacola and advanced flight training at another naval air station.

Doug as a Navy cadet

After high school I reported for duty as a Navy V-12 officer candidate at Gonzaga University in Spokane. At this point the immediate need for pilots was lessening, so the Navy decided that aviators should be commissioned officers. While in the V-12 program, I had a Navy Rank of an Apprentice Seaman, and a pay rate of $21.00 per month.

I completed the minimum required courses at Gonzaga to be eligible to be a commissioned Navy Officer, and I was sent to St. Mary's College in California as a Navy V-5 Aviation Cadet for twenty weeks of pre-flight training. It was there that I learned air navigation, weather, flight planning, Morse code, aerodynamics, officer training, Navy rules and regulations, swimming, physical education, and marching. I now held the rank of Aviation Cadet, with a pay rate of $50.00 per month.

One of the more interesting courses I took during this time, believe it or not, was swimming. It was during my "swimming" course that I was first introduced to the "Dilbert Dunker". This was an airplane cockpit mounted on a rail that dropped into a deep swimming pool. The Cadet was clothed in a regular flight suit and parachute, and when the Dunker hit the water and began to sink, the Cadet had to free himself from the shoulder harness, seat belt, and parachute, and evacuate himself and a one-man life raft from the Dunker cockpit. We then had to inflate the life raft, board it, and await rescue. This was meant to prepare us for a forced landing at sea.

The Dilbert Dunker

Primary Flight Training

Upon completion of my pre-flight training, I was assigned to the Glenview, Illinois Naval Air Station for Primary Flight Training. Added to my $50.00 per month pay rate, was a 50% flight pay, making for a total monthly income of $75.00.

Nearly 9,000 cadets received their primary flight training in Glenview, including names such as Astronaut Neil Armstrong, former President George H. W. Bush, and former President Gerald Ford, to name just a few. During its time, it was the largest primary training facility for the U.S. Navy and when considering the time period that it operated (1923-1995), and the rate at which aviation boomed during that time, one could assume that many pilots still flying today can somehow trace their training and their aviation heritage back to Glenview.

Glenview's Navy Primary Training consisted of four stages. Stage A: Training from dual to solo flights, which included stalls, spins, steep turns, spirals, wheel landings, and solo practice. Stage B: S-turns, precision spins, Pylon 8's (a maneuver in which the aircraft is flown in a figure 8 pattern around two ground references), wingovers, emergencies, and slips to a landing. Stage C: aerobatics, loops, inverted spins, slow roll, Immelmanns (a maneuver often used after an attack on an enemy aircraft to resituate the pilot for a second attack), split S, snap roll, and falling leaf. Stage D: Night flying, strange field procedure, front seat check-out, and cross country flying. Each stage would conclude with a final check ride to ensure that the Cadet was proficient in each of the required areas, and after Stage D was completed, the Cadet was given a Final Primary Check Review, a real indication that the Navy Wings were sprouting!

We trained in a Boeing N2S Stearman, an open cockpit bi-plane. The Cadet would be seated in the back seat of the cockpit with the instructor seated in the front. This could be difficult for a new pilot as the back of the plane sat lower than the front, making it difficult to see. The only communication between Cadet and Instructor was through a Gosport tube. The Gosport tube was a plastic tube which ran from the instructor's facemask, back to a helmet which contained earmuffs through which the Cadet could receive instructions. This provided only a one-way form of communication, providing no means through which the Cadet could speak to the Instructor, so nods or hand signals were given into a mirror which was mounted in the center section of the upper wing. The Cadet might also wiggle the control stick to acknowledge the Instructor's command.

Glenview Naval Air Station (NAS) had two large, round asphalt circles, or "mats" which the Stearmans used for take-off and landing. These allowed the pilots to take off and land into the wind, giving them a 360 degree mat configuration, and making things much easier for the trainees. Larger, faster airplanes would use the regular, numbered runways.

I started my flight training in January, 1945. It being a cold, Illinois winter, we wore sheepskin flying suits. Our training periods would typically last an hour and ten minutes, and when receiving dual instruction, the Cadet was expected to crank the inertial starter and prime the engine. After cranking up the inertial starter (usually two or more times), I would often work up a sweat within the flight suit. Even though the Stearman at Glenview had canopies, the air would grow cold after takeoff, and I would soon be shivering. My sweat would cool, and there were times when the shaking was so bad that it became hard to remain smooth on the controls.

Despite the lingering cold, the canopies were removed in March, but at this point we were running many solo flights. In solo flights, ground personnel would crank the inertial starter for the Cadet, saving them from working up a sweat before flight.

Doug with canopied Stearman

There was only one major accident during my time at Glenview NAS. Two Stearman collided while on approach for night landings; both Cadets were fatally injured.

Intermediate Flight Training
Upon completion of Primary Training at Glenview, I was assigned to Intermediate Flight Training at Pensacola NAS, Florida. While in Florida, we trained in the North American SNJ. The SNJ was a big improvement over the Stearman in that the SNJ had a regular canopy, retractable landing gear, flaps, controllable propeller, and advanced instrumentation and radios. More than 40 countries implemented the SNJ as their trainer during its production run that began in 1935 and did not cease until the 1950s. It took some time to learn all of the plane's complexities, but it was still much easier to fly than the Stearman largely due to the stability and the good cockpit visibility.

Doug with Navy SNJ

Intermediate Training consisted of much of the same elements as Primary Training, but with more advanced instrument training including radio navigation aids, more frequent and longer cross country and night flights, more formation flights, aerobatics and short field training, and more check rides to ensure that we were excelling at the expected rate.

Upon entry to Intermediate Training, we were issued a Blue Instrument Card, and until you qualified for a Green Instrument Card, you were required to clear all flights through the Executive Officer.

One day I decided that I would file a flight plan for an instrument cross-country flight. The weather was expected to be good along my planned route, so I approached the Executive Officer (EO) with my proposed flight plan. He noted my Blue Card, took it and, with a hole-puncher, punched right in the middle of the card.

"Hold it up to the sky, and if the color of the sky matches the color of your card, you will be cleared to go," he said.

Upon completion of Intermediate Flight Training, I received my Commission as an Ensign in the U.S. Navy Reserve, and received my coveted "Navy Wings of Gold"! My base pay was now $150.00 per month, plus 50% flight pay of $75.00 per month, adding to a total of $225.00 per month. On top of that, I now had 296 hours of flight time in my logbook.

Doug in Navy uniform

Carrier Qualification

The significant advancements in aviation during the war led directly to similar leaps in the technology of aircraft carriers. The range provided by the carriers allowed aircraft to be used as focal weapons, a tactic which was illustrated with frightening clarity by the Japanese attack on Pearl Harbor in 1941. Due to these new advances in air-based combat, Carrier Qualification was included as part of our training so after Intermediate Training, I was assigned to a Carrier Qualification course. This consisted of training on a replica carrier deck that was painted on land. Our exercises included the use of a Landing Signal Officer (LSO), carrier landing patterns, formation breaks, wave-offs, and tail-hook procedures.

We then advanced to actual carrier landings and launches. The Navy had a Jeep Carrier based near Pensacola in the Gulf of Mexico, and we would use this for our training. Jeep Carriers were used in the North Atlantic to escort ships to and from Europe, and to protect them from German U-Boats. They typically carried some Grumman TBMs and some Grumman F4Fs to patrol the area and to sink any spotted German U-Boats.

While these Carriers might appear big from the ground, when dropping in for your first real approach the area on which you have to land seems very small. In my first carrier landing, I flew the pattern and approach, following the Landing Signal Officer (LSO) signals. He waved me on so I closed the throttle, and plopped down onto the deck. My tail-hook caught the cable, and the sudden deceleration threw me hard into the shoulder harness as I came to a stop.

The take-off was easier. The carrier had a short hydraulic catapult. When activated, the catapult, along with the acceleration of the plane, would throw me back into my seat as the edge of the deck rushed toward the plane, the carrier fell away and I was flying. After ten or twelve take-offs and landings, we were deemed Carrier Qualified.

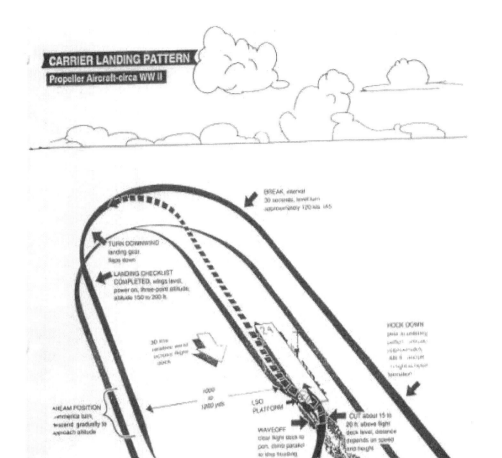

CARRIER LANDING PATTERN
Propeller Aircraft-circa WW II

BREAK, interval
30 seconds, level turn
approximately 120 kts. IAS

TURN DOWNWIND
landing gear
flaps down

LANDING CHECKLIST
COMPLETED, wings level,
power on, three-point attitude,
altitude 150 to 200 ft.

30 kts
relative wind
across flight
deck

HOOK DOWN
prior to entering
landing pattern
(approximately
abeam abeam
of island
structure)

ABEAM POSITION
commence turn,
descend gradually to
approach altitude

1000
to
1200 yds

LSO
PLATFORM

CUT about 15 to
20 ft. above flight
deck level, distance
depends on speed
and height

WAVEOFF
clear flight deck to
port, climb parallel
to ship heading
re-join pattern

90° POSITION, altitude
approximately 90 ft.,
pick up LSO, constant airspeed
7-10 kts. above stalling, power-stall
attitude, follow indications of the
Landing Signal Officer

CARRIER LANDINGS in WW II were more art than
science. All speeds and altitudes were approximate "eye-ball"
measurement and based on pilot's best judgment.

After becoming Carrier Qualified, I was assigned to Grumman Torpedo Bomber Training at the Jacksonville, Florida Naval Air Station. This training was done in a TBM. The TBM was a bit of an adjustment, as it did not have dual controls. The training consisted of a Ground School covering of all systems, handling qualities, stall, approach, takeoff and landing speeds, and an oral exam that entailed sitting in the cockpit while blindfolded and pointing to the different controls and instruments as requested by the instructor.

The TBM is a very stable airplane. It reacts well to control pressures and has good over-the-nose visibility, but it is heavy on the controls. Trainees always learned early on to use the trim tabs and to lighten the stick pressures. In training we focused largely on making torpedo runs, dropping depth charges, formation flying, over-water searches, and also executed many LSO directed landings and approaches.

After TBM training, I was assigned to a TBM squadron at Norfolk NAS in Virginia. I was given several liberties while in Norfolk, and it was a nice town, but my stay coincided with a time of great racial segregation in the south. Being from the Pacific Northwest, I was fairly oblivious to such racism, but I witnessed firsthand the cruelty of the Jim Crow Laws during my time in Virginia.

While in Norfolk, I was assigned to the CVE-14, the Carrier Ticonderoga. The Ticonderoga was one of 24 Essex Class Carriers built during WWII, commissioned in May of 1944, and after serving in several campaigns within the Pacific Theater, had earned five battle stars. After being assigned, we practiced taking off from and landing on a full sized carrier. After practicing within the constraints of the Jeep Carrier in Pensacola, flying from a full sized carrier came easy. The Ticonderoga had a hydraulic catapult which, at first contact, set you back against your headrest, but always seemed to peter out about halfway through the launch.

17

Aircraft Carrier Landing Signals

Propeller Aircraft-Circa WW II

by CAPT John A. Harper, USNR(Ret), LSO, USS Belleau Wood (CVL-24)

FLAPS

MEANING: Flaps are not lowered to landing configuration.

ACTION: Cycle switch to lower flaps to landing configuration.

WHEELS

MEANING: Landing gear is not down and locked.

ACTION: Cycle switch to lower and lock landing gear.

HOOK

MEANING: Tailhook is not down.

ACTION: Cycle switch to lower tailhook.

ROGER

MEANING: Altitude, attitude, airspeed and turn rate perfect!

ACTION: Maintain perfection!

HIGH

MEANING: Altitude above nominal.

ACTION: Drop nose and reduce power to lose altitude. At the "roger" resume altitude by raising nose and adding power.

LOW

MEANING: Altitude below nominal.

ACTION: Add power and raise nose to gain altitude. Hold airspeed. At the "roger" resume level flight by lowering nose and reducing power.

FAST

MEANING: Airspeed high, altitude OK.

ACTION: Reduce airspeed by reducing power and raising nose. At the "roger" add power to hold altitude and airspeed.

SLOW

MEANING: Airspeed low, altitude nose high.

ACTION: Increase speed by adding power and lowering nose while holding altitude. At the "roger" reduce power to hold altitude and airspeed.

LOW DIP

MEANING: Nose low, altitude OK.

ACTION: Raise nose without adding power (yet). Hold altitude and airspeed.

HIGH DIP

MEANING: Altitude slightly above nominal, speed, attitude perfect.

ACTION: Lower and raise nose in one continuous motion without changing power, to descend about five feet without affecting airspeed and attitude.

LEFT

MEANING: Flight path right of nominal.
ACTION: FAR OUT: Bank left or increase left bank angle.

CLOSE IN: Slide left to flight deck centerline.

RIGHT

MEANING: Flight path left of nominal.
ACTION: FAR OUT: Bank right or increase right bank angle.

CLOSE IN: Slide right to flight deck centerline.

WAVE OFF

MEANING: Foul deck or aircraft is not lined up or configured for landing.

ACTION: Apply power and go around to line up for another landing.

MANDATORY SIGNAL!

CUT

MEANING: Altitude and attitude correct, associated arrested landing.

ACTION: Slam throttle to idle, drop nose, aim for flight deck centerline, pull nose up to catch wire (as in high dip).

MANDATORY SIGNAL!

Doug in cockpit of Grumman TBM

Landing on the larger deck was a piece of cake. When the tail-hook attached upon landing, the momentum of the plane would throw you forward into the shoulder harness with the rapid deceleration.

With squadron training complete, the Ticonderoga headed out for the Pacific Theatre. Our destination was the Panama Canal, and on the way down we stopped briefly in Bermuda. To make land in Bermuda, we launched from the Ticonderoga and flew to Hamilton Field.

Bermuda was a beautiful island. Flying over it you could see all of the white roofs dotting the landscape. I later learned that they gathered their fresh water from rainfall collected on those clean, unsullied roofs. Another unique aspect of the island was the fact that there were no automobiles allowed, only bicycles and horse-drawn carriages. The only motorized vehicle I saw during my time in Bermuda was a military jeep leaving Hamilton Field.

After our short stop in Bermuda, we re-boarded the carrier and proceeded to the Panama Canal. It was during this portion of our journey that we learned President Truman had ordered the dropping of the Atomic Bomb on Japan. The war ended days after the second bomb fell on Nagasaki, but still we continued on to the Panama Canal.

Prior to reaching the Canal, eight of us launched our TBMs and flew to France Field near Colon, Panama, on the Caribbean side of the Canal. From there, we taxied about a mile through the jungle to Coco Solo NAS.

Coco Solo was a seaplane base and had no runways, only a ramp from the water to the parking areas, hangars, and crew quarters. Our assignment at Coco Solo was to patrol the Caribbean, looking for German U-Boats. Previous to our arrival, these patrols were being handled by a twin-engine Martin PBM Mariner. This particular aircraft suffered from mechanical issues and was known by many within the station as the "Hangar Queen". Our job was to supplement the search areas of the PBM with our TBMs. Germany had U-Boats based around South America, and with the war having so recently come to an end, we continued to seek them out to ensure that there were no more engagements with the ships entering the Canal Zone.

TBM at Coco Solo NAS Panama

We flew in flights of two. One TBM was armed with a depth charge, and the other with a torpedo. We were assigned square areas in which to search. If we spotted a U-Boat under the water, we were to drop a depth charge to either sink the sub, or force it to surface. If the U-Boat surfaced, we would fire a torpedo to sink it. These searches were conducted until June of 1946, nearly a year after Germany's surrender. No U-Boats were ever spotted.

Tiny Tim Rocket

Towards the end of my service, the Navy had just developed the Tiny Tim Rocket for use in the war. It had the explosive power equal to the broadside fire power of all the turrets on a Battle Ship. To flight test them in the TBM, vertical rails were mounted in the bomb bay, which would allow the rocket to be lowered and then fired well below the airplane's propeller. The Navy had a target barge at Coco Solo, with a large canvas target mounted vertically on top of the barge. We would practice firing the un-armed Tiny Tim Rocket at the target on top of the barge. On one occasion, I fired a Tiny Tim at the target, but somehow it pointed down slightly on the rails, and tracked low and hit the barge at its waterline. That damaged the barge badly and it sank, so I can now say "I sighted ship and sank same." At the war's end, the Navy discontinued the Tiny Tim project.

The Grumman F6F Hellcat

Aside from our scouting assignments around the Canal, we would often pass the time by flying some of the other aircraft stationed at Coco Solo. One in particular was the Grumman F6F fighter plane. We were allowed an operational checkout in the F6F. To be approved, we had to pass ground school on the systems and flight procedures, pass a blindfolded oral checkout, and then away we went. We would taxi the F6F to France Field and take off from there.

The F6F was best known for its role as a rugged, well-designed carrier fighter which was able, after its combat debut in early 1943, to counter the Mitsubishi A6M Zero and help secure air superiority over the Pacific Theater. Such was the quality of the basic simple, straightforward design, that the Hellcat was the least modified fighter of the war, with a total of 12,200 being built in just over two years. During its reign, the Hellcat was credited with destroying 5,223 enemy aircraft.

Doug taxiing Grumman Hellcat in Panama

At this time, the Air Force had several P-47s also based at France Field. We would often get together with their pilots and plan a rendezvous to take flight and either join up or chase tails (meaning to simulate aerial chases and engagements). Their P-47s were much faster than the F6F and could easily outrun us, but the F6F was more maneuverable and could always escape the P-47 when one would get onto our tail. One particular maneuver that I remember worked very well was to roll inverted and dive away from them. They would stay right side up and dive after, but inverted we would lose altitude fast and gain airspeed. Upright, they only built up speed and did not lose altitude as fast, so they would go sailing past without ever being able to attain a shooting position. We would roll upright and, with the additional speed, head for their tail in hopes of getting within shooting range. These exercises were always great fun, and led to some wonderful fellowship between pilots.

Navy Discharge

After the war's end, all servicemen who were not signed up as regular soldiers or sailors were processed for discharge and returned home. Discharge was based on a point system. When you obtained enough points to meet the minimum requirements, you were sent to a discharge center. A serviceman received one point for each month of service, plus an additional point for each month of Foreign Service. At the time, thirty points was the amount needed, and by the end of May, 1946, I had my thirty points.

In June of 1946, I left Panama and traveled to Bremerton, Washington in order to process my Navy discharge and return home to Moran Prairie. I chose not to join the Navy Air Reserve because they met at Sandpoint NAS on Lake Washington near Seattle which was a long trip from Spokane at that time. However, all naval aviators were considered to be on Ready Reserve for five years after discharge.

During the discharge procedure, I applied for civilian pilot ratings through the Civil Aeronautics Authority (CAA) and was issued a Commercial Single Engine Land Rating. A Navy Blue Instrument Card did not qualify me for a CAA Instrument Rating, and the Navy did not train single-engine pilots to a Green Card status.

Chapter 3: Post War Aviation

  The years immediately following World War II were
years of great growth in aviation, particularly in the United
States. When the war ended, the aviation industry in the
United States was the largest manufacturing industry in the
world. In the 62-month period between July 1940 and August
1945, nearly 300,000 aircraft were produced. Never before in
history had an industry developed so rapidly.

  The postwar years also saw general aviation grow to
become a valuable asset. Thousands of former military pilots,
and many other former servicemen who had seen the airplane
perform during World War II, became the market for this
influx of new light aircraft. The GI Bill allowed veterans to
take flight training at government expense, so this not only
resulted in thousands of veterans becoming pilots, but also led
to hundreds of flight schools being opened. General aviation
manufactures, still led by Piper, Cessna and Beech, built
aircraft for both flight training and for private ownership. The
growth in general aviation also included new airports that had
to be built; the training of mechanics and technicians needed
to service the aircraft; the development, production, and

storage of fuel required for these airplanes; and countless other socioeconomic factors which were directly related to this growth.

Seeking to take advantage of this aviation boom, upon my return home I contacted both Northwest Airlines and United Airlines in order to apply for a pilot position. I was still not finished chasing those contrails. They both told me that they had already been contacted by many other applicants, many of whom had piloted heavy, multi-engine bombers and transports and had a thousand hours or more of flight time. Compared to this, my four or five hundred hours of single-engine time and lack of CAA Instrument rating did not nearly qualify me for a pilot job at that time.

So, I took a job as a carpenter and worked on a couple of grain elevators near Spokane. When these jobs were finished, I applied with the U.S. Weather Bureau as a weather observer.

The Weather Bureau awarded me a position in Ellensburg, Washington. Advancements in the weather service industry went almost hand in hand with those in aviation. In 1944, the decision to invade Normandy stemmed from predictions made by the weather services, indicating that the wind and the tides would be right for the operation. This is yet another example of a service that we seem to take for granted today, but like all technology, took years to develop and implement.

I served in Ellensburg for several months before being transferred to Stevenson, Washington. The Stevenson Weather Station was in the Columbia River Gorge, and was built during the early air-mail days. Its location would give the current weather in the Gorge to pilots, indicating if it was above or below the Visual Flight Rules (VFR) ceiling and visibility minimums, which were required to follow the airway beacons to or from Portland. From our weather station, perched upon a rock along the north side of the river, we could see the beacon atop the aptly named Beacon Rock.

25

Stevenson was only about forty miles from Portland, and my cousin, Henry Troh, had an airport and fixed base operation just east of Portland, near Gresham, Oregon. Prior to WWII, Henry had operated a small field just east of this, but when the war broke out, he went to Tulare, California and worked for Tex Rankin, instructing Army Air Corp Cadets in their Primary Flight Training.

After the war, Henry continued training former servicemen under the G.I. Bill, so I signed up for training to qualify for a Flight Instructor Rating. I successfully completed the course and was awarded the rating by the CAA.

The G.I. Bill was yet another advancement of society that I was privy to, but one of a more social importance. What started as the Servicemen's Readjustment Act of 1944 almost never came to pass. The bill was meant to provide assimilation and assistance to the returning veterans, avoiding the missteps of the government subsequent to World War I, which gave returning soldiers only $60 and a train ticket home. The bill not only helped returning soldiers to assimilate, but it also stimulated the economy. Rather than flooding the job market, thousands of veterans went on to get an education or training in a specific field. Many of those who had served as pilots in the war wanted to continue their training after their return home, and under the G.I. Bill, cousin Henry helped many to do this.

I worked for Henry during my days off from Stevenson by instructing students, fueling planes, and replacing airplanes back into their hangars at the end of the day. I earned $3.00 per hour as a flight instructor, and the rest was gratis.

Henry's fleet included Piper J-3 Cubs, a Piper Super Cruiser, Fairchild PT-23s, a Stearman, and his Bird.

The Bird was a biplane with a five cylinder Kinner radial engine. It had an exhaust outlet on each cylinder, which caused a *pop-pop* in both ears upon ignition. Henry later replaced the Kinner with a 220 horsepower, Continental engine.

The Bird had a forward and rear cockpit; the pilot flying from the rear. The front cockpit had a two-person bench seat which faced forward, and a jump seat that faced aft (which was jokingly called the Mother-in-Law Seat). I instructed in all of the aircraft in Henry's fleet, except for the Bird. The Bird was Henry's pride and joy, and only he was allowed to fly it. Later in life, after he had gained confidence in my abilities, he did let me pilot his beloved plane. He had a contract towing banners with it, and I assisted in this several times, flying the Bird over Portland with a banner waving behind me.

In October of 1947, a fellow GI Bill student, Jerry Widmayer, and I purchased one of Henry's Fairchild PT-23s. I had a lot of fun with that plane, giving family members and friends rides and cruising over Stevenson to show off to all of my friends there. On one of those trips to and from Stevenson, I even flew under the Bridge of the Gods, a steel-truss, cantilever bridge which crosses over the Columbia River just below Stevenson.

Later on, when I moved to Meacham, Oregon, I bought Jerry's half of the PT-23, giving me sole ownership of my very first airplane. I kept it on the landing strip at Meacham in the summer, and a hangar at the Pendleton, Oregon airport in the winter. Still being young and adventurous, I would also often rent one of Henry's Piper Cubs to fly up and down the Columbia River, landing on islands and grass strips along the way.

During this time, I made several trips from Lock Haven, Pennsylvania to Portland, ferrying new airplanes from the Piper Factory for either my cousin Henry or Art Whitaker, the Northwest distributor for Piper Aircraft.

The first ferry flight took place in March of 1948. Jerry Widmayer, Harold Allen and I all caught a bus from Portland to Lock Haven. I started out ferrying a new Piper PA-15 Vagabond, while Jerry and Harold flew the new model 90 HP

Piper PA-11. (While in Lock Haven, I also rented a Fairchild PT-19 Ranger and gave Harold a ride in it.)

We left Lock Haven on March 6, 1948, and headed toward Portland with stops in Greenfield, Ohio; Norwalk, Ohio; Macomb, Indiana; Fort Wayne, Indiana; Rochester, Indiana; Kankakee, Illinois; Moline, Illinois; Des Moines, Iowa; Omaha, Nebraska; Grand Island, Nebraska; North Platte, Nebraska; Cheyenne, Wyoming; Laramie, Wyoming; Rawlins, Wyoming; Rock Springs, Wyoming; Montpelier, Idaho; Gooding, Idaho; Ontario, Idaho; LaGrande, Oregon; The Dalles, Oregon; Troh's Skyport (for my cousin Henry); and finally to Art Whitaker at the Portland Airport on March 12, 1948, completing only six days after departing from Lock Haven. This trip gave us a total flying time of 34 hours. While in route to Norwalk, we had to make an unplanned landing in a farmer's field due to ice buildup on the wings, and when flying across Wyoming, the winds out of the west were often so strong that it seemed like we were barely moving. I particularly remember while on approach to Rock Springs, I spotted a herd of antelope and decided to drop down and buzz them. The antelope took off running and actually outran my plane (an impressive feat despite the fact that they are the second fastest land mammal). During that flight, we cruised at about 100mph true airspeed, but with a 50mph headwind.

These planes did not have radios or any other instruments for navigation, other than a magnetic compass and a sectional chart, so navigating our way across the country did not come as easy as it does now. However, this trip took place at the height of the post-war general aviation boom, so every little town across the country had an airport and available fuel. The planes we were transporting carried about three hours-worth of fuel, so we would have to stop fairly frequently. That trip would be more difficult to make today, given the smaller number of airports having available fuel.

After that trip, Jerry Widmayer, Harold Allen and I

were dubbed the "Three Musketeers". Upon our return, Jerry continued his training at Troh's up through the rating of flight instructor. He later flew spraying crops for me one summer in LaGrande, and one in South Dakota. He then got a job operating a fixed base operation in Scappoose, Oregon, and eventually ended up as an instructor for the FAA.

Harold Allen completed his flight training through to commercial status, and then operated a taxi-cab service in the Troutdale area.

My next ferry flight from Lock Haven took place in April of 1949. The "Three Musketeers" were disbanded, as Jerry and Harold were not included in this trip. There were three other pilots, and we ferried four new Piper PA-16 Clippers. We departed Lock Haven on April 14, 1949 and made stops at Byron, Ohio; Goshen, Indiana; Moline, Illinois; Omaha, Nebraska; North Platte, Nebraska; Cheyenne, Wyoming; Rock Springs, Wyoming; Pocatello, Idaho; LaGrande, Oregon; Pendleton, Oregon; and finally to Troh's Skyport. It was a four day trip with 26 hours and 30 minutes of flying time.

My last ferry flight for the Piper Factory took place on March 4, 1955. Norm Desautels and I flew a Piper PA-18 Super Cub from Portland to Lock Haven to pick up a new Piper PA-18A Ag-Plane. The trip out from Portland to Lock Haven took three days, with 22 hours and 55 minutes of flight time. We departed Lock Haven on March 8, 1955; Norm flying the Super-Cub and me flying the new PA-18A. The return trip took five days with 34 hours and 15 minutes of flying time, including some demonstration time along the way. At one point during the trip we were forced to land in a famer's field near Omaha, Nebraska due to bad weather. We waited for about two hours for the weather to improve, and then proceeded on into Omaha. Every ferry flight that I took part in was dead-reckoning via magnetic compass and sectional charts. We used no radio navigation aids.

Meacham, Oregon

I transferred from Stevenson to the Meacham, Oregon weather station, and was promoted to Official in Charge. Meacham was located atop the Oregon Blue Mountains, about halfway between Pendleton and La Grande, Oregon. Like the station in Stevenson, the Meacham weather station was established during the early air mail days and harbored an emergency air strip. The station consisted of a residence house, a weather office building, water storage tanks, and a power generator building.

There were five of us stationed in Meacham and we rotated three eight hour shifts, five days a week. Each man would cover an eight hour shift for five days a week. We had the day shift, 8:00 AM to 4:00 PM, the evening shift, 4:00 PM to midnight, and the graveyard shift, midnight to 8:00 A.M. That provided twenty-four-hour weather coverage every day. We would take turns with the cooking and cleaning, and when on shift, we would send out hourly weather bulletins along with any special weather reports that came about.

Doug at Meacham weather station

The midnight shift was always assigned the voluntary duty of producing a Northwest Region Weather Map. We made these maps using station model symbols from the hourly sequence reports, which were taken from the teletype weather. These reports showed sky cover, wind, temperature, dew point, and current weather, along with ISO-bars depicting high and low pressure areas and frontal activity. Working on these maps was good practice and was always very educational. The knowledge we gained was particularly beneficial for a pilot, as reading and understanding the weather is an essential aspect of flying.

The weather station was about three miles from the town of Meacham. It was accessed via a road which connected with the highway, but this access road was always snowed in during the winter. Because of this, we had to snowshoe or ski the three miles to town. This was a daily trip, one of us having to pick up the mail and any necessary supplies or groceries.

Snow Trail at Meacham Weather Station

31

Fortunately, there were also elk that resided in the area. We would often see them (or their tracks) during excursions to and from town. I got the opportunity to hunt while we were there and once shot an elk for us to eat at the station. Lacking the necessary space, however, we took the meat to town to be cut, wrapped, and stored in a freezer there. While I worked there, Henry Troh flew into Meacham one fall, shot an elk, and flew it home to Gresham.

Doug checking weather instruments

On my days off, I would often leave Meacham on Highway 30, zig-zagging down Cabbage Hill on the north side of the Blue Mountains, and travel on to Pendleton. There was an airstrip just north of Pendleton, an operation called Pendleton Airways that was run by a man named Howard Arthur. I became well acquainted with Howard and went to work for him part time instructing GI students and doing some charter flights. Howard had a North American Navion, a tri-cycle-geared, nose wheel airplane. This essentially means that the undercarriage of the aircraft is arranged in a "tricycle" fashion, with one wheel at the front and two at the back. It was my first time piloting such a plane.

It was during my time at Meacham that I met Bud Veilleux. Bud ran the general store, bar, service station, garage, and wrecker service at Meacham. I started taking Bud flying in Pendleton, and he soon earned his CAA Private Pilot's license. We became close friends, and would later meet up for another ferry flight in April of 1950, in which Bud and I travelled via commercial airline to Lock Haven, then departed on March 28, 1950 flying a Piper PA-20 Pacer, a new four-place model. Bud accompanied me for the cross-country experience, and we made stops in New Castle, Pennsylvania; Des Moines, Iowa; Salt Lake City, Utah; LaGrande, Oregon; Pendleton, Oregon; and Troh's Skyport. It was a four-day trip with 24 hours and 35 minutes of flight time.

Boise, Idaho

The Weather Bureau promoted me to Hydro-Climactic Inspector, based in Boise, Idaho. The job involved inspecting cooperative weather stations in Idaho and Western Montana. I re-painted weather instrument shelters, tested their instrument calibrations, and re-filled mountain snow gauges with a salt-solution antifreeze. It was an interesting job in which I got to meet many interesting people, and had the opportunity to travel through some beautiful, mountainous country. Most of the job was relatively uneventful, save for one minor collision while I was driving down a narrow, winding mountain road. Fortunately, there was only slight damage done to both my vehicle and the pickup that I had hit.

It was during this time that Bud Veilleux, his wife Orlena, and their daughter Jeri also moved to Boise. Bud bought a tractor and did custom tractor work in the area, and during his free time he would sometimes join me for my mountain trips into western Montana to re-charge snow gages. We camped along mountain streams and, after the work was finished, we fished for rainbow and golden trout.

I also flew into Stanley Basin (located in the mountains east of Boise) with a friend from the Boise Weather Bureau to trout fish. This was some of the best trout fishing that I had ever experienced. I later learned that Chuck Yeager, the first pilot to break the sound barrier, flew his Air Force C-47 into Boise and traveled to Stanley Basin to fish. After fishing there myself, I can certainly see why he made the trip.

Bud Veilleux Servicing Snow Gage

While in Boise, I took more flight training under the GI Bill in order to get my Multi-Engine Rating. I trained in a Cessna UC78 Bobcat, which was nicknamed the Bamboo Bomber (it was made almost entirely of wood as metal was a scarce wartime item). It had two Jacob R-755 seven cylinder radial engines, each producing 245 horsepower. It was used as a trainer and a light transport by the Army Air Corp during WWII. As I recall, the engine out procedure required a lot of opposite rudder, which in turn required the pilot to have strong legs. After finishing the training all I needed was an Instrument Rating. Total flight time for the flight training and the rating ride was nine hours and fifty minutes.

Shortly after my multi-engine training, Bud and I heard

that the fixed-base operation in La Grande, Oregon was for sale. Ed McCanse, a local rancher, had just bought out his partner (a Mr. Wagner) and had leased it out. For some reason the lease didn't work out and Ed decided to sell the operation. Since the post-war high on general aviation was abating, Bud and I were able to negotiate a very good price for the complete operation.

LaGrande Air Service, Inc.

The name of our operation was LaGrande Air Service. It was comprised of two J-3 Cub trainers, a Piper PA-11, and a J-3 Cub crop duster/sprayer. We also had the use of Ed McCanse's Stinson Station Wagon for charter work.

Our operation primarily focused on flight training, including GI bill training, charters, and agricultural spraying and dusting. Ag (agriculture) work was expanding rapidly in the Grande Ronde River Valley, as Wagner Seed Co. was raising grass seed in the fertile soils of the valley. On top of that, other farmers in the area were raising peas for seed to be shipped south and used in rotated planting in tobacco and wheat fields, both done during the winter and the spring. Due to all of this, the J-3 Cub was unable to meet our growing needs.

With the concept of aerial application being relatively new (it was originally developed in New Zealand in the 1940s), there were still no available aircraft designed specifically for this purpose. So, we worked with what we had and used our ingenuity to our advantage.

At the time, the government was selling surplus WWII aircraft at very low prices. I had heard of other operators who had bought Stearmans, put P&W R985 HP engines from Vultee BT-13's in them, and then mounted combination dust hoppers and spray tanks in the front cockpit. So, we went to Ogden, Utah where they were selling some of these surplus aircraft.

Doug propping one of two La Grande Air Service Stearmans

We bought two Stearmans for $1,500.00 each (which also included two full tanks of fuel). We flew them both to LaGrande, only to return a week later to buy two BT-13's for $500.00 each (also with full fuel tanks). After flying these back, we began converting our Stearman to dusters/sprayers.

While we were mounting the R985 on one of the Stearman, I flew the other to Yakima, Washington to have Central Aircraft Company install the spray tank in the front cockpit. It was during this flight to Yakima that I noticed the aircraft was very nose heavy. I could make a three-point landing, but the tail would come up to a wheel landing attitude unless I kept the stick back and applied a slight amount of power. We had used the BT-13 motor mount on the first conversion, which extended the heavier R985 engine farther forward on the aircraft. We continued to use that aircraft for the remainder of our time operating LaGrande Air Service, but we made it our workhorse with a hopper/tank configuration. I quickly got used to it and never had any problems and central modified a shorter motor mount for the second Stearman so that it would fly normally.

Doug with BT-13

At the time, the only requirement that the CAA had in modifying ag airplanes was for the pilot to fly it and make an entry in the log book that it was safe to fly and handled okay. I made the entry for both airplanes.

With our BT-13s scrapped out, we put one set of brakes on a Stearman, and one removable fuselage side panel so that it could easily be removed to wash out chemicals from inside the fuselage. We also used the throttle quadrants to operate the R985 engine. Today, those old BT-13s would be very valuable just for parts or restoration.

On top of our spraying and dusting, we also took care of Empire Airlines flights coming in and out of LaGrande, all of them en-route from Boise to Spokane or visa-versa. We did not sell tickets, but would board passengers and mail onto the flights, the mail later to be picked up by the local post office and delivered. Eventually Empire hired a woman from town to take care of those jobs, which really helped us out as it gave us more time to focus on agricultural operations.

Shirley

On December 30, 1950, I went to a dance at the Eagles Lodge in LaGrande. It was there that I met a very pretty girl, and my future wife, Shirley Gerrard. She was introduced to me by Jim Profit, the local refrigerator repairman. We danced the evening away as she told me her family history. Her step-father, Willard Baker, was a carpenter and was in town temporarily to work on a local seed plant. Her mother, Maude Baker and her younger brother, Patrick, were also staying in LaGrande. We formed an immediate connection and at the end of the night I asked her to accompany me to the New Year's Eve dance at the Eagles the very next night. She accepted.

At the time, I was driving a 1947 Mercury Convertible. When I drove up to her hotel the next evening, her brother Pat was in awe of the convertible. Shirley was even prettier than I remembered. We returned to the Eagles and danced our way into 1951, and at the stroke of midnight we had our first kiss. We made time to see each other every day after that, and spent most nights dancing at the Eagles.

On January 5, 1951, I gave Shirley Gerrard her very first airplane ride in our Piper PA-11 although she was reluctant to fly because of a previous experience. When she was younger, she had been in Seattle and was supposed to go flying with one of her girlfriends, but something came up and she couldn't go that day. That very flight ended up crashing and killing her friend. Although she was nervous, I think she enjoyed flying with me, and I certainly enjoyed taking her.

Shirley and I continued to date, spending every day together, and we began to travel the area so that I could introduce her to my friends. In the evenings we would drive to a parking area which overlooked the LaGrande city lights, and we would look at the stars, me pointing out the constellations that I had learned in my celestial navigation classes at Navy Pre-Flight School.

Shirley in La Grande Oregon

We also traveled to Pendleton to meet Howard Arthur and some other acquaintances of mine at Pendleton Airways. I only had a few student flights to conduct at the time, leaving me free to spend time with Shirley, and we spent about eight to ten hours together every single day.

We were married on January 9, 1951, only ten days after our first meeting. Some folks said that our marriage would never last, but as of this writing we have celebrated sixty-five years of a very happy marriage.

Our honeymoon consisted of a trip to Spokane to meet some more friends of mine, then on to Seattle to meet her brothers. We then went to Tigard, Oregon to meet my family and from there to Corvallis, Oregon. We visited Oregon State College to attend Oregon's first Air Applicator School, and its licensing of air applicator pilots. I still have the card from that session. I am listed as Oregon Air Applicator #2. My friend Jerry Widmayer also attended the session, and we would always kid him about being a "third wheel" on our honeymoon.

Shirley and Doug in Portland Oregon

We returned to LaGrande and made ourselves an apartment in the upstairs above the airport office. We had to cut a vent into the ceiling of the downstairs office in order to heat it, and we built a small kitchenette for our meals. The only bathroom was downstairs.

On January 20, 1951, I took Mrs. Shirley Parrott for a ride in the PA-11, and we did a few loops. After this, Shirley decided that she would like to learn how to fly. We started her flying lessons in the PA-11 and all went well until it came time for her spin training. At that time, the CAA required spin training before solo flight. This basically required us to put the aircraft into a spin and recover. For a private pilot's license, it was required that the pilot perform two turns and recover within 20 degrees of the original heading. For commercial pilot's license, it is three turns and recovering within ten degrees. For orientation, the pilot either lined up with a section line, or picked a point on the horizon to start the spin. After practicing a few spins, Shirley decided that she did not want to be a pilot after all.

LaGrande Air Service Operations

The spring following our marriage I stayed busy with student instruction and a few charters, and on March 29th the weed spraying season began. I did some crop dusting using DDT and flying the Piper J-3. The last dusting flight with the Piper was June 14th, and after that we put a dust spreader on the Stearman that had the combo hopper and spray tank. We used it for dusting crops for the remainder of the season, and the other Stearman, which had a spray tank only, we used for weed spraying.

At that time we did not have automatic flaggers or GPS to keep track of where we were on the field, so for spraying we would use flaggers. Our flaggers would pace off a spray swath width after each pass made by the airplane. Shirley and "Pop" Case (Orlena's dad) were our flaggers. We would always start spraying early in the morning to beat the afternoon winds.

I recall times when, after returning from getting another load of spray, I would fly to the field to find Shirley lying down on the ground, sound asleep. I would come in low and fly over her to wake her up (it worked every time). She would stand and shake her fist at me, but would quickly return to her flagging.

We also dusted pea crops with DDT, but I did not need a flagger for this. On each run I would touch a wheel down at the start of the run to mark on the field where to line up for the next swath. I could also dust seed grass fields without flaggers, as they were planted in rows and I could keep track of the rows as I went down the field.

During the spraying and dusting season, we would all be coated with the aroma of chemicals. Our hands would be saturated with the scent of Sulphur dust we used and I remember that whenever we would use real silverware, the utensils would turn black in our hands.

On one particularly hot summer afternoon, Shirley and I went to a movie, taking two seats in the center of the theater.

We soon found ourselves sitting almost entirely by ourselves in the center of the movie hall, the other customers giving us a wide berth as we were still apparently ripe with the scent of the chemicals. On a positive note, we didn't have to worry about anyone sitting right in front of us!

Stearman with modified exhaust stack to prevent igniting sulfur dust

We put in many hours spraying and dusting crops, using everything from 2-4D for weeds, DDT for insects, sulfur dust for weevils, and later on we started using Parathion, an organic phosphate for insect control. Parathion was a deadly chemical and had to be used with great caution. Exposure, either from inhalation or direct contact, could result in nerve damage, loss of balance, and even death. Bud Veilleux handled and mixed the chemicals and loaded the airplane, and he would always use rubber gloves and a World War II gas mask for protection. I would also use a gas mask when applying it, and we always kept anecdote pills nearby in case of exposure.

One day I accidentally grabbed Bud's mask instead of my own, so it didn't have the tight seal that was necessary to block out any chemical inhalation. After about a half an hour of spraying, I began to feel woozy and I lost my sense of speed. I returned to the airport at Enterprise, and Shirley and I went out to Wallowa Lake nearby so that I could get some fresh air. After a few hours I recovered from the symptoms and I went back to work the next day feeling fine, but it was still a big scare for all of us, and the incident made us question the future of insecticides being used in aerial operations. Even DDT was beginning to get a bad name.

Forest Spraying
One summer we were put in charge of spraying sections of forest for spruce budworm. We used liquid DDT with diesel oil as the carrier. Our application rate was one gallon per acre, and the Oregon State Forest Service was to be in charge of the operation.

They had chartered Douglas B-18 WWII bombers from Nevada to do the spraying, along with some BT-13s to take care of the canyons that the bombers could not access. The B-18 was a bomber version of the Douglas DC-3. The BT-13s had a fuel tank installed in the rear cockpit for operating the engine, and used the wing fuel tanks to haul the spray. On one occasion, however, the ground crew accidentally loaded chemical into the fuel tank. There was just enough fuel in the fuel lines to take off, but once in the air a black smoke started spewing from the airplane's exhaust system. The plane was basically running on diesel oil. Fortunately, the pilot made it back to the airport and landed safely, but this was the last use of the BT-13.

Douglas B-18 bombers converted to DDT sprayers

To replace the BT-13, they hired our company and a Stearman operator from Ogden, Utah to use our Stearmans to spray canyons in the Wallowa Mountains. We flew out of LaGrande and Enterprise airports, and to get the right chemical coverage, we would use our altimeters as we flew down the canyons in order to ensure the proper spray width and coverage. For the original pass we would start high and then drop one hundred feet on the altimeter each additional pass, while observing landmarks to ensure proper alignment. The state forester was impressed with our methods and was very pleased with our coverage. This was a very fun operation, and I even got to spray Red's Horse Ranch in the Minam River Canyon.

Red's Horse Ranch

Red's Horse Ranch was a dude ranch and a hunting and fishing lodge. The only way into the ranch (on the ground) was on a two day pack trail, so Red had an airstrip built that ran alongside the river. It was a one way strip, landing upstream and taking off downstream. The canyon was narrow, forcing pilots to land on the end of the strip. There was no room to turn around on a missed approach, and it was too steep upstream to climb out straight. There were a few over-runs on the strip, and one accident that claimed the lives of three people in a Piper PA-16 Clipper.

Most of my trips in and out of Red's were in our PA-11, J-3, or Ed's Stinson Station Wagon. Along with the spraying operations, I would fly in supplies, guests, and workers. During hunting season I would even fly in hunters and return to pick up them and their game. I also flew in other pilots who did not feel comfortable with the mountain airstrip. I would fly them in their airplane, fly it back to LaGrande, and return to pick them up at whatever time Red appointed me. I enjoyed that part of the job as it afforded me the opportunity to fly in many different makes and models of light airplanes, ranging from a Fairchild 24 with a Warner radial engine, to Navions,

Stinsons, Pipers, etc.

On top of all of our duties at Red's, during our first full year at LaGrande Air Service we flew forest fire patrols, did many charters, lots of student instruction (some in their own airplanes which was quite a variety), seeded burned forest lands, and did aerial photo sessions. All of our operations were both fun and profitable, making for a really great experience during that year.

CAA, Texas A&M Ag Plane

On September 23, 1951, Shirley and I flew to Weiser, Idaho to observe and fly the CAAs AG-1, a plane which was specially designed by Texas A&M for agriculture work. It had a cockpit that sat high to increase visibility, and it carried the

Doug flying CAA AG-1

spray or dust in the wing, outboard of the pilot. This was favorable in case of an accident, and it also made it easier for the ground crews to load. I got the opportunity to fly it around the Weiser airport, and made a few dry spray runs along with a couple landings and takeoffs. It handled very well and had excellent visibility and a comfortable cockpit. Unfortunately it never went into production, but many Ag planes designed and built since then have used many of the same ideas.

45

United Airlines

While I always enjoyed our time spraying and dusting with LaGrande, we never could fully overcome our anxieties about working with such toxic chemicals. So, I applied for a pilot position with United Airlines and was accepted in January of 1952.

I reported to United at Denver, Colorado, but I did not have a CAA Instrument Rating and was sent to Clinton Aviation at the Denver airport to train for the rating. They used a Cessna 140 for instrument training, and covered very basic instruments, such as needle and ball, airspeed, magnetic compass, clock with sweep second hand, altimeter, and rate of climb indicator. At that time those were the only instruments that the CAA allowed for a flight check. There were no artificial horizons or ADFs. The radios were low frequency for two-way radio communications, and also low frequency for range approaches and en-route navigation. During this training, United conducted a thirteen-hour Link Trainer Course to assist with radio navigation and approaches. A Link Trainer, also known as a "Blue Box" or "Pilot Trainer", was basically a flight simulator used to teach pilots how to properly fly by instruments. The simulator would respond to the pilot's controls and give an accurate reading on the instruments. Upon completion of my twenty hours of instrument training, along with the successful rating ride, I was assigned to United's training center at Denver Stapleton Airport on March 1, 1952.

At Denver Stapleton Airport I was given training in the Douglas DC-3, and after eleven hours of training in the DC-3 and another seven in the Link Trainer, I was qualified for a co-pilot position. It was then that United assigned me to their Newark, New Jersey pilot base. Shirley and I had hoped for a west coast assignment, so I was forced to request a ninety day leave of absence in order to return to LaGrande and finish our operations there. I later informed United that I would not be returning to fly for them. What I did not realize at the time was that I had a great seniority date with United, and how important the pilot's seniority date was in selecting his pilot base, aircraft to fly, schedules to fly, vacations times, etc. Seniority dates were assigned at the end of the pilot's initial flight training. Thus, a pilot was junior to all pilots hired ahead of him or her, and senior to all pilots hired after them. This realization came later during my time with Northwest Airlines.

Back to LaGrande

In September we traded off the J-3s and the PA-11 for a four place Piper PA-22 Tri-Pacer. That fall we did a lot of flying in and out of Red's Horse Ranch, and charters to Lords Flat in eastern Oregon for elk hunting parties.

During some time off, Bud, Orlena, Shirley and I flew into Lords Flat to camp out and do some hunting of our own. One day, while Bud and I were off scouting for elk, Shirley picked up a shotgun at camp and went out to shoot some dinner. She ended up shooting a grouse, her first time firing a shotgun and harvesting wild game. Admittedly, this first hunt was somewhat illegal as Shirley did not have a license, but Shirley and Orlena cooked up the grouse and it was delicious. Bud and I never did shoot an elk on that trip.

Refusing to be "out-hunted" by my wife, Bud and I later returned to Lords Flat. I shot a bull elk up on the top of the flat, but he ran a short distance before tumbling off the top and down a deep draw. Bud and I had to quarter the elk and pack it back up to the top, and after all of that work we both swore that if something similar were to ever happen again, we would just camp out at the bottom of the draw, eat the elk right then and there, and walk out with full stomachs and empty packs.

Chapter 4: A New Venture

   One cannot look at the history of aviation as we know it today, without considering the incredible expanse and implementation of the airline. Today, we take for granted the fact that we can purchase a ticket online with a few clicks, drive to the airport and hop onto an airplane with hundreds of other passengers, and cruise around the world, stopping at nearly any destination that we can imagine. While it might be difficult for some people to imagine, this was not always so.

   It was in 1925, nearly a hundred years ago as of this writing that the airlines were first set in motion. The Air Mail Act of 1925 expedited the development of the airline industry by allowing the postmaster to contract with private airlines in order to deliver mail. Shortly thereafter, the Air Commerce Act gave the Secretary of Commerce power to establish airways, certify aircraft, license pilots, and issue and enforce air traffic regulations. The first commercial airlines included Pan American, Western Air Express, and Ford Transport Service. Within 10 years, many modern-day airlines, such as United and Northwest had emerged as major players.

Northwest Airlines

Northwest Airlines was originally founded as Northwest Airways by Colonel Lewis Brittin in 1926. The original fleet consisted of two rented, open cockpit bi-planes, and its sole duty was delivering mail from the Twin Cities to Chicago.

It wasn't until July of 1927 that Northwest flew its first passenger flight to Chicago. To purchase a ticket was $40, equivalent to nearly $500 in today's world, and the flight took 12 ½ hours, with stops in La Crosse, Madison, and Milwaukee. During this time, the pilot would report for duty wearing goggles, leather helmet, and long, leather trench-coats. Unfortunately I was still a bit young to take part in the leather helmet and goggles era of Northwest.

It wasn't until January of 1953 that I entered the scene, applying for a pilot position at both Western and Northwest Airlines. Northwest responded and assigned me to a co-pilot ground school class, starting February 15 of that year. Shirley and I flew the Tri-Pacer from LaGrande to Minneapolis, where the class was to be held. It was a fun flight, with stops in Missoula, Billings, Miles City, Bismarck, and Alexandria. Shirley even flew a couple of legs over eastern Montana and into the Dakotas, following the section line due east while I pretended to be sleeping.

Doug and Piper Tri-pacer

After I completed the ground school, we returned to LaGrande. We took a different route home, stopping in Sioux Falls, North Platte, Cheyenne, Rock Springs, Salt Lake City, and Boise. After returning home, I passed the time until my Northwest flight training date by doing some instructing and some crop spraying.

At that time, Northwest had domestic routes from Seattle and Portland through Minneapolis, Chicago, Milwaukee, Detroit, Washington D.C., and New York, with many stops in between. They also had international flights to the Orient, departing from Seattle with a stop in Anchorage. These flights went to Tokyo, Seoul, Shanghai, and from Tokyo to Okinawa, Taipei, and Manila.

During WWII, Northwest flew military flights across Canada and into Alaska, and because of the sparsely populated country of northern Canada and the winter snow cover, Northwest painted the vertical fin, rudder, and the wing tips red. This was to help locate any airplanes that might have to land or crash in the snow-covered wilderness, and led to the moniker: The Northwest Big Red Tail.

After the war, Northwest Airlines had continued military contracts to fly troops and supplies into South Korea. They even furnished the crew for the United Nations DC-3 in that area. This military activity led to Northwest hiring more pilots, myself included. My official hiring date was March 30, 1953, and I was given a seniority number of 452. I was not aware at the time what exactly a seniority number meant, but I was soon to find out, as it controlled most of my career with Northwest.

Included in Northwest's fleet were the DC-3, DC-4, and the Boeing 377 Stratocruiser. After the war, Northwest purchased 25 Martin 202s to replace its DC-3s. The Martin 202 was a transport version of the Martin B26, a WWII medium twin-engine bomber. One of the requirements to meet CAA's transport standards was a minimum propeller-to-ground clearance of nine inches. To meet this requirement, Martin increased the landing gear strut length by pumping it up just enough to get the required clearance. This made the gear very stiff which caused damage to the wing sections upon landings, and Northwest lost five of the 25 Martin 202s to fatal accidents; some, but not all being caused by structural failure. Because of this, the pilots union voted to not fly them, so the airline sold the remaining twenty 202s, and replaced them with DC-3s and some additional DC-4s. This situation placed Northwest Airlines into deep financial trouble. I still remember seeing signs on all of the cockpit doors that read: "This Aircraft is mortgaged to Banker's Trust of New York".

Northwest Airlines DC-3

Northwest flew both Shirley and I back to Minneapolis, and my first training flight was in a DC-3 on March 3, 1953, making that day my pilot seniority date with Northwest Airlines. First year co-pilot pay was $350.00 per month, and meal allowance while away from the pilot's base was $1.00 for breakfast, $1.50 for lunch, $2.50 for dinner, and $1.50 for a midnight snack. We were only allowed three meals per duty period.

I trained for five hours and ten minutes in the DC-3 before my first co-pilot flight on March 28, 1953, which departed from Minneapolis with a set destination of Billings, MT and included stops in Fargo, Valley City, Bismarck, and Miles City.

Northwest Airlines DC-4

My training for the DC-4 began on April 13, 1953, and after just three hours and fifty minutes I was allowed to co-pilot. The Douglas DC-4 is a four engine, propeller driven airliner. It was used in service during WWII, and after 1945 several civil airlines worldwide were using the DC-4. My first co-pilot flight on a DC-4 went from Minneapolis to Billings with a stop in Fargo, and took place on April 20, 1953. It was during this co-pilot training time that I flew the Link Trainer (the previously mentioned flight simulator) for six hours.

Minneapolis was the pilot base for most of the domestic destinations that Northwest had at the time. These destinations included Billings, Chicago, Pittsburg, Washington DC, and several other stops in between. I still remember how busy Chicago Midway Airport was. It was a challenge just to get through on the radio for your IFR Clearance (which essentially ensures that conditions are safe for landing). The controllers really had to speak fast, and I recall one Braniff pilot who spoke with a slow, Texas drawl, saying to the controller, "You'll have to slow down your talkin', my ears can't hear as fast as you talk."

Doug in early Northwest Airlines uniform

First Billings, Montana layover

I can still remember our very first layover in Billings, Montana. Our flight arrived at the Billings Logan Field in the late afternoon, and on our Billings layovers Northwest would always place their pilots in the Babcock Apartments. These were located above the Babcock Theater, and at that time both captain and co-pilot would share a room. The stewardess had her own room, or roomed with a stewardess from another flight.

After dropping off our things at the apartment, I went across the street to a drugstore to pick up a pack of gum. I had a ten dollar bill (about all I needed for a one day layover), so I picked out my gum and gave the clerk my money. The change that I got in return was all in silver. This was during the time period when Montana used silver dollars rather than dollar bills, and after filling my pockets with these silver dollars, I almost had to consider picking up a pair of suspenders along with my gum.

When I returned to Minneapolis, I went to the terminal restaurant for a snack. Shirley had found a job there so she took my order and brought me a hamburger. I paid for the

53

meal with a silver dollar, and left her a second as a tip. She was very impressed by this, and kept that silver dollar for many years after.

Northwest also had a pilot base in Portland, Oregon which was flying DC-3s and DC-4s. The DC-3s flew from Portland to Billings, making all of the stops, and the DC-4s flew to Minneapolis, also with stops in between. The senior pilots in Portland also got the privilege of flying to Honolulu in the DC-4. I bid for a position in the Portland base, it being closer to home, and I was awarded a co-pilot position.

Aerial Navigation at the Time

I found that the DC-3s were much more fun to fly, and I'll always remember how challenging some of the trips into Billings were. We flew mostly Visual Flight Rules (VFR), which means that, within the required weather conditions, the pilot is granted governance over the aircraft upon approach to the landing area. When we filed for Instrument Flight Rules (IFR), it was along colored airways. Colored airways were basically airways which were categorized based on their headings. Green and Red indicated east or west headings and Amber and Blue indicated north or south headings.

Low frequency ranges consisted of four quadrants, each sending out aural signals. One quadrant would transmit an A signal, which was a *dit dah* in Morse code. The next quadrant would transmit an N signal, or a *dah dit*. This was done by the other two quadrants with the same A and N codes. Where the signals overlapped, the A and N would change to a steady tone. This was called the beam, thus there would be four legs protruding from each station. The stations would be lined up along the course between the airports along the airway, with the aural beams guiding pilots along specified airways. It was called navigating by ear. The center of the quadrant had no signal, and was appropriately titled the Cone of Silence. When you reached the Cone of Silence, you knew that you were directly over the station.

Most stations also had a marker beacon which would transmit a steady, higher-pitched aural tone, and a steady white marker light through the cone, transmitting on 75 megacycles, called the "Z" marker. That was a much more concrete indicator that you were directly over the station.

These stations not only provided en-route navigation, but also provided radio guidance for instrument approaches into airports. The instrument approaches also had 75 megacycle beacons, which were located along the airways that approached the airport. Those markers provided a positive point to begin an en-route descent on arrival, or a minimum crossing altitude for departure.

Along with the aural navigation, we would also navigate along lighted airways. These were marked by a series of 50' towers, each with white, rotating beacons placed atop a 70' long, concrete, painted yellow, course arrow. These towers were placed every ten miles along the route.

Each beacon tower also had red course lights which were lined up with the airway course. The course lights flashed a Morse code signal that established its position. These were located every ten miles on the airways. The code began in the west and proceeded east for the duration of ten beacons, or one hundred miles, and then it started over again. The first beacon flashed the Morse code for the letter W (*dit dah dah*) and the second flashed a U (*dit dit dah*) and this would continue on through the letter sequence of V, H, R, K, D, B, G, and M, at which point it would start over with W. We had a little saying to help us remember the sequence: "When Undertaking Very Hard Routes Keep Directions By Good Methods". They were also made to coincide with the colored airways. These lighted airways were built from coast to coast during the late 1920s, and were originally meant to assist the early airmail planes.

Even when flying VFR, we would use beacons a lot during night flights. This wasn't as much for navigation as it was to help us with our descents. By knowing their location and elevation, we would know when to start a descent into the destination airport. The DC-3s and DC-4s were not pressurized, so we would always try to plan our descents so as not to exceed 300 feet per minute and prevent ear distress for our passengers. The beacons would help us to maintain this.

Airports themselves were identified with a rotating beacon which had a steady white light on one side, and a steady green light on the other. This appeared as a flash of white, followed by a flash of green. Military airports had smaller beacons, and the green side had two steady green lights instead of one, which made them appear as a flash of white followed by two flashes of green.

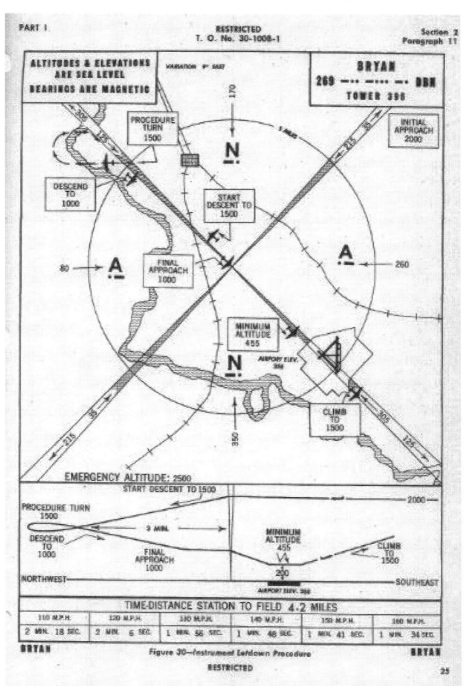

Low Frequency Range Instrument "Letdown" procedure

Lighted Airway Beacon Code

West to East a Beacon every ten miles, after tenth
Beacon the code started over.

Beacon course light code. (Morse Code)

Beacon:
1. W .–   When
2. U ..–   Undertaking
3. V ...–   Very
4. H ....   Hard
5. R .–.   Routes,
6. K –.–   Keep
7. D –..   Directions
8. B –...   By
9. G ––.   Good
10. M ––   Methods

A Typical Flight from Portland to Billings, MT

A typical flight out of Portland to Billings made stops at Yakima, Spokane, Kalispell, Missoula, Helena, Butte, Bozeman, and finally Billings. From Billings, a Minneapolis-based crew would fly the plane on to Miles City, Bismarck, Aberdeen, Jamestown, Fargo, and Minneapolis.

Flying out of Portland, we would fly east up the Columbia River to Hood River, then northeast to Yakima. If it was Instrument Flight Rules (IFR), we had to fly on low frequency ranges to The Dalles, and then north to Yakima. I specifically remember the flight to Yakima for several reasons. One was that the Yakima tower had one of the first female tower controllers. She had a voice like "Miss Monitor" (a character played by Theodora Thurman on a popular NBC radio show in the 1950s), and was a sweet voice to hear in aviation at the time. I also recall, when turning to final from base you would fly over the drive-in theater.

Another aspect that made Yakima a memorable stop was the fact that they sold Washington Delicious Apples in the terminal, and we would always stock up on our return flights.

After Yakima we proceeded to Spokane's Geiger Field, and from there we would fly to Kalispell. Since Kalispell lacked navigation aids at that time, we had to fly in using VFR. If the weather was VFR from Spokane to Kalispell, we would fly over Coeur D' Alene, then on across the mountains to the Flathead Valley. The only report that we were required to make during this direct leg was when entering the ADIZ, or Air Defense Identification Zone. After WWII there were areas that were not covered by defense radar, and flights moving through the area were required to report by radio when entering and leaving these areas.

I remember telling the captain on my first flight into Kalispell from Spokane, upon entering the Flathead Valley, that it must be Shangri La, it was such a beautiful area.

If ever during this leg the weather was not VFR, we

filed IFR to Missoula and made an instrument approach to Missoula. Then, if the weather from Missoula to Kalispell was good enough, we would proceed VFR north over Flathead Lake and on to Kalispell from there. I recall on one particular trip from Missoula to Kalispell during the winter, I asked a pilot who had just made the trip from Kalispell south to Missoula how the visibility was coming down the lake. He jokingly radioed back that it was marginal, but I could follow the tracks that he made on the lake.

Radio Communications

At that time all communications with Air Traffic Control (ATC) centers, position reports, ATC clearances, etc. were done through company radio, then passed on to the center via ground lines. We never spoke directly to the en-route centers. Our only direct communications with CAA facilities were through tower and ground control, who would forward ATC clearances to departing aircraft, and who would also close IFR flight plans upon the arrival of any aircraft. Non-airline flights communicated with Interstate Airway Communications (INSAC) stations, which would direct communications to centers via ground lines. INSAC stations were located at all airports that had CAA personnel assigned to communicate with aircraft passing over. They would transmit any weather observations placed on the hourly teletype circuit by the Weather Bureau. Information including light briefings, flight planning, weather sequence reports, forecasts, etc. was available at INSAC guard stations, which were later renamed FSS, or Flight Service Stations. All company radios consisted of day and night time, High Frequency (HF) communications, and Very High Frequency (VHF) for local communications.

We would use the local VHF communications for *very important business* when flying into Missoula from Kalispell. Missoula had a very nice restaurant in the terminal building, and if it was lunch time, we would radio ahead and have the

Missoula agent order some hamburgers and milkshakes to be ready upon our arrival. After landing, we would race to the restaurant, pick up and pay for our food and race back to the airplane, all in the time it took to unload and load passengers and airmail and to refuel the plane if necessary. We would eat our meals after departure, en-route to Helena.

The route from Missoula climbed past Jumbo Mountain, up the Clark Fork River Valley, over Drummond, then over the Avon Intersection and across the Continental Divide, through McDonald Pass and into Helena. Descending into Helena, we would use the smelter stack in east Helena as a reference point to turn into the airport. When lined up with the runway, during poor visibility, we would precede past a pile of junked cars about three fourths of a mile from the airport, and start our final descent to the runway at that point. We had many visual landmarks to guide us (often more attractive than a pile of junked cars) along our route through the mountains, as we were often flying VFR.

When departing Helena en-route to Butte VFR, we climbed over McDonald Pass and on through Elk Park, then past Meaderville and the Columbia Gardens, an amusement park with a Ferris wheel and a rollercoaster, and then we would take a left toward the Butte Airport. If the weather was IFR, we would make an instrument climb out of Helena, then head south to Whitehall and west to Butte, all via the Instrument Procedure.

As with many things in life, the little details are what stand out in my memories of flying across Montana. For example, I remember one of the best steak dinners that I have ever eaten was at a small restaurant in the Meaderville part of Butte. I also recall the Anaconda Copper Co. working on the mountain west of Butte at the time. It was nicknamed the "Richest Hill on Earth", but later, when pit mining took the place of underground mining, the "Richest Hill" was displaced by the "Deepest Hole on Earth". It was sad to see this change. I also recall that Bozeman had a very beautiful airport, with paved runways and one grass runway. We always enjoyed using the grass runway, as it made for very smooth landings. Bozeman also had a very nice terminal building as the station manager was a talented gardener. It was always interesting to see the different plants that he used to decorate the terminal area.

When departing Bozeman for Billings, we would cross the Bozeman Pass, flying over Livingston and on into the Billings Logan Airport. If the winds were strong along the route, we would pass south of Livingston next to the mountains to avoid the serious turbulence that frequently occurred on the airway over the Livingston low frequency range.

The Billings Airport is located above the Yellowstone Rims, on the north side of Billings. It sits about 200 feet above the city. Bob Hope once visited Billings for a show, and his remark about the airport's location was, "This is the first time that I have ever landed at an airport and had to parachute into town!"

Dick Logan was the airport manager in Billings, and he met every flight that came in during the day. Sometimes, if we landed later in the evening, Dick would be *very* cheerful and happy to see us, as he would often wait for the later arrivals in the airport bar. The Logan family had sold the land for the airport to the city of Billings, and later donated more, thus the name Billings Logan Airport.

On one particular DC-3 flight into Billings, it was just after dark and we were lined up for landing on the main runway. We were just about to touch down, when, in the glow of the landing lights, we spotted several antelope on the runway in front of us. We aborted the landing, looped around, and on the next approach the antelope were nowhere to be seen. The airport now has game fences around the runways to prevent deer, antelope, and other large game animals from entering the area.

Crews from Minneapolis took the flight on East from Billings, stopping at Miles City, Montana, Bismarck, North Dakota, Jamestown, North Dakota, Fargo, North Dakota, and on into Minneapolis.

Seattle crews that flew from the coast and across the mountains to Billings were called "Mountain Men", and the Minneapolis crews flying on east to Minneapolis, were called "Flat Landers".

Flying the DC-3

The DC-3 was a relatively easy airplane to fly. A fixed-wing, propeller-driven airliner, its cruise speed and its range revolutionized air transport in the 1930s and 40s. Its impact on the industry arguably makes it one of the most influential transport aircrafts ever made.

From a pilot's perspective, the DC-3 had reasonable climb performance, and was easily trimmed for cruise. It was not pressurized, so our cruise altitudes were low across the mountains. In the heat of summer, it would be really bumpy along this route and passengers were often airsick. This earned the DC-3 the unfortunate moniker, "The Vomit Comet". We had at least one particular stewardess that would get sick on every single flight. She was almost ready to quit, but resolved to overcome her airsickness and keep her job, a goal that she did eventually achieve!

The DC-3 required constant elevator trim in cruise flight. Whenever a stewardess walked to the back of the plane, it would take nose-down trim to re-balance the aircraft, and conversely, when she would walk from back to front it would take nose-up trim to balance the aircraft.

At that time, the qualifications required of a stewardess were that they be single and under the age of 32. If they were married or surpassed the maximum age during their employment, they were let go. They also had to keep a certain weight-to-height ratio, and were subject to monthly weight checks. If they exceeded that weight, they were grounded until they were able to lose the excess weight.

With the sensitive elevator trim on the DC-3, we would sometimes tease the stewardess, saying that it took three or more trim marks to balance the airplane every time she walked to the back of the cabin, and that she'd better watch it or the airline would put her on "weight watch suspension". Remarks like this usually resulted in no coffee or cold coffee for the rest of the flight. They always had their ways of getting back at us.

The DC-3 was a conventional gear airplane, that is to say it had a tail wheel. The tail wheel was a full swivel type, and we would lock it straight ahead when we were lined up for takeoff and leave it locked until after landing, and prior to taxiing to the terminal. We always landed on the main gear with the tail up in a near level flight attitude, and lowered the tail as we slowed down after touching down on the runway. During this transition from a tail up attitude to touching down on the runway, the rudder would be blanked out by the wings and fuselage, so if the airplane started to turn during this transition, the rudder was useless. To control the airplane at this point, we would use the ailerons. The aileron is the hinged flight control surface, usually forming part of the trailing edge of each wing. To stop a turn, we would turn the ailerons into the direction of the turn. For example, if we wanted to stop a turn to the left, we would turn the ailerons as if we wanted to bank left. This would lower the right aileron, causing drag on the right wing, which would straighten out the landing roll. This tactic, though counter-intuitive, was always very effective and kept us lined up with the runway during rollout.

While all pilots would use similar tactics, each pilot had unique ways of personalizing the DC-3's controls. One captain would always take off his shoes and put on moccasins during flight in order to get a better feel for the input to the rudders. Another would put a piece of masking tape on every switch that he turned on or off. This would help him remember to return them to normal when he was done with them or after he had parked. Eventually, better checklists and crew coordination eliminated the need for masking tape.

Between the main cabin area and the cockpit of the DC-3s, there was a cargo space, some radio racks, and a Janitrol, gas-powered cabin heater. There was an access door for the cargo space on the forward right side of the fuselage. The vacuum tube radios of that time kept the area quite warm.

We carried some unique cargo in this space at times, including live baby chickens, and on one flight we even had some minks. The minks were pretty smelly. There was another flight from Spokane to Missoula in which we hauled homing pigeons in the cargo space. There was a competition among the pigeons' owners to see whose pigeon would be the first to arrive back home in Spokane after being released for an over-the-mountains flight from Missoula.

To maintain all of these facets of the aircraft, Northwest issued co-pilots a tool kit to carry in their flight bags with a pair of pliers, screw drivers, and a crescent wrench. We seldom had to use any of the tools, but the Janitrol cabin heater could be contrary at times, so we would remedy this by hitting the unit with our trusty crescent wrench.

Icing over the Cascade and Rocky Mountains

Aircraft icing conditions were a common aspect of flying the route from Seattle and Portland to Billings, especially during the winter months. Ice along the leading edge of the wing caused a significant increase in stall speed. However, both the DC-3 and DC-4 had de-icing boots mounted on the leading edge of the wings, the horizontal stabilizer, and on the vertical stabilizer. They operated on pneumatic air and were made of rubber, with air passages that would swell and cause the ice to break away and fall off. We usually operated the boots during descent into warmer air. If operated during icing conditions, the boots would only crack the ice without removing it, allowing more ice to buildup in the cracks. The boots would then inflate only into the bridged area underneath the ice.

The DC-4 had a long wire, high frequency antenna that extended from over the cockpit to the vertical stabilizer. When encountering icing conditions, this wire would accumulate a small amount of ice and put forth a low hum. We used this as our ice warning device.

On one of my eastbound flights from Spokane to Missoula, we were flying at an assigned IFR altitude of 9,000 feet and we encountered some moderate icing. During our descent into Missoula we were able to de-ice the wing and tail leading edges, and landed without incident. But as we passed over Mullan Pass, we met a westbound Northwest flight that was traveling from Missoula to Spokane at an IFR assigned altitude of 10,000 feet. This flight encountered heavy icing conditions and had been unable to clear the wings and tail of the ice before approaching Geiger Field at Spokane. The Captain later stated that it took Maximum Except Take Off (METO) power to maintain a velocity above stall speed in order to fly the approach to descend and land.

Over Water Ditch Training

Northwest had many overwater flights. All pilots and cabin crew members were required to be qualified for these overwater flights, most of which were routed across the north Pacific. This meant that the water temperature was very cold, so boarding the life raft and putting up the cover were very important to survival. A passenger left in the icy water would have only minutes before death, but on the raft survivors would be able to share body temperature. Each human body generates heat equivalent to a 100 Watt lightbulb, so when huddled on the life raft they would have a much higher chance of surviving.

SAFETY In matter of seconds raft will support 20 occupants. Small section remains uninflated to enable those in water to clamber aboard. Others jump from dock, simulating airplane, to test tough rubber.

Life raft deployment training

The qualifications consisted of ground school and the launching of life rafts. In Portland, the life raft launch training was done at Blue Lake, northeast of Portland.

Incidents in Portland

During this time period, when commercial airlines were still a relatively novel commodity, there was a competition between airlines for the service that they offered. That being the onboard meals, equipment type, departure and arrival schedules, time en-route, etc.

The fares were set by the Civil Aeronautics Board, and individual airlines did their best to ensure that their passengers were treated well in order to keep their reviews and their profits up. An example of this for Northwest was that during a non-stop flight from Portland to Chicago on a Boeing Stratocruiser, a passenger arrived at the airport a little late. This passenger happened to be a good friend of mine, Mr.

Harold Wagner. Harold was president of Scoop-Mobile, a dirt-moving machine manufacturer, and he was a partner with my cousin, Henry Troh at Troh's Skyport. On this particular day, the aircraft had already taxied to the end of the runway and was running up to check engines when Harold arrived. However, a Northwest agent called the flight on a company radio and asked him to delay his takeoff. The flight taxied off the runway and parked, and the agent loaded Mr. Wagner and his bags into a pickup, drove him out to the airplane, and loaded him through an outside door that led to the downstairs passenger lounge of the aircraft. The flight took off with only a slight delay. With the extensive security measures and budgeting issues in today's market, it is hard to imagine that such a thing ever occurred.

My First Meeting with Donald Nyrop

During this time, Donald Nyrop was the new president and CEO of Northwest Airlines. The first time I met him was in Portland. I was filling out a flight plan from Portland to Billings, and Mr. Nyrop came in and introduced himself to all of us, even a lowly DC-3 pilot such as myself. It was shortly after that incident that I was furloughed. I would run into Mr. Nyrop again several years later, and was very impressed when he recognized me and called me by name.

My furlough from Northwest began on September 30, 1953, giving me my first real indication of just how important a seniority number was. During my furlough, I went back to instruct full time for my cousin, Hank Troh. It was at this time, on March 16, 1954 to be exact, that I solo-trained Hank's daughter, Lorraine. She is still flying to this day. Also, during this time period of flying for Hank, I flew a charter in a PA-22 Tri Pacer carrying Melvyn Douglas, a two-time Oscar winning actor, from Portland to Tacoma, Washington. I still remember that the weather during this flight consisted of low ceilings and rain, typical weather for autumn in the Oregon/Washington area. I made it direct into Tacoma, but on the return flight it was night, so I had to detour around Olympia and Kelso, Washington to the Columbia River and then on into Troh's Skyport.

In the spring of 1954, we purchased a small travel trailer and camped out in LaGrande. We continued our LaGrande Air Service operation, but moved out of our small apartment above the office at LaGrande Airport, as a new operator had already leased the airport facilities. We built an airstrip and hangar at Island City, Oregon, just a couple miles east of LaGrande, and spent that spring doing some more agriculture work, along with a few charters and some student instruction.

To help advertise our operations and let our client base know that we were still operating as an agricultural flight service, we set up a display at the county fair. I flew the Stearman to the fair, landing on a country road near the fair grounds and then taxiing into the display area that we had reserved.

Stearman at County Fair

Our advertisements apparently had an impact, and on May 19, 1954 I flew our Stearman spray plane to Missoula, Montana for a job, and the next day to Presho, South Dakota. Bud Veillieux accompanied me flying in our PA-18. We had lined up some crop spraying jobs in the Presho area where Bud grew up. We stayed busy spraying crops in Presho and around Chamberlin, South Dakota until June 25, 1954.

Advertising Handout for County Fair

It was during our work in South Dakota that I got the opportunity to fly the PA-18 over Mt. Rushmore, which is an awe-inspiring sight from the air. Also, while at the Presho Airport, Bud and I got to meet Joe Foss. Joe was a WWII Marine Ace Fighter Pilot, and he had flown into Presho in a Piper PA-11 to campaign for the governor of South Dakota. Joe Foss was the leading Ace Fighter of the Marine Corp during WWII, and was credited with shooting down 26 Japanese aircrafts. Mr. Foss subsequently won the election and became Governor of South Dakota.

We finished our work in Presho on June 25, 1954. Before returning home, I flew the PA-18 to St. Paul, Minnesota in order to check on my status with Northwest Airlines. My furlough was still ongoing with the company, so Bud and I returned to Portland, making stops in Rapid City; Sheridan, Wyoming; Billings, Montana; Bozeman, Montana; Missoula, Montana; Spokane, Washington; Pendleton, Oregon; and on into Portland, with a total flying time of 14 hours and 35 minutes.

After South Dakota, I returned to work for Henry Troh. The conditions of my return, however, were disheartening. On May 26, 1954, while I was away in Presho, Henry's wife Ruth and his son Henry Pete had both been killed in an aircraft accident near Gooding, Idaho. They had been flying a new Tri-Pacer from Lock Haven, Pennsylvania to Portland when their plane went down. Their loss weighed heavily on both Henry and his operation.

Fortunately, there was a bit of happy news to offset the loss. I met my beautiful wife Shirley at the Skyport, and received the news that she was pregnant with our first child.

TV Antennas

I continued instructing and helping Hank out on the weekends, but during the week I worked part time for Rollie Dryden. Rollie was an early student of Hank Troh, from prior to WWII. He was diagnosed with Polio after he learned how to fly, but he continued to pilot, even with the handicap. All of the airplanes that he flew were tail-wheel airplanes, and we were always impressed with his abilities to overcome the effects of the polio.

Rollie had a radio and television shop in Gresham, Oregon, a service that was a bit of a specialty as TV was still new to the area. My main job with Rollie was putting up TV antennas. A man named Herb Grubbs, a former flight instructor for Hank Troh during the peak of the GI Bill training, was also working for Rollie. Herb would often help

71

me install antennas. I was the man on the roof, pointing and raising or lowering the antenna until Herb, who would monitor the television inside, came out of the house and gave me the thumbs up. The Gresham area was surrounded by low-lying hills, and those homes that were hoping to receive Channel 27 out of Portland (which was transmitted on an ultra-high frequency signal) would need a fair amount of finagling in order to get a signal. We would often have to return to the same house several times, as any weather would affect the reception.

It was tedious work at times, but working with Herb was beneficial for me, as he had also instructed cadets during WWII and was able to give me some of my instruction toward a Flight Instructor rating.

On September 5, 1954, our first son Joe was born. He was a big baby, weighing ten pounds, eight ounces, and measuring 24 ½ inches in length. Shirley and I were both very proud parents, and Joe was immediately embraced and spoiled by all of the other pilots at Troh's Skyport. I gave Joe his first airplane ride on September 19, 1954, when Joe was only two weeks old. This became a family tradition, as our next two sons, Don and Jeff, received the same, ceremonial flight at two weeks of age.

The folks around Troh's were more like a family than they were customers or co-workers. Hank's sister, Gladys, ran a restaurant upstairs above the office in the main hangar at Troh's, and on weekends we would all gather there for what almost felt like family reunions. Everyone there was addicted to the art of flying, most with their own airplanes based at Troh's, and our weekend activities would often consist of competition flying, such as spot landings or closest landing over an obstacle, and we would sometimes even take group flights to the Oregon Coast. As previously stated, these good folks all welcomed Joe into the family, even setting up a pool to guess the date and time of his birth (which Dick Ott, Hank's mechanic, ultimately won) and throwing a baby shower for him. It was a great place to start a family.

Helicopter Training

During December of 1954, I decided to begin flight training in a Hiller Helicopter. Having only been around since 1939, the helicopter was still a relatively new vehicle in the world of aviation, but we believed that it would be very useful as a spray and dusting aircraft, especially in the small fields of the Grande Ronde Valley.

As I proceeded with the training, however, I learned just how expensive it was to operate a helicopter. It would have required the sale of both of our Stearmans just to make the down payment on a new helicopter, and we would need another full time mechanic to keep it flying, as a helicopter required more than twice the maintenance of a conventional airplane. So, after about six hours of training, I discontinued the venture and we gave up on the idea of converting to helicopters. This was a bit regrettable, as the training was quite fun. I always hoped to return and finish, but never did get around to it.

In March of 1955, I teamed up with Norm Desautels, traveling to Lock Haven, Pennsylvania in order to pick up a new Piper PA-18A. Norm and I went in 50/50 as partners in a new agriculture, crop spraying and dusting operation, and had decided it was time to buy a new plane. I returned to LaGrande with the new PA-18A, and we dusted and sprayed all of that summer. Meanwhile, Norm and Jerry Widmayer flew our old PA-18 to Presho, South Dakota to spray crops there. All of us had a good season, but we chose to discontinue the partnership at the end of the summer. I kept the new PA-18A, and Norm took the old one plus some cash. Norm went on to work for Pan-Am in Seattle as a ground crewman, and I was finally called back to Northwest.

On a side note, I also got the opportunity to fly a Coll Air Ag plane in April of that year. It was a very good performing airplane, but it was not readily available at that time, and was quite expensive.

Back to Northwest

I was recalled to fly for Northwest in August of 1955. I was now based in Seattle, which meant that I would have to drive back and forth to Seattle from Portland for my scheduled flights. I piloted mostly DC-3 flights from Seattle or Portland to Spokane, with stops in Yakima.

My stint with Northwest did not last for long, because in October of 1955, a Northwest Airlines DC-3 landed long at Yakima, going past the end of the runway, through the airport fence, and across the road before coming to a stop in a ditch. One of the passengers on board was Edward R. Murrow, the WWII correspondent and news broadcaster. He was apparently riding in the jump seat in the cockpit, which I am sure was quite a thrill for him. Fortunately, nobody was injured, but the aircraft was badly damaged and taken out of service for repairs. Since they were now short one airplane, they had an excess of pilots, and I was again furloughed.

I went back to my old standby job at Troh's Skyport. This consisted of more charter work, along with some more antenna work for Rollie. Shirley was also working as a waitress at Bill's Steakhouse, and we luckily had some money put away in savings, so we survived the second furlough just fine.

On April 30, 1956 I was again recalled to the Seattle pilot base for Northwest. I had to go through the DC-3 and DC-4 re-qualification courses, and spent some more time with the Link Trainer. We continued to live in Portland, so I had to commute back and forth from Seattle for all of my flights. I continued working for Hank on my days off, instructing, running charters, and towing banners.

On July 8, 1956, on a trip from Seattle to Spokane in a DC-4, the captain let me fly from the left seat. This was my first time taking the lead pilot position for Northwest, a good feeling even though I was still getting co-pilot pay.

At that time, Northwest had check lists and standardized procedures, but most captains also had their own procedures, and check lists were sometimes ignored. As a co-pilot, I kept a log of each captain's individual procedures, writing them down in a little notebook for future flights so that I could stay on good terms with each of the pilots. We all had our favorite captains to fly with, but because of my low seniority date, it was difficult for me to always fly with the captains that I admired.

With all of the furlough time, it took me nearly three years to get off of my first year probation. I was now on the second year co-pilot pay scale, with a base pay of $230.00 per month, plus 30% of the captain's hourly, gross weight pay, mountainous pay, and mileage pay on the equipment flown.

Gross weight was 1 and ¾ cents per pound. The DC-3 was 25,000 lbs., and the DC-4 was 73,000 lbs. The mileage pay was determined by the speed of the aircraft, and was computed as either scheduled time from block to block, or actual time from block to block, whichever was greater (the DC-3 was 155mph and the DC-4 was 250 mph). Hourly rates for the DC-3 were $4.60 in the day, $6.90 at night, $5.60 during the day over mountains, and $8.90 during the night over mountains. A DC-3 captain's total monthly pay was approximately $850.00, and a second year co-pilot for the DC-3 received $484.00. It was a big boost from a first year co-pilot pay of $350.00 per month.

On April 20, 1957, we finally moved to Normandy Park, near the Seattle Tacoma Airport so that I no longer had to drive back and forth from Portland. I was flying the DC-3 the majority of the time, and had a series of flights that flew to Spokane. We would often stay over in Spokane in order to fly trips to Portland and back. The Spokane to Portland flight included a long, afternoon layover in Portland, so during those layovers I would go out to Troh's Skyport and work for Hank, sometimes giving me an extra three hours of flight time per day. I would also often bring my captain or a stewardess along with me to fly in Hank's open cockpit Stearman. I remember one captain that wanted to check out in a Super Cub, and after a few sessions he completed the check out. I think that he was hooked after his first session, as he said that he was going to stick with it until he could land the Super Cub as short as he could a DC-3. He eventually went on to buy a Super Cub and flew it for many years, even teaching his son to fly it.

In February and March of 1958, I checked out as a co-pilot in the DC-6B and DC-7C. I would later fly the DC-6B on the line for quite a long period of time, but I never did fly the DC-7C on the line.

Northwest's very first flight simulator was for the DC6-B, and was an exact cockpit version of that aircraft. It did not include motion, but was similar to the Link Trainer in that it had a "crab" to follow the flight path of the simulator. The "crab" followed the trainer inputs across an instrument approach chart, leaving a mark on the chart that followed the route of flight exactly, so any mistakes made were obvious. The simulator did make it much easier to adapt to the DC6-B cockpit and procedures when we entered actual flight training.

Spokane Pilot Base

In April of 1958, Northwest opened a new pilot base in Spokane. All DC-3s and DC-4s were to fly out of Spokane instead of Seattle. I bid the new base as senior co-pilot, a position which also had to be qualified as captain. The position would require serving both as co-pilot and as reserve captain. To help further my progression with the company, in April 30 of that year I completed my training for an Airline Transport Pilot Rating and a DC-3 Type Rating. The total time for DC-3 checkout was 12 hours and 20 minutes. On December 30, I also completed the DC-4 Type Rating, and the total time for checkout was 10 hours and 10 minutes.

I also had to route qualify into all of Northwest's

airports along the route between Seattle and Portland, to Minneapolis, and on to Chicago Midway Airport. This was accomplished by riding into all of the airports as an observer, meaning you rode as extra crew in the cockpit. I also had to qualify into Troutdale, which was a twenty minute, round trip flight from Portland. The stop in Troutdale was a simple touch and go. On top of these observations, we were required to complete more Link Trainer instrument approaches into each of the airports. The total Link Trainer time to meet this requirement was eight hours, giving me a total of 86 hours spent in Link Trainers.

The Link Trainer for this particular training was equipped with basic flight instruments, including artificial horizon, and radio navigation included low frequency radio ranges, Automatic Direction Finder (ADF), Instrument Landing System (ILS), and VHF Omnidirectional Range(VOR). It was also equipped with a "crab" in order to mark any mistakes made on approach. Northwest's Link Trainer at this point was also very old and well worn. They had a bellows system that allowed them to bank in turns and pitch up and down for climbs and descents, but the bellows on the trainer in Seattle were so worn that they flopped the trainer to one side or the other. To counter this, the Link had side straps that could be fastened in order to keep it upright, and could only turn with no pitch or bank. Later, as new simulators were designed, the Link Trainer was retired.

I was granted the position in Spokane, and we left Seattle in May of 1958. On June 18 of that year, I was flying the DC-3 as a co-pilot on a turnaround trip from Spokane to Portland and back. It was an afternoon trip which was scheduled to return at about 9:00pm. At this time, Shirley was expecting our second child, and when I left that afternoon, she appeared to be doing fine. When I returned that evening, however, our next door neighbor met me at our house and informed me that Shirley was in the hospital with our new baby boy. He had been kind enough to take her to the hospital

77

when she went into labor, and he and his wife were even babysitting Joe that night. I quickly changed out of my uniform and into my street clothes, and proceeded to the hospital to see Shirley and to meet our new son. Both were doing just fine, and we now had two boys, Joseph and Donald.

After Don was born, Shirley and I decided we needed a bigger house. We moved across town to a house near Wandermere on the north side of Spokane. Our third son Jeff was born on August 25, 1959, and fortunately I was home and able to take Shirley to the hospital. We were now a family of five, and all three sons were initiated into the world of aviation at two weeks old.

Al Gillis

Oftentimes, during my layovers in Billings, I would spend time with a friend of mine named Al Gillis, the owner of Gillis Aviation at the Billings Airport. I would also pick up Piper parts from Gillis and take them to Hank Troh, or bring parts to Al from Art Whitaker, the northwest Piper distributer in Portland. On one particular trip, I was flying a DC-4 from Spokane to Billings and ended up with a three-hour layover in Billings. During the layover, Al decided to show off his new Piper Comanche. It was a low wing, single engine, retractable gear, four-place airplane. He offered me a ride, so I loaded up in the left seat and away we went. We did some local aerial work before returning to the airport, at which point I made my first approach and landing in a Comanche. It sat pretty low, and after just having flown in a DC-4 with a cockpit that sits nearly two stories off the ground it took a bit of adjusting. Thinking we were too low, I asked Al to check that we had the landing gear down and locked. He ensured me that it was, and also added, "Hang in there, it will touch down soon!" He was right, and despite my reservations we made a very smooth landing.

I later flew Comanches fairly frequently and got used

to the airplane's low profile. Al Gillis lived well into his 90s, and after his death in August of 2003, I flew his ashes to Great Falls, Montana where he was born and raised. I made the trip in an open cockpit, Stearman bi-plane, and his good friend Keith Wallace sat in the front cockpit with Al's ashes. It was an honor to be a part of the ceremony, and I remembered Al fondly as we made his last flight.

Some Memorable Incidents

On another instance during my time with Northwest, I was on a layover in Billings on a return trip to Spokane in a DC-4, when we got word that a severe thunderstorm was approaching the area. I called the Northwest dispatch in Minneapolis to get clearance to fly the DC-4 away from the airport until the storm had passed. They were reluctant at first, but approved my request, and we got off the ground just barely ahead of the approaching storm. We held north of the airport, staying clear of the storm's path for about 45 minutes.

After the weather had cleared, we returned to the airport to find the runways painted white with hail. I made a slow approach, touching down as close as I could to the end of the runway and holding the nose up for more drag. The plane stopped with some runway left to spare, and we taxied slowly and cautiously into the gate. As we passed the general aviation area, we saw many light aircraft that had been badly damaged. Several of the hangars had also been damaged, and even the terminal building had some broken windows. Had we not made the decision to fly the DC-4 out of the area, it would not have been airworthy for the trip back to Spokane.

Whether it was a storm or a buildup of ice, it seemed there was always something to keep me on my toes during my time with Northwest. One interesting aspect of flying the DC-4s was the complex fuel systems that they bore. All of Northwest's DC-4s had been military-54s or R5Ds at one time, which meant that no two were exactly alike. Most of them had eight fuel tanks, but some had six, and one had only four tanks. Depending on the length of the flight, fuel was loaded only into the tanks that were necessary to complete the flight. On short flights only four tanks might be filled, while on longer flights all eight of them would be filled. The burnout procedure always had to be followed very closely to ensure that a tank was never run dry (which could lead to the engine quitting for lack of fuel) but it could be difficult to monitor this since the planes were all different, and on top of that the fuel gauges on the DC-4s were not reliable. The fueling crew would often dip a measure stick into the tanks to determine the exact amount before takeoff, but on one occasion the crew forgot to do this, and when I landed at my destination we found that there were only 54 gallons of fuel left in the number one tank.

I also had the opposite problem, in which I had to circle around the airport before landing to burn the fuel and get the landing gross weight down to an acceptable level. It was in a six tank DC-4 and the number one tank had been overfilled, but the dump valve was inoperable.

On a separate incident, after taking off from Helena en-route to Billings, our number four engine failed. We feathered it and I decided to proceed on to Billings rather than return to Helena or to stop in Butte or Bozeman. I knew that Billings was the most suitable airport because of the frequent turbulence and strong cross-winds around Bozeman and Butte, and I also knew that Billings had a very good maintenance and ground crew. It was also easier to get parts in Billings, so getting the aircraft back into service from Billings would be a much faster process.

ALPA

To this day, the Airline Pilots Association (ALPA) is the world's largest airline pilot union. It has been around since the early 1930s and currently advocates for more than 52,000 pilots. It originated during a time when pilots (particularly air mail pilots) were seen as an expendable commodity. The position of the airlines at those times was essentially "fly at all costs, during any weather, just get our product delivered!" Many pilots joined ALPA's cause in the 1940s, during the war, in hopes of creating an independent aviation safety board. In the early 1950s, the new pilot base at Spokane was assigned an ALPA council number 144, and I was elected co-pilot representative. I was designated as a delegate at the 16th ALPA Board of Directors meeting in Miami.

Fortunately, there were very few problems between management and the pilot group at Spokane, aside from a few minor scheduling gripes, so one of my primary duties as an ALPA representative was working with new co-pilots on their approval forms. Most new hires were first assigned to the Spokane pilot base, and all new co-pilots were on probation for their first twelve months of employment as a pilot. To get through the process, they were required to get the approval of their captains. Some captains were very lax about this, while others were far too demanding. I helped several of the new co-pilots navigate this process, and many of them went on to have successful careers with Northwest.

In working through all of these processes together, the Spokane pilot group (consisting of about 50 pilots) grew very close. To further our relationships, we would often spend days off challenging one another on some of Spokane's many golf courses.

My last DC-3 Flight

On September 18, 1958, I made my last flight in a DC-3. I was captain on Northwest Airlines Flight 612, from Portland to Spokane. It was after this that Northwest replaced all of the DC-3 passenger flights with DC-4s. My time logged in a DC-3 reached 2,281 hours. It was always one of my favorite airplanes to pilot.

After retiring the DC-3, Northwest began looking into finding locations for a stopover on its North Pacific flights to Japan. In July and August of 1958, it developed a contract with a construction company that was converting Shemya Island, a small island at the end of the Aleutian Chain, back into a US Air Force Base. It had been a military field during WWII, and after the war ended Northwest leased the island as a stopover. They had their own Ground Controlled Approach (GCA) at Shemya; the only other radio navigation aid on the island was a low frequency, non-directional beacon.

To aid the conversion process, we were assigned to fly a DC-4 Freighter to Shemya with supplies and construction materials. Most of these flights were non-stop between Anchorage and Shemya, but some had to make en-route stops for fuel at Cold Bay, Alaska, the last point on the main land.

Shemya Island is one of the last islands in the Aleutian Chain, and while it sounds like a place for adventure, our layovers in Shemya was never overly eventful. It is only two miles wide by four miles long, and we would usually spend our days combing the beaches for shells or Japanese fishing net floats. It lies between the North Pacific Ocean and the Bering Sea, and the difference in temperature between these two bodies of water creates thick fog, especially when the wind is blowing from the warmer Pacific across the Bering Sea. The fog would get so thick at times that it became difficult to find your way around on land, so they had a rope along the trail from the barracks to the mess hall to ensure that nobody got lost on this 2x4 mile island.

Needless to say, the fog made for some interesting approaches. There were no radio approach aids in Shemya, just the Ground Controlled Approach (GCA), which was a controller guiding you onto and along the approach path to the runway. He would give you a heading and an altitude to start the approach, and then would direct you right or left to stay on the approach course to the runway. Once you were lined up, he would have you descend along a flight path down to the runway touchdown point. This was done by first getting an altitude assignment, then giving directions to either begin descent, stop descent, increase descent etc., until you either had the runway in sight or had reached the missed approach altitude.

Added to the fog, the winds at Shemya seldom lined up with the runway, and were most often strong cross winds. With a cross wind, the nose of the airplane was not pointed at the runway on approach. This forced pilots to go against their natural reaction of pointing the nose toward the runway, but with the winds they would then be blown off course and have to make a missed approach. Many of us found that the best way to overcome the situation was to have one pilot fly the GCA approach, and the other pilot look out the windshield for the runway. This gave him a chance to see what the drift angle was, then take over and fly the airplane visually onto the runway when the time came, making the landing with the correct crab angle.

Flight Engineer Strike

In October of 1960, Northwest's flight engineers went on strike. The airline industry was shifting to all jet-powered aircraft, and Northwest had purchased a Douglas DC-8, a four engine jet that was supposed to be capable of nonstop flight from Seattle to Tokyo. The DC-8 required a third crew member in the role of Flight Engineer. The pilots insisted that the third crewmember in a jet aircraft should be pilot qualified, but Northwest decided that it would be too expensive to train flight engineers to be co-pilot qualified. It was less expensive to train a co-pilot to be a flight engineer. Thus, the bitter flight engineer strike began. This same issue arose all over the airline industry, leaving it in shambles.

When the strike began, Northwest continued to fly its piston-powered fleet. My last flight as a DC-4 captain was on October 14, 1960; a flight from Billings to Spokane. After leaving Missoula, the company radio called us and informed my co-pilot that he was furloughed because of the strike. On our descent into Spokane, the co-pilot called for the approach check. The weather was clear with unlimited visibility, but we were both a bit distracted after getting the news concerning the strike. While doing the approach check, I failed to set the hydraulic valve control in the down position, and as we approached for landing the co-pilot called for the gear down. Due to the lack of hydraulic pressure, the gear did not go down. We proceeded with a missed approach, and before our next approach we had figured out what was wrong. We repeated the approach with all landing checks done properly, and the co-pilot landed smoothly. This was my last flight as captain of a DC-4, and my last captain flight in general for a quite a while. I had logged 862 hours as captain.

I continued to fly as co-pilot on the DC-4 for the remainder of 1960. My last DC-4 flight ever (not as a captain) was from Seattle to Spokane on Christmas day, 1960. My total time logged in a DC-4 is 1,963 hours. It was about this time that Northwest discontinued the DC-4.

When the Flight Engineer's strike first started, Northwest switched to flying DC-6B aircraft out of the Spokane pilot base. In May of 1961, the Spokane base was closed, and the pilots stationed there had a choice of bidding either the Minneapolis base or the Seattle base. I bid co-pilot at the Seattle base, and was assigned a second officer position there.

After my transfer, I began ground school for a flight engineer rating. This meant that I was essentially working toward qualification as the flight crew member who is responsible for the aircraft's engines and other systems during flight. On May 8, 1961, I started flight training in the DC-6B for the flight engineer rating. After just 2 hours and 45 minutes on the DC-6B panel, I passed the rating ride. It was May 10, just two days after I had started the training, and I now had a flight engineer rating for reciprocal engine powered aircraft.

Northwest Airline's second officers had to be pilot qualified and flight engineer qualified (a requirement that led to the aforementioned strike). The second officer's seat faced the systems and pressurization panel in the cockpit, and during takeoff and landing he could turn his seat forward to monitor the power settings and the engine instruments.

After that I attended four weeks of ground school for the DC-8 second officer position, and the turbo jet powered flight engineer rating. After twelve and a half hours on the DC-8 panel, I received my turbo jet powered Flight Engineer rating.

I was now in the Jet Age.

Chapter 5: The Jet Age

The term Jet Age was coined in the late 1940s, and at that time the only jet-powered aircrafts were military, most of which were fighters. The first jet airliner to take wing was the British aircraft, de Havilland Comet in 1949. It went into service in 1952 and was the first to offer regular, transatlantic service in 1958. When the Boeing 707 was put into service on the route from New York to London in 1958, this became the first year in history that more passengers made the transatlantic trip by air than by sea.

My jet age essentially began with more training. The four weeks of ground school training for our first jet airplane was much more detailed and extensive than previous qualifications I had gone through. There were more thorough explanations of the systems on the jet airplane, which in some cases were more complex than the systems we had learned for propeller driven planes. All of us being new to the jet, it quickly became clear that we had a lot to learn about the aircraft and its systems.

Operating jet engines was quite different than operating piston engines. Jet engines consist of an inlet compressor and an exhaust turbine. They bring air in, add fuel, compress it, ignite it, and it is expelled as thrust. The engine instruments at that time consisted of EPR (or engine pressure ratio, which indicates the ratio of turbine discharge pressure to compressor inlet pressure), an N1 indicator which indicates the percent of RPM low pressure compressor, the N2 indicator which indicates gas temperature in the turbines, and the fuel flow indicator which indicates metered fuel flow to the engine in pounds per hour. Power was set by advancing the throttles to the desired EPR, and thereafter the NI, N2, EGT (Exhaust Gas Temperature), and Fuel Flow were automatic and just needed to be monitored. This was a bit different from piston engine operation, where RPM was set with the propeller control, manifold pressure was set with the throttle, and fuel flow was set using the mixture control.

The jet also flew much higher and had a more complex pressurization system, a factor that made it more fitting for transcontinental travel. It included emergency oxygen mask deployment for passengers should the cabin altitude exceeded 10,000 feet. This could only occur in the event of a loss of cabin pressurization from engine bleed air intake into the cabin, or the failure of a cabin window or a crack or opening in the fuselage. In the case of a loss of cabin pressure at high altitudes, the resulting lack of oxygen would lead to unconsciousness. This could happen in a very short amount of time, so the cockpit crew had oxygen masks readily available. If one pilot departed the cockpit, the remaining pilot would put on his oxygen mask as a safety measure until the other pilot returned. This ensured that there would always be a conscious pilot present in the cockpit in the event of a loss of pressure.

Part of the second officer qualification on the DC-8 was some right seat time, three landings and takeoffs, and to ride along as an observer on scheduled line flights. I did this on two round trip flights from Seattle to New York, giving me a total of 22 hours and 30 minutes of flight time. Northwest did not have a DC-8 simulator, so all of the airplane training was done in the actual aircraft. After this, I was fully qualified to act as a DC-8 second officer.

Even with the seemingly constant advancements in technology, the airlines still had competition. Still being a relatively new industry, they had to compete with the railroads for passengers. The airlines' main selling point was their speed. It took significantly less time to fly somewhere than it did to ride the rails. However, the railroad remained in the competition by marketing their dining cars, Pullman cars (or sleeping cars), wide seats, and generally superior service. To keep up, the airlines then had to offer some answer to these extra services, so during the propeller era, the airlines did

Northwest airlines Douglas DC-8

meal service during flight. The food was pre-prepared in ground based kitchens, and then loaded onto the aircraft's flight kitchen where it was kept warm in an electric oven. The only downside to this was the fact that propeller-driven aircraft could not always climb high enough to get above the weather-created turbulence. They could only cruise at or below 25,000 feet MSL (Mean Sea Level), not always high enough to top a thunderstorm. When turbulence did become a problem, the meals could not be served, thus giving an extra leg up to the railroad.

With the introduction of the jet, the airlines became much harder for the passenger trains to compete with. Jets could cruise at altitudes up to 39,000 feet MSL, enabling them to top most bad weather and any turbulence that might be associated with it. They were also equipped with better meal kitchens, capable of preparing food in-flight rather than just warming pre-cooked meals. They could also offer better beverage services, more comfortable seating, and nicer in-flight amenities.

Not only did the jet fly higher, but it was faster. The jets average speed was 500 mph, versus the propeller transport's 300 mph. Jets were also less noisy, with less piston engine drone and propeller vibration, and it could make much longer non-stop flights. With fewer engine failures, better braking, and more reliable systems (i.e. hydraulic, pressurization, electrical etc.), they were also much safer than their propeller-driven counter parts.

Needless to say, it wasn't long after the jet airliners were put into scheduled operation in most cities across the country, that the railroads began cancelling their passenger services. I remember that Montana alone had three major railroads running across the state, and all ceased taking passengers. Now there is only one passenger train still operating in Montana, and that is AMTRAC, which cuts across the northern part of the state.

Paul Soderlind
Paul Soderlind was, at the time, the Flight Operations and Research Director for Northwest (the FORD unit as he jokingly called it). He was a Montana boy, raised in the small town of Rapelje, west of Billings. He learned to fly in Billings, and soon thereafter hired on with Northwest Airlines as a co-pilot. He flew some of the Northwest northern region flights

at the beginning of WWII, and later joined the Navy as a transport pilot. He returned to Northwest after the war, and flew line some before becoming a check pilot, and later being appointed the Director of Flight Operations.

Paul's responsibility as Director of Flight Operations was to develop procedures and operating standards for flight crews, a task he had long been trying to institute for Northwest. As I mentioned earlier, some crews did not always follow the procedures or checklists very closely, but with the advent of the jet and all of its complexities, flight crews were forced to strictly follow all of Paul's procedures and checklists. Paul referred to this as SOPA, or Standard Operating Procedures Amplified.

The more complex jets required crew procedures that covered every aspect of a unified crew operating and flying the airplane. The captain and co-pilot worked with flight dispatch in planning the flight, which included routing, fuel requirements, altitudes, alternate airports, etc. While they were taking care of these things, the second officer was doing the aircraft walk-around inspection, cabin inspection, cockpit inspection, and logbook and maintenance review.

Once all of the cockpit crew members were in their seats, the instruments were checked and the navigation routing was set up, and the pre-start checklist was read. After start, the pre-taxi checklist was read, and prior to takeoff the pre-takeoff checklist was read. The pilot that was going to be flying for the day would then set the takeoff power, backed up by the second pilot and monitored by the second officer. During takeoff roll, the pilot that was not flying would call out the air speeds, V1, V2, V Rotate, and the climb speed. After takeoff the climb check was read. When reaching cruising altitude, the second officer monitored the engine power, while the pilot who was not flying did all of the radio communications, and the pilot flying maintained the course. At the end of the flight, prior to descent, the descent checklist was read, and during the descent, the pilot not flying called out the altitudes at 2,000 and 1,000 feet above the altitude that the flight was cleared to descend to. Prior to approach, airspeed bugs (movable arrows) were set for approach and landing, the approach procedure was reviewed by the crew, and the approach check was read. Prior to landing the landing check was read, and during final approach the pilot that was not flying called out airspeeds and altitudes.

After touchdown, the pilot put the engine into reverse thrust, and the support pilot continued to call out airspeeds. An after-landing checklist was then read, and the captain then taxied to the gate as the co-pilot took care of all communications with ground control and company radio. Once parked, the parking checklist was read.

After several deadly jet crashes caused by poor or non-existing crew procedures, Paul ensured that his were the best in the industry. He covered every aspect of flight, including engine out on takeoff, in route engine failure, and turbulence encounters, along with every other possible emergency. This long preceded the FAA's call for Crew Resource Management (CRM) programs, and with Paul's leadership and his development of SOPA, Northwest Airlines, who at one time had one of the worst accident records in the industry, became the safest airline not only in the US, but in the world.

Flying to the Orient

After completing second officer training in the DC-8, I started doing line flights from Seattle to Honolulu, New York, Minneapolis, Chicago, and other domestic locations. I was also flying co-pilot on the DC-6B on the Seattle to Spokane turnaround, and on flights to Billings and beyond. Getting back into the DC-6B was both easy and enjoyable, and I logged a total of 461 hours in it.

Northwest had started its flights to the Orient in 1947, with flights from the Twin Cities to Tokyo, Seoul, Shanghai, and Manila. This expansion to Asia and the launch of their transcontinental flights led to the "golden age" of Northwest.

In November of 1961, I flew my first flight to the Orient. It was in the DC-8C as a second officer, and we traveled from Seattle to Anchorage to the Tokyo Haneda Airport. The comfort and speed of the DC-8C jet was a giant step forward for transportation across the North Pacific, especially when compared to the piston-powered flights in the DC-7C and DC-6B, both of which flew at lower altitudes and were required to make more in route stops.

The DC-8C had Pratt and Whitney JT4A-9 jet engines, and was supposed to be able to fly non-stop from Seattle to Tokyo. However, with a full payload and the required fuel that it would take to make the trip, the jet was unable to fly that distance without stopping to refuel. This was due largely to the westerly winds encountered when flying to Tokyo, but the return trip west could be made without stops.

I continued to fly as second officer on the DC-8 trips to the Orient. Along with that, I would sometimes make flights from Seattle to New York with a layover in New York, then from New York to Anchorage, and after a layover in Anchorage we would return to New York and then Seattle. About half of my flight time during this period was logged as co-pilot in the DC-6B.

In March of 1963 I qualified as S/O (second officer) on the Boeing 720B. The first Northwest Airlines Boeing jet was the 707-320B. The 720 B was a shorter version of the 707-320B, but had the same Fan-Jet engines as the 707-320B. This made it something of a Hot-Rod! Northwest used the 720B to fly shorter routes out of Tokyo, and to fly on Seattle to Anchorage turnarounds. On one such turnaround, I flew to King Salmon rather than Anchorage, as I was carrying a group of commercial fisherman.

I flew with one captain named Russ Sorkness, a check and training pilot, who would allow the co-pilot and the S/O to swap seats. Thus, on August 4, 1963, I flew my first scheduled jet flight on a DC-8C as a pilot, flying in the right seat on a round trip flight from Tokyo to Taipei with a stop in

Okinawa. I was allowed several more right-seat flights with Russ during that quarter, and I really appreciated the co-pilot time that he provided me.

I was lucky enough to work with Russ for several flights because at that time pilots bid for quarterly international schedules, so you would end up flying with the same crew for three months. This was done because the monthly flight limitation of 85 hours could not always be followed with the longer international flights. Quarterly schedules were designed to follow the 85-hour monthly limitation as closely as possible, but if the 85 hours was exceeded, the extra time could be carried over to the next month.

In October of 1963, Northwest started operating the 707-320B on flights to the Orient, replacing the DC-8C. Because of this I started getting some right seat time on the 707-320B. The DC-8C was mostly used on military charter flights and I still got to fly it on co-pilot trips out of Seattle. I loved flying the DC-8C on those shorter flights with more takeoffs and landings.

On our flights to the Orient, we would always end up with long layovers (36 hours or more) in Tokyo prior to flying back to Seattle. We stayed at the Ginza Tokyu Hotel near the Ginza business area of downtown Tokyo. This was a very modern hotel at the time, sitting at ten stories high (the maximum height allowed due to the earthquake danger in Japan), and harboring some fine dining, barber shops, and gift shops. It was a very popular place for both businessmen and tourists.

I always really enjoyed exploring downtown Tokyo during my layovers. The city was not very well laid out, so trying to find where I was going was always an adventure. The streets were not straight and were not arranged in square blocks, so at times you would think that you were walking around the block, but would end up in a completely different location.

Once I'd learned how to navigate the city, I would often walk up the hill to the Tokyo Tower and the Masonic Hall located nearby. I learned that General Douglas McArthur was a Mason and was instrumental in establishing Masonry in Japan after the war, and that one of our flight dispatchers, Shigeaki Morita, was a Master of the Tokyo Yuai Lodge No. 11 during the year of 1968. Since I was also a Master Mason, Mr. Morita would often invite me to attend his Lodge. I would have loved to accept his offer and compare their ceremony with ours, but my layovers in Tokyo never coincided with their meeting nights.

Also, on my walks around Tokyo, I met a Japanese student who came up to me and ask me to speak English with him. We went to a local tea house, found a table and ordered some tea and simply conversed in English. Afterwards he politely bowed, said goodbye, and we went our separate ways.

One day, while at home between Orient flights, I got a call from Jerry Whitney who lived in Athena, Oregon. Jerry had sold us chemicals for our ag-operations at LaGrande Air Service, and I had not spoken to Jerry since we had shut down our operations in LaGrande.

Jerry was now a business partner with Ed Miley in Athena and they had started the Pacific Basin Trading Company (PABATCO). He was importing Hodaka motorcycles from Japan, a sporty little motor cycle with a two-cycle engine that made it very lightweight and efficient. However, Jerry was having communication problems with the Japanese regarding the Hodaka's development for sales in the US, so he asked me if I would be willing to act as an intermediary during my time in Tokyo. I agreed to give it a try.

Prior to my next Tokyo visit, Jerry sent me a list of items to discuss with Hodaka. My contact in Tokyo was a Mr. Alex Hata, Hodaka's director of exports. After our first meeting, Alex and I had many more meetings, usually in my hotel room, in order to iron out any communication problems that were too complicated to deal with in writing.

I remember one problem in particular came from the fact that Hodaka had changed the transmission oil dipstick from an aluminum stick to plastic. The plastic stick would come loose after the engine got hot, and would fall into the transmission gears. After many attempts at written communication, Hodaka could still not understand what the problem was.

On my next trip to Tokyo, I met with Mr. Hata and a Hodaka engineer, and after discussing the problem for a couple of hours they were both nodding in understanding, but I got the inkling that they still did not comprehend the issue. I suggested that we go to Hodaka's nearest shipping warehouse in Tokyo and view an actual motorcycle and they both agreed. When we arrived, I walked over to one of the bikes and removed the dipstick. I pointed to it and used hand motions to demonstrate the problem for them. Both of their expressions brightened, and they said, "Ah so, deep steek." They finally understood the problem and got it quickly resolved.

One summer, after our many business meetings, Alex Hata came to the U.S. to visit PABATCO, and during his visit he came to our house and I took him on a flight in a Super Cub over Mt. Rainier. It was his first ever flight in a small airplane and he was completely in awe over the whole experience. He generously stated that "this mountain is much bigger than Japan's Mt. Fuji."

Even though I was being trained on the bigger, jet airliners, I still spent plenty of time flying light aircraft. In February of 1964, I ferried a Piper PA-18 Super Cub from Cut Bank, Montana to Kent, Washington for Joe Kennedy. Joe was the previously mentioned, Northwest Captain who wanted to land a Super Cub as short as he could land a DC-3. During a layover, I took Joe out to Troh's and checked him out in a Super Cub. It took him a while to get the Super Cub slowed down for a landing, hence his eagerness to master the landing to a point where he could land them as short as he could a DC-3. On subsequent layovers, Joe would come and practice in the Super Cub, and it was these layovers that led to him purchasing the Super Cub from Cut Bank.

I flew his new airplane to the Kent airport, where Joe had a hangar. On February 22, 1964, I gave Joe dual instruction in his new PA-18. He did great, and actually did land it shorter than a DC-3. Because I had helped him, Joe let me fly his Super Cub whenever I wanted to, the only stipulation being that I had to return it to the hangar with a full tank of gas.

I tried to take advantage of every opportunity I had to fly, testing out different makes and models of airplanes. I would often rent a Waco UPF biplane from the Renton airport, fly it out to our farm in Kent, then throttle back and fly over the neighbor's place and yell, "Get to work!"

In April of 1964, Don Leonard, another Northwest Captain, and I went into a partnership on a Cessna 310B twin engine airplane. I spent a lot of time in that airplane, flying the family on trips to Disney Land in California, trips to visit my sister in California, and on many trips to Oregon. I traded my share of the 310B to a retired Northwest pilot, C. Opsahl, on May 27, 1966. I traded him for his Cessna 182, and I also purchased a hangar near Joe Kennedy's at the Kent Airport. I sold the 182 in October of 1969 and bought a Citabria 7KCAB, a single engine aerobatic airplane.

On September 30, 1965, I qualified for a single engine seaplane rating. A fellow Northwest pilot, John Paquet, gave me five hours in a Taylorcraft BC-12D float plane on Lake Washington and on Lake Union in Seattle. John owned a Republic Seabee, which he would often fly into Lake Tapps, south of Seattle, and he allowed me to book some more time in it.

Doug and boys with 1958 Cessna 310B

Our friend and fellow pilot, Don Leonard, had a cabin and a dock on Lake Tapps, and John would often pull water-skiers behind his Seabee. The fun eventually came to a stop when a Sheriff showed up and informed John that, while it wasn't necessarily illegal to pull water-skiers with an airplane, the neighbors had complained about the noise. The sheriff "strongly suggested" that we stop, so in the interest of being a good neighbor, we put an end to our airplane-based water sports.

My last flight as second officer was on August 23, 1964 on a 707-320B from Tokyo to Seattle. I ended up with 2,164 hours as a flight engineer/ second officer. Most pilots checked out as co-pilot as soon as their seniority allowed, very few wanting to remain second officer or flight engineers for their entire career.

I checked out as a co-pilot on the Boeing 720B and Boeing 707-320B on August 26, 1964. It was a great feeling to get back into the pilot's seat again and do some real flying. Northwest was now flying jet aircraft on all of its routes. As co-pilot, I flew domestic and international schedules. Northwest also had a Military Airlift Contract (MAC) flying troops to Vietnam and other Pacific destinations, but most of my co-pilot flights were to the Orient.

Northwest Airlines 707

On one of my first 707 co-pilot trips into Tokyo Haneda Airport, the weather was changing rapidly with fog forming. The weather was still holding when we landed and visibility was good, so we proceeded to the Ginza Toku Hotel. While eating dinner, we noticed several ambulances and police cars rushing toward the airport. Shortly after our arrival, a Canadian Pacific DC-8 had crashed short of the runway. The minimum visibility for the approach was one half mile, and the minimum ceiling was 200 feet. The pilot had obviously descended below the 200 foot minimum and had landed in the bay. The fog may have been accompanied with a wind shear condition, which may have caused the airplane to suddenly lose speed and altitude and drop into the bay. Several deaths and many injuries resulted from the crash.

The next morning, we were on a flight from Tokyo to Seoul, Korea. The fog had cleared and the weather was beautiful. A British Airways 707 took off just ahead of us, en-route to Hong Kong. They flew south of Mount Fuji, while our route took us well north of the mountain. We could see the lenticular clouds over the top of the mountain, which are an indication of strong winds and turbulence, creating a standing wave of strong, vertical up and down drafts.

That day, the British Airways 707 flew too close to Mt. Fuji, trying to give passengers a better view of the mountain. Evidently they flew into the standing wave and could not climb out of it, causing the aircraft to crash into the mountain and killing all on board. It was an eerie feeling, piloting a flight that was bookended by two fatal crashes. I was always aware of the risks involved in flying, and took all necessary precautions to avoid them.

Fortunately, aviation safety was improving very fast with the introduction of jet powered aircraft. However, as with any new technology, we were still learning the nuances. The faster and higher flying jets created some new challenges; one of them being climbing into standing waves which are high altitude, high velocity winds occurring over mountains. Due to incidents such as the British Airways crash, Northwest began to develop procedures to recognize and circumvent these waves. There are many locations in which standing waves were common so these areas were marked on our en-route charts, and if the conditions were right to create a standing wave, flight crews were notified so that they could re-route flights around them. It was not uncommon, while flying in those areas, to get a call from United Airlines, asking for the locations of the mountain waves. Northwest Airlines, under Paul Soderlind's direction, was still ahead of the rest of the industry in safety practices.

Operating a 707 out of the Tokyo Haneda Airport runway at a maximum gross takeoff weight barely met the minimum takeoff and climb requirements for the 707, so NWA received FAA approval for a clearway takeoff from Haneda Airport's main runway which headed out over Tokyo Bay. A clearway is an area beyond the paved runway, free of obstructions and under the control of the airport authorities. The length of the clearway may be included in the length of the takeoff distance available. Even with the clearway, a Northwest dispatcher had to stand atop a terminal roof with a pair of binoculars to view the harbor and ensure that there were no ships in the way of our takeoff.

On one of these clearway takeoffs, I was co-pilot, and as we were initially climbing out, a seagull hit the captain's windshield. The bird splattered, making such a mess that we could not see out. The captain told me to take the plane and continue the climb while he operated the windshield wiper to try and clear away the mess. It did clear up enough for us to continue on to Seattle, and fortunately for us, Boeing had tested their windshields to ensure that they could withstand a bird strike. I had heard that they did this by firing a five-pound chicken at the windshield using an air-powered canon. However, they tested them, our windshield held up throughout the flight and sustained no damage.

During this period of my career with Northwest, my family and I traveled as pass riders all over the U.S., the Orient, and Hawaii. On one such trip to the Orient, Shirley and I took our eleven-year-old son, Joe along with us. I outlined the trip, planning stops at many of the different sites I had visited during my layovers. My friend, Alex Hata, helped me with all of the railroad tickets and hotel reservations, and Joe's fifth grade teacher agreed to allow him to go on the extended trip without being counted absent if Joe would give an oral report about his travels upon his return. We saw to it that Joe took notes on all of the locations we visited, and his report turned out quite well. I still have a copy of it to this day. His teacher commented that it was "Very accurate and impressive." (See Joe's report in APPENDIX 1)

Joe feeding beer to a Kobe Beef steer

Jet Captain
The bidding for pilot positions was based on a pilot's seniority. The pilot's date of hire placed him on the seniority list and whenever a position opened up the first hired was the most senior pilot on the list. With my seniority at the time it appeared that it would be a long while before I would be able to hold a captain's position in Seattle. However, my seniority was ample enough to hold a captain position on the Boeing 727 in Minneapolis.

I bid for the position and on November 11, 1966 I began training on the Boeing 727. The 727 was a three engine jet, and I completed the training on November 25, 1966. I now had three Type Ratings on my Airline Transport Pilot certificate: the DC-3, DC-4, and the 727.

Northwest Airlines Boeing 727

The 727 was replacing the DC-6B, DC-7C and the Lockheed Electra aircraft on Northwest's domestic routes. It carried around 70 passengers, had a three-man crew, and cruised at the same speeds as the Boeing 707, which was Mach 0.82 (Mach is the speed of sound, and 0.82 is the percentage of the speed of sound).

The Boeing 727 was also a very comfortable airplane, was easy to fly, and was very popular with passengers. Northwest's 727s were in a two class configuration; twenty first class seats and about fifty tourist section seats. The cabin crew consisted of five flight attendants and the in-flight service was excellent. The kitchen was efficient, with both ovens and refrigeration.

On January 2, 1967, I started flying as captain on the 727 out of Minneapolis. They were all domestic flights, most flying to Washington D.C. with stops in Cleveland, Detroit, and Pittsburg. Later, I also captained flights from Minneapolis to Seattle, Chicago, and Portland, with stops in Spokane. I enjoyed the short, domestic flights as they afforded many takeoffs and landings, a real challenge to one's pilot skills.

Also some flights through the Montana mountain stations. It is interesting to compare some of the scheduled flight time between the DC-3 and 727 on certain segments of those flights. All the DC-3 flights were scheduled as VFR. The 727 had to be scheduled IFR, meaning that all IFR departure and arrival procedures had to be flown. Some examples:

- Missoula to Helena DC-3 50 minutes, 727 35 minutes
- Helena to Butte DC-3 35 minutes, 727 45 minutes
- Butte to Bozeman DC-3 35minutes, 727 40 minutes
- Bozeman to Billings DC-3 55 minutes, 727 34 minutes

The DC-3 was faster on short flight segments.

I found a home to rent on Lake Minnetonka, so Shirley and the boys flew on passes to Minneapolis with our black lab, Baron. The boys enrolled in school and we began to make a life for ourselves in Minnesota. It was February when we first moved into the lake house, which was small but comfortable. We had never seen the home without the cover of winter, so it was fun to see what the melting snows revealed as the year progressed. Suddenly there were benches, a barbeque pit, and a dock with a pontoon boat. The boat and the dock were included with the house rental, and when the ice melted off of the lake I bought a small outboard engine to use on the boat. We would use the boat to visit our other pilot friends who also had houses on the lake, and the boys would often take it out to go fishing. We had a lot of fun in that house, and made a lot of great memories.

I had one incident on the 727 during this time. The 727 had a Drum Altimeter, and there had been trouble with that altimeter throughout the industry. I was on a flight from Washington D.C. to Detroit with a stop in Pittsburg. The weather going into Pittsburg was overcast at 2,100 feet, with visibility at 10 miles and some light snow showers. The temperature was only 21 degrees Fahrenheit, with wind at 14 knots and an altimeter setting of 30.24.

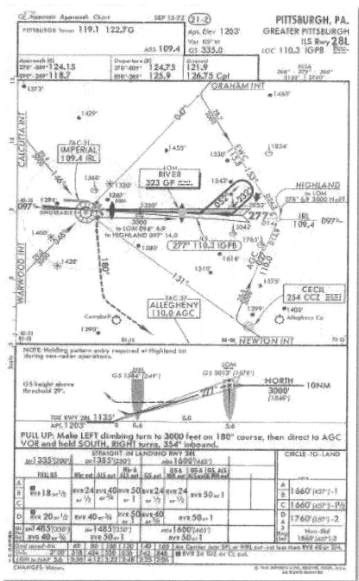

Pittsburg ILS 28L Approach

Pittsburg Approach Control cleared us to descend to 3,000 feet, and vectored us to the Runway 28L Localizer. During the vector, tower advised us that they observed our

Precision Airborne Radar (PAR) altitude was at 2,000 feet. We questioned them as to whether the PAR altitude was above sea level or above the ground. They replied that it was above sea level. Both of our altimeters indicated 3,000 feet MSL, or Mean (average) Sea Level. We were still in the clouds that were 2,100 feet above the airport, which had an elevation of 1,182 feet. We knew there was something wrong, because if we were at 2,000 feet MSL, we should have been well below the clouds, and only about 1,000 feet about the ground.

We were cleared for an ILS approach to runway 28 Left. Pittsburg Approach Control followed our approach on their PAR. We broke in and out of the clouds, with both altimeters reading 3,000 feet MSL prior to crossing the outer marker. We then followed the ILS localizer course and VASI (Visual Approach Slope Indicator) to the runway.

Once on the ground, both altimeters read 1,181 feet MSL, which was the elevation of the airport. We proceeded on to our next stop in Cleveland, then on to Detroit. An FAA official met our flight upon arrival in Detroit. He had been alerted of our situation in Pittsburg and was making a routine check to determine if the aircraft's altimetry was air worthy. After discussing it with us, he was satisfied that the aircraft was okay and could continue. The flight data tapes were removed and sent to Northwest Flight Operations.

Paul Soderlind later viewed the tapes and sent me a letter, stating that it was an excellent approach, and that I would have passed a six month check with a 4.0!

We later learned that the problem was with the Pittsburg approach radar. They had the PAR shut down for maintenance after that incident, but still had later incidents in which the approaching aircrafts were shown to be lower than they actually were.

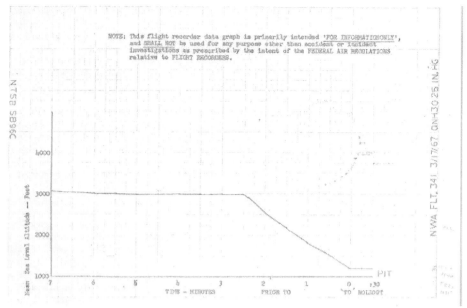

Flight recorder data of approach to Pittsburg

I was fortunate to have only the one incident during my time on the 727. My last Boeing 727 flight was on May 30, 1967, from O'Hare to Minneapolis. I logged 654 hours in that airplane.

On May 1, 1967, I was senior enough to bid and get a Boeing 707/720B captain position in Seattle. The 707 paid better than the 727 because they had a heavier gross weight, which was a part of the pay calculation. The 707 also flew international routes that provided an international pay override.

Being based in Seattle again gave our family the opportunity to return to our place in Kent, Washington. I had purchased a new car during our time in Minneapolis, so we rented a U-Haul trailer, loaded up all of our things including Baron who rode in a kennel in the trailer, then headed west back to Kent.

It has been said that a mile of highway will take you a mile, but a mile of runway can take you anywhere. However, having always flown on most of our family trips, it was a nice change of pace to hit the highway and drive across the country. We made several stops in South Dakota, including the Bad Lands, the famous Corn Palace, and Wall Drug. The highlight of the trip, however, was when we entered Wyoming and saw the Big Horn Mountains for the first time. We stopped and all got out of the car so that we could admire them. Being from the west coast and the Cascade Mountain area, we had really missed the mountains during our time in the flat country of the Midwest. It was as if the mountains were welcoming us back home.

On May 4, 1967, I logged a two hour, six-month check in the Transdyne Trainer, which had replaced the Link Trainer. On May 12, I went to Miami for 707/720B flight training, and by May 22 I had completed 17 hours of flight training and passed my FAA check ride, receiving a Boeing 707 and Boeing 720 Type Ratings. I now had Type Ratings in a Douglas DC-3, DC-4, and Boeing 727, 707, and 720. In Seattle on June 5, I also received my night qualification for the 720B. The night qualification familiarized the pilot with the cockpit and external aircraft lighting procedures for flying after dark.

I had enjoyed my time as Second Officer in the Orient, so I was eager to get back to international flights. Flying into Hong Kong required special airport qualification, unlike other destinations where pilots only needed simulator qualifications. Hong Kong required the simulator, plus a deadhead flight into Hong Kong. The first flight into the city required a check pilot to accompany, and I completed my Hong Kong Captain qualification in October of 1967.

Landing and takeoff procedures were always interesting in Hong Kong. The Hong Kong Airport runway 13 was 10,932 feet long, and extended from the mainland into the bay. It had a displaced threshold of 1,790 feet to clear some residential buildings, and landing before the threshold was prohibited. That area could only be used for starting a takeoff, so runway 13 was thus used for both landing and takeoff.

The runway 13 ILS (Instrument Landing System) angled toward the runway, with the localizer course of 088 degrees to the middle marker, located 1.7 miles from the end of the runway. The middle marker also acted as the visual point to start a right turn to line up with Runway 13. The decision height over the middle marker was 675 feet, and if the runway was not in sight at that point, a climbing right turn was immediately required for the missed approach.

What made it very unique were the two very large billboard-sized checkerboard patterns painted on the hill just north of the middle marker. From the checkerboards, a right turn was made to line up with runway 13, and the approach was continued visually until landing. While on that approach, you could see houses and apartments on the hillside off your left wing, and they sometimes seemed close enough that you could look into their windows.

Doug in left seat of 707

On June 11, 1967, I flew my first 707 as captain. It was a Military Airlift Command (MAC) flight from Seattle to Tacoma, then to Yokota, Japan. The flight time was 10 hours and 40 minutes, and it was also a line check flight. The check pilot signed me off, and I was now officially an aircraft captain, with all of the responsibilities associated with being in command. It was a moment to be proud of.

My "First Flight Curse" Begins

On June 13, 1967, I reported to Yokota Air Force Base for my first solo flight as a 707 Captain. It was another MAC flight from Yokota to Cam Ranh Bay, Vietnam.

The 707 configuration for MAC flights was 165 seats, all one class. The troops boarded with their military packs and proceeded to their assigned seats. They had all begun their trip at McChord Air Force Base near Tacoma, and they all deplaned once they arrived in Yokota. I boarded the aircraft, put my flight bag in the cockpit, and proceeded through the cabin for an inspection. None of the flight attendants were on board yet, and as I returned to the front of the cabin, visiting with the purser (the officer who kept the accounts), I heard a small *poof.* I looked across the cabin and saw smoke rising from under the front right passenger seat. I went down the passenger stairs to alert the ground crew. The co-pilot was still in his seat and left the aircraft after I told him that I had seen smoke. The second officer had been doing his cabin inspection, and the smoke became so dense that he could not see and had to follow the armrests to the front of the cabin in order to find the door and exit the plane.

After I got on the ramp, I quickly found the other cabin attendants to ensure that they were all accounted for. The fire quickly became very intense and burned through the top of the cabin. The Air Force fire crew showed up to fight the fire, and the fire chief suggested they move the airplane off the ramp to let it burn. However, the co-pilot had set the parking break prior to his exit, so there was no way to get the plane off of the ramp. Luckily, the fire did not spread to the other airplanes or equipment on the ramp. The fire was eventually extinguished although several of the fire fighters suffered from smoke inhalation.

707 following fire started by leaking oxygen bottle

It was later determined that the cause of the fire was a leaking oxygen bottle located in the forward baggage compartment. There must have been some grease or some type of combustible material in line with the oxygen leak. As the aircraft was brand new, the oxygen system had not yet been serviced, and it was a mystery as to how the foreign material could have gotten into the compartment.

Needless to say, the flight was canceled and I was grounded until I had completed a debriefing on the incident. So, without my first solo flight as captain of the 707 completed, I returned to Seattle the next day.

Boeing sent a crew to Yokota to restore the aircraft, and it returned to the line. While the incident had prevented my first solo flight as captain, there were some good safety procedures that resulted from the fire:

1. Aisle lights were installed on all aircraft to assist in evacuation with dense smoke in the cabin.
2. The main cabin door escape chute will not be in place until the aircraft has left the gate. If installed before pushback, if an attempt is made to open the door from either the outside or the inside, the escape chute could blow into the jet way, obstructing the door from fully opening.

Fire damage can be seen on top of 707 fuselage

It was June 21, 1967 when I finally did make my first solo flight on the 707. It was a flight from Seattle to McChord, to Yokota, and on June 23 I made the trip from Yokota to Cam Ranh Bay, South Vietnam, and then on to Da Nang. I flew many MAC flights into Vietnam during that time.

Military Airlift Command

During the Vietnam War troops were transported overseas and returned back to the United States by air, unlike WWII when overseas transportation was done via troop ships, forcing the troops to endure a much longer trip home. Most U.S. International Airlines furnished aircraft and crews for Military Airlift Command (MAC) flights. Northwest Airlines, being the major trans-Pacific carrier, had by far the most MAC flights across the Pacific to Vietnam. Northwest flight crews were qualified to use Doppler Navigation across the North Pacific Ocean, and had ground facilities in the Orient to support the MAC. They provided 165 passenger Boeing 707-320B's for this service.

All total, I flew 107 MAC flights in and out of Vietnam. Most of my flights originated from McChord Air Force Base near Tacoma, Washington, with destinations such as Saigon, Cam Ranh Bay, and Da Nang in South Vietnam. Some of my flights were also flown out of Travis Air Force Base and El Toro Naval Air Station, both in California. Most were routed through Elmendorf Air Force Base in Anchorage, Alaska, then across the Aleutian Chain to Yokota, Japan, then on to Okinawa, Japan, and from there we would make the final stops in Vietnam.

Observing the troops that we were hauling was always interesting. When they boarded in the U.S. they were always anxious and melancholy, uncertain about what lie ahead of them. When they boarded in Vietnam it was just the opposite: all smiles and eager to get home. When landing back in the U.S. there would always be a loud cheer from the troops (even if you made a hard landing). Many of them would even kneel over and kiss the tarmac after they de-planed. That's really happiness to be back in the good old U.S.A.!!
It was also interesting to observe the different behaviors between the different military branches. When boarding the aircraft, the Army troops would meander to their assigned seats, taking quite a bit of time to get seated and settled down. The Marines, however, marched aboard and moved down the aisle to their seats without hesitation.

Although they seemed more oriented and disciplined, the Marines were not without their blunders. This was made clear by one memorable flight out of El Toro N.A.S. with a load of Marines. I flew from Seattle to the Mc Chord AFB in Tacoma to pick up troops to go to Travis AFB, then ferry the airplane to El Toro NAS to pick up a load of Marines destined for Vietnam. We had a delay in Tacoma before heading for Travis, then another delay in Travis, all of which was adding to our on-duty time. We loaded the Marines at El Toro, and were on our way to Elmendorf for fuel before proceeding on to Yokota.

HEADQUARTERS MILITARY AIRLIFT COMMAND

UNITED STATES AIR FORCE

CERTIFICATE OF

RECOGNITION and APPRECIATION

BE IT KNOWN TO ALL WHO SHALL SEE THESE PRESENTS, THAT:

DOUGLAS H. PARROTT

While in the employ of   Northwest Orient Airlines, Inc.   as a   Captain , between   July 21,   19 65 and   November 9,   1969 did perform an outstanding service to the United States of America by participating in sustained aerial support of the United States Armed Forces engaged in combat operations within the Republic of South Vietnam. In recognition of completing   Thirty-eight-102   Contract Airlift Logistical Support Missions for the Military Airlift Command, I extend to you my heartiest congratulations and award to you this certificate as a token of appreciation.

Given under my hand at Scott Air Force Base, Illinois this 7th day of   July   19 70 .

JACK J. CATTON, General, USAF
Commander

Military Airlift Command Certificate of Appreciation

Prior to landing at Elmendorf, we informed the company that we could not go beyond Elmendorf without the minimum requirement of eight hours of crew rest. The company agreed, so we landed at Elmendorf. Once on the ground, the company provided transportation to the hotel in Anchorage for the Marines as well as the flight crew.

The next morning, we reported back to Elmendorf, made out our flight plan and were ready to board with the troops. The airplane had been moved to a different position on the airport, which was about a mile from the terminal. It was a cool, rainy Anchorage morning, with wet roads and tarmac. They had a van to take the crew to the airplane, and busses to haul the Marines. We soon learned, however, that during the layover some of the Marines had gone into town to celebrate; a few of them celebrating their way right into a jail cell. They were released by the Anchorage police with a warning and arrived at the airport properly dressed in their Marine uniforms. The Sergeant in charge of the Platoon was a big guy with a gruff, commanding voice, and when they brought the buses around for the Marines to ride to the airplane, the Sergeant lined them up and shouted, "We are not going to ride." He then had them line up in marching order and shouted, "They will march to the airplane in double time." He then moved in front of the platoon, hollered, "Forward March – Double Time!" and led them all the way to the plane in double time. The experience was a real indication as to why Marines are so tough and well disciplined.

When they arrived at the airplane, they marched down the aisle and into their seats. The rest of the flight was uneventful, and we got them to their destination in "double time".

ALPA Airline Pilots Association

On September 18, 1967, I was elected Master Executive Chairman (MEC) for the Northwest Airlines Pilot group. I had served three terms as Senior Co-Pilot Representative of Spokane Council 144, Senior Copilot Representative of Seattle Council 54, and MEC Senior Copilot. I also served as Council 54 Grievance Committee Chairman, and had attended three ALPA Board of Directors meetings. I served on the MEC Check and Training Committee, met with the National Board concerning Jet Crew Complement, and was a member of

Headquarters Neutral Panel for Merger Agreements.

My first activities as MEC Chairman were directed at educating myself in regard to the problems facing Northwest pilots, and exploring the various problem areas that existed between the company and the pilots.

I spent some time at ALPA headquarters and had some pleasant meetings with ALPA President, Charles Ruby. We considered "beefing up" our home office staff, which would result in improved services for our members, as well as provide more assistance to the local elected officers in solving the problems that might arise between the company and our pilot group.

I also met with Northwest Airlines officials in order to discuss a few of our mutual problems. I told them that I was hopeful that any problems between ALPA and the company could be resolved by sincere, honest discussions and a minimum amount of threats or litigation from either side. They were all in agreement and also hoped that we could resolve the many problems that existed between the pilot group and the company. This was merely the beginning of my "education".

One of the major problems was with the captain checkout of former flight engineers. The MEC proposed a letter of agreement that would allow former flight engineers the opportunity to check out as captain, and also allowed them to remain as permanent co-pilots or second officers. Many former flight engineers did not want to upgrade to co-pilot or captain due to their limited experience. There was a deadline by which they had to make up their minds about whether or not to accept or reject the captain checkout, placing pressure on those pilots to make a decision. As an aside, this particular group of pilots, while being represented by the International Association of Machinists, had already signed an agreement with the company that stated they had the option to not check out as captain. ALPA had no part in this agreement.

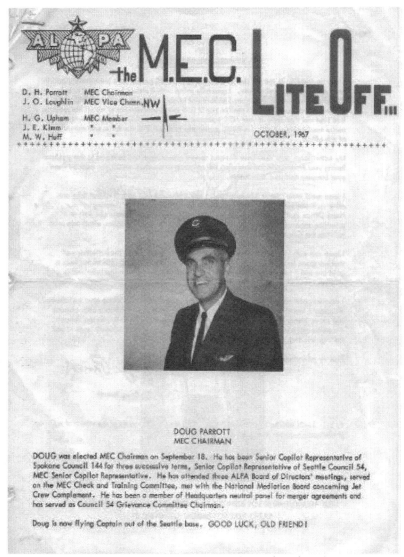

the M.E.C. LITE OFF...

D. H. Parrott — MEC Chairman
J. O. Loughlin — MEC Vice Chrmn. NW

H. G. Upham — MEC Member
J. E. Kimm — " "
M. W. Huff — " "

OCTOBER, 1967

DOUG PARROTT
MEC CHAIRMAN

DOUG was elected MEC Chairman on September 18. He has been Senior Copilot Representative of Spokane Council 144 for three successive terms, Senior Copilot Representative of Seattle Council 54, MEC Senior Copilot Representative. He has attended three ALPA Board of Directors' meetings, served on the MEC Check and Training Committee, met with the National Mediation Board concerning Jet Crew Complement. He has been a member of Headquarters neutral panel for merger agreements and has served as Council 54 Grievance Committee Chairman.

Doug is now flying Captain out of the Seattle base. GOOD LUCK, OLD FRIEND!

ALPA Newsletter Announcing Doug's Election as MEC

Once the pilots achieved seniority, however, they were covered by the APLA contract. With this in mind, we worked with the company to resolve the problem and give this group of pilots the rights that were consistent with their working agreement.

There were also efforts to establish a System Board of Adjustment to resolve grievances. We had not had a System Board of Adjustment in a long while, and there was a huge backlog of unsettled grievances. Both the company and the MEC supported establishing a System Board, and it was necessary to contact the National Mediation Board to assign a neutral party to hear the grievances.

On top of these issues, there was the unresolved "Rall/Lee" case. This case involved the dismissal of Captain Rall and First Officer Lee in Honolulu, consequent to the Captain reporting for flight while under the influence of alcohol.

Captain Rall had been scheduled to dead-head back to Seattle, but the company had rescheduled him to cover as captain for a Military Charter Flight. Not expecting to pilot, the captain had been out drinking the night before. He had reported for the flight the following morning, and the co-pilot had flown while Captain Rall slept in the right seat. Some of the military men had observed the situation and reported it to the company.

ALPA defended Captain Rall and First Officer Lee through the System Board. The company took the case to court. ALPA agreed to financially assist the pilots until the court's decision had been made. The courts ruled against the pilots, and both were terminated.

Most of the previously mentioned issues were resolved by April of 1968. The first issue, involving the flight engineers and co-pilots checking out as captain, was resolved by giving these pilots the choice to either check out as captain, or to remain as a co-pilot or second officer.

A System Board of Adjustment was finally established in order to deal with employee grievances, and 30 grievances were resolved almost immediately. Other, long standing grievances were prepared for future System Board action.

Another dispute came about after NWA purchased the

newest Boeing 707, the 320B. It was heavier than previous 707s, and therefore required higher gross weight pay. The company scheduled it for flight without an agreement with ALPA on new pay rates, and 32 pilots were fired for refusing to fly it.

The ALPA pilot group made a special assessment of its members in order to loan the 32 fired pilots the pay that they were losing due to the dispute. The NWA MEC negotiated directly with management to settle the issue, and to return the 32 pilots to work. The company also agreed to correct their personnel records so that they would show no breaks in service, and to negotiate pay rates for the new aircraft before putting them into service. I am quite sure that, had we gone to a civil court or the System Board, we would not have had as good of results, so this was another success for the Air Line Pilots Association.

National Labor Board Decision 83

September 1933 the Air Line Pilots Association petitioned the National Labor Board to mediate pay disputes with a number of airlines over air mail flying pay rates. The pay rates had been arbitrary. Each airline set its own rates which varied between airlines, and were increased or decreased at the will of the individual airline.

The National Labor Board realizing that the industry was rapidly changing, with the addition of hauling passengers, ruled that *"pilot pay should be based on productivity."* Productivity was based on the speed and weight of the aircraft being flown. They also ruled that night flying and miles flown should receive additional pay. They set monthly base pay rates. They determined that eighty-five hours should be the monthly maximum flight time. We used this ruling to establish the pay rates for the Boeing 747. Quite a change with larger faster aircraft, even using higher productivity pilots pay rates.

1940 DC-3	1986 B747
160 MPH	525 MPH
21 Passengers	400 Passengers
19 trips to haul 400 passengers	1 trip to haul 400 passengers
Capt. $11.75/hour	Capt. $175.72/hour
F/O $2.95/hour	F/O $114.22/hour
	S/O $96.65/hour
Crew $14.70/hour	Crew $386.59/hour
Flight time – 20 hours	Flight time – 5 hours
$294.00/trip	$1,932.95/trip
X 19 trips = $5,586.00 crew costs for 400 passengers	X 1 trip = $1,932.95 crew costs for 400 passengers
$266.00 crew cost per passenger	$4.83 crew cost per passenger

Flight crew cost comparison to carry 400 passengers from Seattle to New York.

Contract Negotiations

On April 30, 1968, we moved into a long series of contract negotiations. It took all of that year to establish mediators, the process being dragged out by several cancellations of negotiations and recesses. The company was simply unwilling to cooperate with ALPA.

One of the important aspects of the changes that ALPA was trying to institute was the monthly hours and duty hours. Other airlines differed in this area. United had a maximum of 85 flight hours per month, and a trip hour credit of one hour pay for each three hours on duty. Pan Am had strict rules on duty times. They had to double crews on trans-Pacific flights in order to meet the requirements, so it looked like a parade when the uniformed crew deplaned in Tokyo. Trans World Airlines had reduced monthly hours to a maximum of 75 hours and a trip hour credit of one hour pay for each four hours on duty.

The Northwest contract at the time was similar to United's in regards to the monthly hours and trip hour credit. Our goal was to change it to 75 hours maximum monthly flying and a trip hour credit of one hour pay for each four hours on duty.

Northwest's company negotiator, Homer Kinney, had previously told NWA management that ALPA's proposed change would require the hiring of 100 additional pilots. Del Plue, a first officer who was also a part of the NWA ALPA Negotiating Committee, and I looked at all of the current pilot schedules that had been built with the current contract. The proposed monthly hours and duty regulations projected a requirement of less than 10 new pilots. The big factor was the reduction of trip hour credit from one hour pay and credit for every three hours on duty, to one hour pay and credit for each four hours on duty. One for three required eight hours pay for every 24 hours scheduled away from home, and since eight hours in 24 is the maximum legal flight time allowed under the Federal Air Regulations, it was nearly impossible to schedule a pilot to fly actual hours using the one for three contracts. One for four allowed six hours in 24, making it easier to build pilot schedules without any penalty time. This would require fewer pilots, which would then offset the reduction in monthly hours. We also constructed a phase procedure for the new hours, so as not to disrupt existing schedules while the new rules were being implemented.

On March 4, 1969, I made an appointment to meet with Mr. Nyrop to present this information to him directly. Donald Nyrop was the previously mentioned President of Northwest Airlines (who had an acute ability for remembering names and faces). Also at this meeting was Mr. Benjamin Griggs Jr., Vice President Assistant to the President. Mr. Nyrop briefly looked over the material that Del and I had compiled, and then changed the subject to discuss investments. He recommended land as the best investment, as it was being used at a fast pace and no new land could be created. Despite the lack of resolution regarding the real issues at hand, I did later take his advice and, in 1973, purchased a cattle ranch near Roundup, Montana. . .

On January 15, 1969, ALPA directed the Northwest pilots to strictly adhere to the Standard Operating Procedures Amplified (SOPA), and to take extra precaution on all NWA flights during this period of contract negotiation strife. One complaint regarding the new, amplified operating procedures was that they would sometimes cause flight delays and extra flight time. Some crews were accused of taxiing too slowly, causing flights behind them to be delayed. ALPA reprimanded them, and it took a while before the company acknowledged any positive effects of the SOPA operation. The best benefit was the extra encouragement for safe aircraft operation during a period of low pilot morale.

On May 26, 1969, ALPA set a strike date of June 13, 1969. Northwest was informed that absolutely no flights would be flown after the deadline, including Military Air Charter flights. It was shortly after the strike date was set that Mr. Leveret Edwards, Chairman of the National Mediation Board, requested that ALPA and the company meet in Fort Worth, Texas for mediation.

Mr. Edwards himself served as the mediator. He started by taking our current Red Book (contract), starting on the first page, and going through it page by page to ensure that both sides agreed on every aspect. When we came to a page or an item that either side disagreed on, both sides would put forth their arguments for their desired change, then we would move on. After he had guided us through the entire book, he returned to the unresolved items to see if they could be resolved at that time. Many of these items were resolved under Mr. Edwards' guidance, but at the end of the day there were still enough left unresolved to warrant further negotiations.

On the day before the strike, Mr. Edwards brought the company and the ALPA representatives together to try and work out the remaining contract issues. The company gave very few offers, and as the deadline approached, Mr. Edwards was forced to travel back and forth between the two parties, trying to reach an agreement. There were no offers accepted by the company or by ALPA, so at midnight the strike officially began. The pilots collectively walked off of the job, and the airline was shut down.

At around 3:00 a.m. that night, Northwest came forward with some new offers. ALPA studied and accepted them, but there were still items left unresolved, so the strike remained in effect. It was then that Northwest's top management became involved. Another offer was made by the company, ALPA accepted, and the strike was ended after only six hours. It took only six hours to end a process that had taken 16 months and 18 days from start to finish.

With the new compromise, our hours were set at 80 per month with duty times, 1 for 3.5 trip hour credits, new pay rates, and retro-active pay to name a few significant changes. It was a long, hard battle, but NWA was well known for its protracted negotiations. There would be more negotiation struggles in the future, as well as more, longer strikes, although this particular six-hour strike was the first ever pilots' strike at NWA. (See APPENDIX 2)

SOPA SAM
THE NEGOTIATIN' MAN

THE BALLAD OF SOPA SAM,
THE NEGOTIATIN' MAN.

Now Sopa Sam was a negotiatin' man,
hard workin, loyal and such;
Who worked on the spread of Dry Rot Ned,
well known for his miserly touch.

For years and years in this vale of tears,
Sopa labored without a word,
While pokes all round got more feed and found,
for pushin a much smaller herd.

Ol' Dry Rot had, a very bad
foreman of dour demeanor,
Horrible Homer his name, sayin' No
his game, and no rattler born that was meaner.

After all those years of blood, sweat and tears
and watchin' ol' Dry Rot get rich,
Sopa slowed down one day and to hisself did say,
"For a raise I'll make a pitch."

So to Homer he went, but his nose was all bent,
For Homer's one word was No –
Though he pleaded and shouted and mumbled and pouted
For his raise there was no where to go.

Back home on the range, with heavy heart
(He felt he'd been sorely abused),
Ol' Sopa thought that surely he ought,
To no longer be so poorly used.

So he challenged Homer to a shoot-out Spree,
at the G.O. Coral it was to be.
Then He strapped on his guns and his big black hat,
The time had come, and that was that!

They met right there as the sun did sink,
They both slapped leather and quick as a wink,
Ol' Sopa had Homer in his sights,
and he was caught dead to rights.

But Sopa Sam was a negotiatin' man.
Hard working, loyal and such,
and Though he had Homer in his sights,
He didn't want to shoot him, much.

Midnite came and the end drew nigh,
And Homer quaked at Sopa's eye.
To save his life he talked away and
Six hours later he'd had his say.
Then Sopa put his guns away
Cause he'd finally got his raise in pay.

Now Sopa's back pushin' that great big herd.
Ol' Dry Rot's still gettin' rich.
and Homer's practicing on his one word,
But Sopa still has his pitch.
For if things ever again must come to that,
He's still wearin' his guns,
and his big Black Hat.

Meeting Charles A. Lindbergh

Without a doubt, the most memorable affair
that I ever had the honor to attend, as chairman at the NWA
MEC, was held on April 21, 1969 in Washington D.C. An
Honorary Membership in the Airline Pilots Association was
presented to the renowned aviator, Charles A. Lindbergh.
Northwest Airlines ALPA Council 1 presented the idea as a
resolution to the ALPA Board of Directors 20th biennial
meeting in November, 1968, and the resolution was met with
unanimous approval. Retired Northwest Airlines captain,
Harry McKee, then the ALPA Director of Public Relations,
made all of the arrangements for the presentation and acted as
Master of Ceremonies for the evening.

Charles Lindberg, Charles Ruby, Doug

Some other NWA pilots in attendance were Harry Upham, Chairman of NWA Council 1, Chuck Hagen, Lee Smith, Walt Bullock, Homer Cole, and John Huber. Also attending was Jimmy Doolittle, a reserve officer in the United States Army Air Corp who was called back into duty during World War II in order to lead the famous Doolittle Raid, in which B-25B bombers were flown from an aircraft carrier to perform a long-range, retaliatory raid on Japan after Pearl Harbor. Other famous aviators present were Bud Gurney, "Snuffy Smith" (who taught Lindbergh to fly), retired United Airlines Captain Harold Gray, Chairman of the Board of Pan American, Charles Ruby, President of ALPA, Ken Lane (who had actually fueled the Spirit of St. Louis), along with numerous other aviation pioneers who attended to speak on behalf of General Lindbergh and the Airline Pilots Association. I was awed by the number of renowned aviators in attendance and was very humbled to be in the presence of such industry pioneers.

I am quite sure that I was not the only person to be humbled by the experience. General Lindbergh belonged to only three organizations, the Army Navy Club, the Quiet Birdmen and after that night, the Airline Pilots Association. For a man of such high integrity and ideals to choose to be a part of our organization, made every member feel extremely proud to be associated with ALPA.

Several of the aviation greats in attendance gave some very enlightening, interesting talks, but to me Lindbergh's farsighted speech for the future of aviation was the most profound. He spoke about supersonic transport, indicating that it was not really the long distance, trans-oceanic airliner of the future. Instead, he argued that sub-orbital aircraft would one day be used for those long haul routes. He cited some very convincing scientific studies to support his theory, and as of this writing, supersonic transport crafts are long gone. It will be very interesting to see if Mr. Lindbergh's vision of the future of aviation comes to fruition.

More ALPA Work

On May 6 through May 9 of 1969, the Executive Board of ALPA met in Washington D.C. This was the first meeting of this newly constituted body made up of MEC Chairmen from all of the airlines represented by ALPA. The Board was created at the Board of Directors meeting in Miami in November, 1968. It was to meet every six months in order to make ALPA policy, to interpret the constitution and by-laws, and to monitor the general affairs of the association.

At this first meeting, I presented an agenda item which requested headquarters to see more timely administration of the Railway Labor Act by the National Mediation Board. The Railway Labor Act is a United States federal law that governs labor relations within the airlines and the railroad. The act seeks to substitute bargaining, arbitration, and mediation for strikes as a means of resolving labor disputes. Since ALPA had recently used labor strikes to effectively achieve its demands, speaking for the Railway Act was no easy feat, but after warding off the over-ripe tomatoes and eggs, our resolution passed unanimously (and with no eggs or rotten vegetables on my face).

I was also given the opportunity at this meeting to present an item submitted by the Continental Airlines MEC and the Flying Tigers Airlines MEC, which would permit the members of ALPA to participate in the financing of our new office building in Washington D.C. by providing interest bearing building bonds to be made available for membership subscription. This was also passed unanimously.

After being elected for a second term as MEC Chairman during our long, drawn out contract negotiations, I accepted on the condition that I would resign as soon as a new contract was approved. We now had a new contract, better relations with management, a System Board to make decisions regarding pilot grievances, as well as several long standing issues resolved. It had been a great experience, and I had learned many important lessons and met some really great people. With my newly acquired knowledge and friends, I stepped down as MEC Chairman; my term lasted from October 1, 1967 to August 1, 1969. (APPENDIX 3)

AIR LINE PILOTS ASSOCIATION
MEMORY BUILDING, 1329 "F" STREET, N.W.
WASHINGTON, D.C. 20004
(203) 347-2311

AFFILIATED WITH AFL-CIO

INT'L

April 9, 1969

Mr. D. H. Parrott
24442 - 156th Street, S. E.
Kent, Washington 98031

Dear Mr. Parrott:

On April 21st, a Monday, at the Sheraton Carlton Hotel, formal address, 923 16th N. W. or 16th & K, N. W. in Washington D. C. there will be a gathering of close personal friends and other select pilot personnel to honor General Charles A. Lindbergh who is being presented an honorary membership in the Air Line Pilots Association.

This event will start at 5:30 p.m. promptly with a cocktail party, continuing until 6:30 p.m. Dinner at 7:00 and the balance of the evening to be vested in the ceremony surrounding this presentation.

We are most happy to extend this invitation and should there be any change in your plans, would appreciate your notifying me at our Washington, D. C. office located at 1329 E Street, N. W., Munsey Building, 20004. Reservations have been made for you at the Sheraton Carlton. Because of the limited number attending this affair, this letter is your authorized admission and should accompany you and be presented on request at the Sheraton Carlton.

I am sure you will find the effort to attend this function well worth your while as the gathering of close friends of General Lindbergh in one place at one time possibly will not occur again.

Warmest personal regards.

Sincerely yours,

AIR LINE PILOTS ASSOCIATION

Capt. Harry H. McKee, Director
Public Relations

HHMcK/vrp

"SCHEDULE WITH SAFETY"

Invitation to ceremony with Charles Lindberg's autograph

128

Back in the Cockpit

After spending so much time working on negotiations with the company, it always felt good to get back in the pilot's seat. On December 19th and 20th of 1968, I had a two hour warm up session and a four hour proficiency check in Northwest's first Boeing 707 simulator. It did not have motion or visual references, and the engine out training was almost negative training when losing an engine on takeoff. The necessary rudder input was also excessive. If you were to use that much rudder in a real airplane, you would be heading way off of the runway. That was one of my few experiences in that simulator, as most of my flight checks were done in a real airplane.

On January 12, 1969, I had a charter flight in a 720B, flying the Guthrie Theatre Group from New York to Los Angeles. It was an overnight flight, was late for departure, and consequently, most of the passengers had been waiting in the bar. We eventually loaded them and all of their instruments for takeoff. Once we'd reached cruising altitude, the lead flight attendant came to the cockpit and complained about the passengers' drunken conduct. Apparently they were refusing to take their seat and were demanding more drinks. I instructed her to go back and take a seat and to be prepared for some "turbulence".

After moving the controls back and forth to simulate rough air, I turned on the seatbelt sign and made a PA announcement that some flights ahead of us were experiencing some turbulence, and requested that all passengers return to their seats. About a half an hour later, with only a few instances of self-induced turbulence, the flight attendant came back and reported that the passengers had all gone to sleep.

The remainder of the flight to L.A. was quiet and peaceful, and we even received a few compliments from the passengers about the great flight upon their departure. Being a captain often entailed more than just flying the plane.

Captain Parrott and 707-320B

During this time period, revenue flights had to have about 65% of their load factor in order to break even. Whenever there were open seats, airline employees and their families had pass privileges, so I would often get a first class pass for one of my sons to accompany me on domestic flights. At that time I could also bring them up to the cockpit to sit in the jump seat or "flight observer's seat". On December 30, 1967, my youngest son Jeff joined me on a flight to Minneapolis. We toured the twin cities and enjoyed the sights, even visiting the Northwest Airlines Dispatch and Flight Planning facility. I made a similar trip with my middle son, Don, in July of 1968, and on October 10, 1969, my oldest son, Joe, joined me on a flight to Washington D.C., where we visited the Smithsonian and viewed the Lunar Rock. It was great to have opportunities to travel with all of my sons and give them the experience of seeing new places.

On June 28, 1969, Northwest accepted a contract with the Air Force to provide air freight service to several of its mid-Pacific islands. We provided a 707 freighter and a flight crew of three for that operation, and the crew did their own dispatching and weight and balance computations. It was really a "barnstorming" operation. Our first flight for them was on June 29, 1969 out of Hickam Air Force Base in Hawaii, to Midway Island and then back to Hickam.

Midway Island was an interesting place. It was very small and the airport covered most of the island's surface. After we had landed and unloaded our freight, we taxied for our takeoff and our return to Hickam AFB in Hawaii. As we taxied out, we were joined on the taxiway by several Albatross (the actual bird, not the aircraft). They waddled along, moving slowly, and finally began beating their wings frantically, trying to take off. They finally got airborne and were off. I later learned that Albatross can fly out to sea and stay airborne for days — a more proficient aviator than even our jets!

The next day, on June 30, we flew from Hickam to Eniwetok Atoll in the Marshall Islands, with stops at Johnston Island and Kwajalein. During our layover at Eniwetok we ate and slept in the Air Force facilities, and that evening we were able to join the Air Force personnel at an outdoor movie theater. The next morning, we returned to Hickam with stops in Kwajalein and Johnston Island, and while we were taxiing for takeoff at Kwajalein, we were told to hold on the run up area because there was an incoming test missile from Vandenberg Air Force Base, California. It wasn't long before we saw the missile, and watched it splash down in the center of the bay.

We made one more flight from Hickam to Kwajalein and back on July 2, for a total of 29 hours' flight time during that four-day operation.

Doppler Navigation Instructor
In March of 1970, I checked out as an instructor for Doppler navigation. Doppler radar was the first on board,

pilot only navigation (it did not depend on ground based aids). It consisted of four vertical radar legs, and as they traveled across the surface they would return a course direction and speed using the Doppler Effect. In essence, we would bounce a microwave signal off of a desired target, and would analyze the changes in the wave after it had returned to determine the target's velocity and range in relation to the radar.

When over smooth waters, the radar legs would often drop out and we would resort to using Long Range Air Navigation (LORAN) signals to plot our position and update the Doppler computer. We could also use our on-board radar to plot our position off of the Kurile Islands along our North Pacific route. Our radar was capable of plotting a line of position and distance in relation to the island. Programming the flight check points into the computer and updating them was the primary function of the flight crew.

Prior to Doppler, flights across the Pacific and to the Orient required a professional navigator in order to maintain the proper flight path, but with Doppler the pilots did the navigation. During all of my flights as co-pilot and captain in the 707, the Doppler was used to navigate, so I was familiar with how it worked. Since we had expanded our Pacific routes and added the Boeing 747, all of which required new co-pilots and captains, the airline was in need of more Doppler training for those that were new to the technology.

On March 10, 1970, I made my first flight as a Doppler Instructor on a Boeing 707 freighter from Seattle to Tokyo with a stop in Anchorage. The flight went well and the pilots did great.

On a later flight as Doppler Instructor, I was in the jump seat of another 707 freighter when the side cockpit window cracked during our ascent out of Anchorage. We turned the airplane around and returned to the airport, fearing that the window would fail completely and depressurize the aircraft. The Anchorage maintenance crew

132

replaced the cracked window and we took off again and headed for Tokyo. That was the only pressurization scare during my career as a jet pilot, and I was very thankful that Boeing had installed double windows.

Cub Captain Training

On June 1, 1970, the chief pilot assigned me as a Cub Captain Instructor. Northwest had a new program for initial captain qualification training, in which the new captain would bid a monthly schedule and would then act as captain on those trips, but with a senior captain acting as co-pilot. Most of these trips were a short haul, and I ended up doing this for three new captains. It was a very enjoyable, rewarding assignment, helping those up-and-coming captains to reach their potential.

One of my proudest moments as a pilot instructor, however, came on September 5, 1970. It was my oldest son, Joe's, *sixteenth birthday*, and I had been instructing him in our Citabria for over a year. On his birthday, I signed him off for solo flight at the airport in Auburn, Washington. We had done all of his training out of the Kent airport, but it was too windy there that day, so we flew to Auburn. It was an amazing experience seeing my passion for flight getting passed down to my first son, and I truly enjoyed watching the Citabria take off and return safely after a successful first solo flight.

Air Vietnam

On December 19, 1970, I departed Seattle on a freighter flight to Tokyo with an overnight stop in Anchorage. Upon arrival in Tokyo, I was assigned as one of the three captains to fly Air Vietnam flights for the next two months.

Air Vietnam was a South Vietnam scheduled air carrier, and they had a number of routes out of Saigon to other points in South Vietnam, and to other points in East Asia. They flew all of those routes in a Boeing 727, but their 727 was in a maintenance shop in Hong Kong for major maintenance and overhaul, so they contracted Northwest Airlines to fly those routes until its airplane was back in operation.

Northwest furnished a Boeing 707-320B, three flight crews, and a maintenance crew chief to operate its routes. Air Vietnam furnished flight attendants, dispatchers, and all of the ground personnel.

On December 23, 1970, I flew my first Air Vietnam flight from Hong Kong to Saigon, South Vietnam. That day happened to be TET, or the Chinese New Year, so upon reaching the Caravel Hotel in downtown Saigon (which was to be our home for the next two months), we were welcomed by fireworks and dancing in the streets. It was quite an experience for a country boy from Washington!

Doug (left) in Saigon

Even when there weren't ongoing TET celebrations, Saigon was a lively place. It was densely populated; the streets congested with bicycles and pedestrians carrying buckets and other various packages. Our hotel faced the town square and on one side of the square was the Capitol Building. Around the rest of the square were several restaurants and shops, and the restaurants actually served some very good meals. I always enjoyed walking through the square, checking out the shops, and getting away from the congestion of the streets.

On one of these walks through the square, I noticed a large group of well-dressed Vietnamese standing on the steps of the Capitol Building. I watched as the local police came and asked them to leave and the group then dispersed peaceably. The next day, after a flight to Hong Kong, I picked up a Hong Kong newspaper and read an associated press story about a riotous protest at the Capitol Building in Saigon the previous day — evidence that the press anywhere can so often skew the facts in order to sell papers.

As another means to pass the time in Saigon, I also joined a French Club. Vietnam had been a French territory before the war, and the club was Le Cercle Sportif Saigonnais (The Saigon Sports Circle). Some of the flight crew members had been invited to join, and the meetings made for some very interesting conversations. They were all U.S. citizens, trained by the U.S. FAA and assigned to Saigon.

One of the international flights that Air Vietnam offered was into Singapore, and I truly enjoyed the flights into Singapore. It was a beautiful country with friendly people and some fine hotels and restaurants. There was one hotel in particular that had a very nice lounge and restaurant, and we would always meet there and listen as a musical group played popular tunes from the past and present. I would often ask them to play "Harbor Lights" — Shirley's and my favorite song when we were dating. On subsequent trips into Singapore, whenever the group saw me enter the lounge, they would play "Harbor Lights".

While on a trip to the Orient with Shirley and the boys several years later, we stopped in Singapore and stayed at the same hotel. We unpacked, cleaned up, and headed down to the lounge, and when the musical group saw me, they immediately started to play our song. Shirley was amazed, as was I, that they still remembered me and my song after all those years.

Doug with Air Vietnam flight attendants

Unfortunately, due to the scheduling of our flights overseas, I was unable to make it home for Christmas in 1970. Shirley was disappointed that I would not be home on Christmas day with her and the boys. I was able to call her on an overseas telephone to wish them a Merry Christmas, but it was difficult to talk with the delay and the static. I finally arrived home on December 30, and although it was late, we all enjoyed our Christmas celebration together. While I was home, Shirley and I flew the Citabria for two hours over the snow-covered Cascade Mountains. The beauty of the mountains nearly made up for my absence, and we did our best to enjoy each day until my return to Saigon on January 9th.

The domestic flights for Air Vietnam were usually

between Saigon and Danang, near the border of North and South Vietnam. Those flights were always full, and oftentimes were even overfull. Our 707 had twenty seats in the first class section and one hundred seats in coach, so the Vietnamese, being small people, would often sit two to a seat in the first class section. This made it hard to know exactly how many passengers were on board, and most would stand on the seats and crouch down to fasten the seatbelt around them (their regulations were obviously more lax than in the U.S.). This made for some very dirty seats, but we left the seating arrangement to the cabin attendants as long as we knew that our weight and balance were within limits.

It was always interesting to see their carry-on luggage. On flights going north to Danang, the passengers often carried fruits and vegetables, and on their return flights to Saigon they would be carrying tools and other hardware that they had acquired from the military surplus stores in Danang.

The Vietnam War was still going on at this time, with the Viet Cong active in the Saigon area. They would sometimes fire at incoming jet transports with small arms, but the bigger jets were going faster than they appeared, so the shots were always behind the airplane. I only know of one hit—a Pan Am 707 that landed with a small arms hole in one of its engine nacelles.

On January 16, 1971, we took off from Saigon on a flight to Danang, and during takeoff we heard a loud thump. The 707 landing gear would always give a bit of thump when retracting into the wheel wells, so we didn't think anything of it. We immediately got a call from the Saigon Control Tower asking if we were okay, and they informed us that two rockets had been fired at the airplane and gone off just behind us. Fortunately for us, and for everyone on board, the Viet Cong had not led us enough and missed their target. A few minutes later, the Tower called and reported that the local military had located the Viet Cong who had fired the rockets and wiped them out.

On February 2, 1971, during our return flight to Saigon from Kuala Lumpur, we experienced a hydraulic failure. We went through the check list for such an incident, manually lowered the landing gear, and made a no flap landing in Saigon. We stopped the airplane on the runway and waited for a tug to tow us to the parking ramp. Once again, Paul Soderlind's Standard Operating Procedures had worked perfectly.

On flights from Saigon to Bangkok, we would stop in Phnom Penh, Cambodia to drop off and pick up passengers and cargo. The Phnom Penh airport had been built by the Russians, and the paved runways were always rough. The Russian influence was also made known by a Russian Antonov AN-2, a very large cabin single engine biplane parked on one of the ramps. It was about the size of a Ford tri-motor.

On one trip to Phnom Penh, I went into the terminal building to take a look around, and came upon a small shop that specialized in souvenir goods. Shirley liked to collect spoons from all of the places that we had visited or that I had flown to, so I asked the man running the shop if he had any souvenir spoons from Phnom Penh, Cambodia. He did not have any that day, so I told him that I would be returning the next day and he said that he would bring a spoon from his home.

That night the terminal building was gutted by a fire. The fire had been started after the Khmer Rouge, a group of militants dedicated to the communist party in Cambodia, had shelled the area. I went inside, and there he was — in a makeshift stand, selling his wares. I approached his stand, and when he saw me he held up the spoon. I gave him an extra good tip, wished him well, and went on my way. That was my last trip to Phnom Penh.

As far as the military usage of aviation goes, thinking changed a great deal between the end of WWII and Vietnam. Since WWII, the U.S. had been working on designing aircraft for jet-age nuclear retaliation against superpowers. The tactics used in the Vietnam War forced changes. They simply had the wrong planes and the wrong kind of training for that type of war.

The on-again off-again bombing patterns forced them to shift the usage of their B-52 Bombers. Vietnam was also the last time that the US sent a significant number of propeller-driven, fixed wing aircraft into combat, making it the end of an aviation era. This made way for the mass implementation of helicopters in military operations. It was essentially a complete makeover of the United States Air Force, shifting from a focus on massive, nuclear-force retaliation after WWII, to a more wide-spread, multifunctional force that was able to operate across the entire spectrum of military aviation.

From December 23, 1970 to February 14, 1971, I flew over 150 hours for Air Vietnam, most of them from Saigon to Danang. I never witnessed combat firsthand, but I did experience the residual effects, both as a pilot and as an American citizen. I returned home on February 15th, much to Shirley's and my relief, and our family life returned to normal.

Note from Air Vietnam Chief of Flight Operations

Back Home

Although it was very nice to be back in the United States and the flights that I was more accustomed to, even the domestic flights were not without incident. I remember one instance when I was a captain on a return flight from Newark to Seattle, and on the final leg of the flight we had a complaint from one of the first class passengers.

A college student had boarded with a first class ticket on his way home from spring break. He was wearing a sleeveless, V-neck shirt, and seated next to him was a business man wearing a suit and tie; a more common attire for passengers at that time. The business man complained about having to sit next to "hairy armpits" so the stewardess went out to the passenger agent to ask for a possible change in seating assignment for the student. The plane was full, so the young man was asked to deplane. When he refused, I was asked to go speak to the boy and have him removed. I informed him that his checked bag would be brought to him in the terminal, where he could get properly dressed and take the next flight to Seattle. The first class passengers all thanked me for removing the boy from the flight, as his hairy armpits were simply not welcome. Needless to say, it was a much different world then than it is today.

Another incident that I can recall from one of my domestic flights was on a Boeing 720B during a non-stop flight from Seattle to the Dulles Airport in Washington D.C. After reaching our cruising altitude, I made a public service announcement as we crossed over Miles City, announcing the Yellowstone River below us. Immediately after the announcement, the lead flight attendant came to the cockpit and informed me that we had a family onboard that were supposedly returning to Great Falls, Montana from Portland Oregon. They had been mistakenly boarded onto our flight, and when they heard that we were over Miles City, they knew that the plane was well past Great Falls.

The family had a six-month old baby with a serious

respiratory condition that required a special formula medication. The passengers had only brought enough medication for the expected two-hour flight to Great Falls, and the remainder of the medication was in their checked bags, which were on their way to Great Falls. The baby appeared to be feverish and flushed, and was very fussy and cranky. Considering the baby's condition, we diverted our flight back to Great Falls, and upon landing, all of the passengers were de-planed and escorted to the nearest restaurant where the airline provided them with a free meal and drinks.

None of the passengers complained, and Northwest actually received some complimentary letters from some of those passengers for the extra service provided for the family. This was a clear indication of a time in airline history when good service was an airline's best competitive tool.

While we didn't always have sickly infants or under-dressed college students on board, we often had Washington State Senators Warren Magnuson and Henry "Scoop" Jackson on the flight from Seattle to Washington D.C. Warren Magnuson would board at Dulles with the assistance of his aides, and he would sleep for the entire flight before being assisted off the airplane in Seattle. Jackson, on the other hand, would always bring a briefcase full of paperwork to attend to.

In May of 1972, Northwest combined Flight 78, a non-stop flight from Seattle to D.C., (an 8 hour and 20-minute flight) with a flight from Dulles Airport to Anchorage, Alaska with a stop at the New York JFK airport. I really enjoyed making that flight, as it included a layover in Washington D.C., and we had some friends from Kent who were living in that area. The man of the family was flying as a captain for United, and I would sometimes pick up some Alaska King Crab in Anchorage to deliver during my layover at Dulles. I am pretty sure that they also appreciated me being on that particular route.

Bob Reeve

Bob Reeve was the founder and president of Reeve Aleutian Airways headquartered in Anchorage, Alaska. The airline pioneered routes from Anchorage along the Aleutian Island Chain as far as Attu Island; the very end of the Alaska Aleutian Chain. This is the most western point of the United States.

Reeve was a barnstormer during the 1920's before joining Pan American-Grace Airways in South America. There he piloted a Ford Trimotor on the famous "Airmail Route 9" from Lima to Santiago, Chile. At 1,900 miles it was the longest aviation route in the world at the time. Tails of Alaskan mining treasure prompted Reeve to head north in 1932. He stowed away on a steamship and arrived in Valdez Alaska with twenty cents to his name. Bob discovered a wrecked Eaglerock aircraft and went to work for the owner repairing it for one dollar a day. When repairs were complete, Reeve leased the airplane from the owner and went into the air charter business. From this modest beginning, Bob Reeve built Reeve Aleutian Airways with scheduled service along the Aleutian Chain and chartered flights to all points in Alaska.

Often when I had an Anchorage layover, I would go to the Reeve offices and visit with Bob Reeve. His daughter Janice Reeve Ogle was now the CEO of Reeve Aleutian Airways. Bob was getting up in years, but still came to his office every day. He was always fun to visit with, and swap flying tales.

On one trip, I bought a new book "Glacier Pilot" which was the story of Bob Reeve. I took it to his office on June 16, 1972, and he autographed it for me. A really elaborate autograph, he not only signed it but included a hand drawn picture of a biplane flying over high Alaskan mountains. I will now quote his autograph, "*A warm welcome back and Aloha to that Tiger of the Skies Capt. Doug Parrott – with my great esteem and all good wishes to you and yours is our fine NWA forever sparkling lines – good fringe benefits (earned) and all happy landings! "Bob Reeve"*

On one of my visits he offered me free transportation on Reeve Aleutian Airways. I later took him up on that offer. My next door neighbor in Kent, Ed Meisenheimer, a pilot for United Airlines, and I flew to Anchorage to fly to Cold Bay, Alaska to go goose hunting. We boarded Reeve Aleutian Airways flight 55, a Lockheed Electra, to Cold Bay, Alaska. Bob Reeve had arranged for us to stay in the Reeve crew barracks at Cold Bay, and to eat at their mess hall. The barracks were comfortable and the food was great.

Ed and I got up early the next morning, with shotguns in hand and walked across some tidelands to an area that was loaded with geese. We got a few and returned to the barracks. As we crossed the tidelands we noticed the huge tracks of a Kodiak bear.

When we got up the next morning we noticed some muddy bear tracks on the side of the barracks, about eight feet up. As we walked to the hunting area the next morning, we really watched over our shoulder for any sign of one of those huge Kodiak bears. Luckily we didn't see any. We did get a whole bunch more geese.

Reeve Aleutian Airways had a flight from Cold Bay to St. Paul Island. They flew the Grumman Widgeon, a two engine amphibian, to carry the mail to the natives living there. The pilot, Dave Kruger, asked me if I would like to ride along and I eagerly accepted. It was a low level flight across the tundra, and on across the sea. On the way across the tundra, a huge Kodiak bear stood up on his hind legs and waved his front legs at us as if trying to knock us down. As we got close to him, he got down on all four and ran really fast. I wouldn't want him chasing me, there is no way that I could out run him.

When we arrived at St. Paul Island, we landed in the bay, then water taxied to the shore, and with extra power ended up on the shore. The natives were there to greet us. It was like Christmas for them to get their mail, which consisted mostly of mail order packages, from Sears and other mail order companies.

We unloaded, and the natives pushed the airplane back into the bay, we then taxied out and took off for our return to Cold Bay.

The next day we flew back to Anchorage and home with bags loaded with geese. It took a couple of days after I returned home to clean all of those geese and put them in the freezer. It was an adventure that neither Ed nor I will ever forget!

1972 NWA Pilot Strike

Northwest Airline Pilots went on strike again on the first of July, 1972. It was only the second strike (the first since the previously mentioning strike over pilot contracts), and it lasted for three months. Some pilots chose to cross the picket lines this time, adding some "scabs" to our pilots list.

During this time, while waiting for the strike to end so I could get back to work, my sons happened to go on a fifty-mile hike across the Cascade Mountains with their Boy Scout troop. I had always been very active with the troop, being a committee member and a Merit Badge councilor, but I was unable to join them for the hike that summer because if the strike happened to come to an end during that time, I would be getting called back to work.

Since I could not join in, Lee Imlay, another NWA captain whose son was also active in Boy Scouts, and I decided that we would fly my Citabria over the hiking trail and drop the boys some ice cream. We packed the ice cream in canvas bags with some dry ice and loaded it into the plane. Flying over the Cascades and following the trail, we eventually spotted the troop. We circled them to get their attention and then made our first drop—a bar of soap attached to a small parachute. The package landed next to the troop, and we laughed as they opened it up and shook their fists at us. We then commenced to dropping the real treat, and while they were happy for the gift, they had to wait about three hours before they could enjoy it because the dry ice had frozen it solid.

After the drop, I climbed to a higher altitude and made a victory roll and a loop. The roll went fine, but the loop stalled out at the top in the thinner air and became more of an Immelmann maneuver.

Pilots Promoting "Neighborly" Program

A group of Seattle based Northwest pilots organized a program which covered a variety of talks to schools and business groups promoting Northwest Airlines and the airline industry in its efforts of noise abatement and other public concerns with aviation. Northwest pilots bought billboard advertising: *Fly with us, your neighbors*

Pilot Sponsored Billboard

NORTHWEST AIRLINES, INC.

MINNEAPOLIS-ST. PAUL INTERNATIONAL AIRPORT

ST. PAUL, MINNESOTA 55111

OFFICE OF
THE PRESIDENT

May 17, 1972

Dear Mr Parrott:

The article from the Seattle Post-Intelligencer
telling of your promotion program has just come across
my desk.

I appreciate your interest and your efforts in
telling the Seattle area what Northwest Airlines and
its employee group means to that economy. It can be
very effective in our mutual goal of filling seats
and providing job security.

My personal thanks and best wishes.

Sincerely,

Donald W. Nyrop

TO: Captain Don Leonard
     First Officer Marv Peterson
     Second Officer Jim Fernandez
     Captain Doug Parrott
     Captain Bob Bates
     Captain David Beardslee

Letter from Northwest CEO, Donald Nyrop

The Ranch

Shortly before the strike, Mr. Nyrop had set up an employee stock option plan, and I had enrolled to the maximum amount. My hope was to save enough money to someday invest in a ranch in Montana, heeding Mr. Nyrop's advice about property investment. I was worried that he would discontinue the plan in light of the pilots' strike, but fortunately he kept it in place. This plan worked out very well for us, as the FAA required airline pilots to cease flying on scheduled airlines after the age of sixty. Since sixty was far too young to quit working, Shirley and I had decided that it would be great to start a new career as owners and operators of a small ranch.

Shirley and I toured parts of Idaho, eastern Washington, and western and central Montanan in search of a suitable ranch for sale. Having made many stops in Montana on the DC-3 and DC-4 flights, I had a decent idea of some places that would suit our needs. Many of these areas, however, were being developed and the population was increasing at an alarming rate.

We signed up with the United Farm Services and requested listings in south-central Montana. They soon informed us of a ranch near Roundup, so my son Jeff and I got passes on a Northwest flight to Billings, then rented a car and met the Farm Service Agent in Roundup. He took us out to the ranch and showed us around, and we were both very impressed.

I later brought Shirley out to tour the ranch, and she remarked on the lack of trees in the area. I assured her that there were plenty of trees in the Bull Mountains and the Musselshell Valley and that the ranch was located along the Musselshell River and had an abundance of cottonwoods.

We purchased the ranch in the spring of 1972, and provisionally leased it to the son of the agent who had shown it to us.

That summer, we hosted an exchange student from

Japan. His name was Kazuhiro Shiomi, and he told us that he had come over to "discover America". Since Kazuhiro can be an awkward name in America, he agreed to the nickname of Chris, for Christopher Columbus, and to this day he is still known by my family as Chris Shiomi.

Shortly after his arrival, we drove to Roundup to show him the ranch. He was jet-lagged and slept most of the way, missing the beautiful scenery of the mountains and awaking just in time to witness the dry, treeless area west of Harlowton. We asked Chris what he thought, and he drew in a deep breath and responded, "Velly Ronesome".

Luckily, we made another trip later that summer so that Chris could see the real Montana country, and this time we even brought a trailer with two new Hodaka motorcycles. Ed Miley of PABATCO had let us trade two old bikes for new ones, as a gesture of thanks for my efforts in communicating for the company in Japan.

The pilot strike ended on October 1, 1972. I was glad for the return to work, as it afforded me the opportunity to take Chris with me on several flights. We made several trips throughout the U.S. so that Chris could "discover America". The family and I took Chris to Disney Land in California, New York City, and Washington D.C., where we were fortunate enough to witness Ronald Reagan campaigning on the Capitol Steps. Chris probably saw more of America than most Americans do, and I am glad for the opportunity to show him around.

On May 2, 1973, I gave Chris his first flying lesson in our Citabria. It was just an introductory lesson with very little hands on flying, but I think that he truly enjoyed it.

Douglas DC-10

July 31, 1973 was my last 707 flight. Ironically, it was a two hour, six-month check ride, but fortunately I passed with flying colors. My total flight time logged in the 707 was 6,723 hours, and I now had enough seniority to fly the DC-10 out of the Minneapolis pilot base.

Shortly before my last 707 flight, on July 29, I had my first DC-10 simulator flight. It was the first simulator that Northwest owned with a visual feature. There was a moving camera mounted on a wall which had a pictorial map of the area. There were a lot of problems with the camera, and they discontinued its use during my training session. Other than that, it was a very good simulator. I logged eleven hours and thirty minutes in the simulator before starting my flight training in the DC-10.

Northwest Airlines DC-10

The DC-10 is a three engine, wide body jet. Its most distinguishing feature is the two turbofan engines mounted on underwing pylons and a third engine at the base of the vertical stabilizer. It was a successor to the DC-8, and was first introduced in 1970.

The DC-10 had the latest instrumentation, which was almost identical to the instrumentation NWA had installed in the 747. The biggest difference was that it had a V-Bar on the artificial horizon instead of cross bars, which made an ILS approach much easier. An artificial horizon is an instrument that is used to inform the pilot of the airplane's orientation in relation to the Earth's horizon. We used it during climb, cruise, descent and approach, and during climb and descent the altitude that you were climbing or descending to would be entered, and the V-Bar would return you to level flight at the pre-selected altitude. This made hand flying much easier, and made it easier to monitor the auto-pilot.

The DC-10 also had an Inertial Navigation System (INS). It consisted of three units that synchronized the aircraft's position, the same system that NWA used to navigate the Boeing 747s. Northwest also installed the same 747 Pratt and Whitney engine cores on the DC-10. They wanted only one type of engine stored outside of the U.S. mainland. The reason they wanted this consistency was to ensure that, should an airplane need an engine replacement in Tokyo, the same engine core would be available whether it was a DC-10 or a 747. Due to the extra weight of the additional fuel load Northwest also had to install a center landing gear on the DC-10.

Another training requirement that was unique to the DC-10, was being able to compute a "Drift Down Point". This entailed calculating a "point of no return" when flying long distances over water, which meant the point at which the airplane had burned too much fuel to return to its original point of takeoff. Since the DC-10 had only three engines, in the event that one of them failed and a descent to a lower altitude was required to maintain flight, an operation which required a higher fuel burnout, we had to be able to compute the point at which such operations might become risky.

My flight training in the DC-10 was done at Moses Lake, Washington. After eleven hours of training, including my six month check, I was ready for my first flight from Minneapolis to Fort Lauderdale, Florida. After twelve hours of safety pilot time, including a line check, I was cleared to go on scheduled trips without a check pilot.

My first solo trip in the DC-10 was on August 31, 1973. I flew from Portland to Cleveland with a stop at O'Hare. Upon landing in Cleveland, the number two engine overheated and flamed out after going into reverse. This was yet another "first flight" in a new aircraft that ended in misfortune. I was at least happy that the entire airplane didn't burn like the 707 in Yokota.

More General Aviation Flying

On October 9, 1973, my son Don and I flew the Citabria from Kent to our ranch in Roundup. Keeping the family tradition alive, on June 18th of the next year, his sixteenth birthday, Don flew his first solo flight in the Citabria and did an excellent job. It was a great feeling to watch my second son take to the skies.

In the summer of 1974, my nephew Greg Parrott, son of my brother Gene, came to visit us in Roundup. I gave him dual instruction in the Citabria, and he made his first solo flight on June 30, 1974. A few days later, Greg's parents, Gene and Shirley, came to Roundup to visit and to pick up Greg. We went to the airport to show Gene the airplane that Greg had been flying. Greg and I went up for a short flight, and Gene was shocked when we landed, I got out of the plane, and Greg took off by himself. We now had another "flying Parrott" to add to the list.

Before Gene and his family left Roundup to return to Seattle, I gave Greg more dual instruction, some local and some cross-country. Greg went on to fly in the service and for the Government. He later became a helicopter pilot.

In October of 1974 I gave flight instruction to Scott Imlay in the Citabria. Scott is the son of Lee Imlay. Scott is also an Eagle Scout, and was on the hike in the Cascades when Lee and I dropped them the ice cream. Scott was a glider pilot. On October 26, 1974 Scott made his first solo flight in the Citabria. I gave him another three hours of instruction after his first solo flight. Scott went on to get his private pilot's license. Later on Scott competed in many glider events in Eastern Washington State.

After buying the ranch, the family and I moved to the town of Roundup. We kept the ranch leased out until we had everything settled and our new ranch house construction finished. We chose to build on a hill between Highway 12 and the Musselshell River. It had a single, lonely Ponderosa pine on it, and a beautiful view of the Musselshell River Valley. Just below the hill, there was a long flat area north of some irrigated alfalfa fields. It was an ideal spot for a landing strip. I hired a contractor to level the strip, and I planted it with Fairway Crested Wheat Grass. The landing strip was completed before we had even started building the house (first things first!) and Don and I made the first landing on our new ranch on October 6, 1974.

We started construction on our new home in the spring of 1974, and officially moved into the house in January of 1975.

DC-10 Trips

Most of my DC-10 flights were domestic, which included trips to Alaska. One of my favorite trips was a multi-stop flight from Seattle to Newark, with stops in Spokane, Great Falls, Billings, Chicago, and Detroit. It was a very popular flight, running nearly full on most trips.

As always, there were a few trips that were more eventful than others, a truth that kept my job that much more entertaining. On a return trip out of Newark to Detroit, a first class passenger became very drunk and began to offend the other passengers with his childish antics. The stewardess informed me of the problem after landing in Detroit, so I went back to tell the man that he would have to de-plane in Detroit. He refused and started to rant and rave, so I went into the terminal and requested the assistance of a terminal guard. He was removed from the aircraft, his ranting continuing into the terminal. He began to demand that his luggage be brought to him, but I told him I would not allow him to delay the flight any longer, and that his luggage would be returned to Detroit on the next flight from Chicago. The passengers were very grateful for the removal of the drunk, some even writing to Northwest and praising my actions.

152

NORTHWEST AIRLINES, INC.
MINNEAPOLIS-ST. PAUL INTERNATIONAL AIRPORT
ST. PAUL, MINNESOTA 55111

OFFICE OF
THE PRESIDENT

January 7, 1974

Dear Doug Parrott:

I am pleased to send on to you the following comments from Mr. Robert L. Waligunda of Princeton, New Jersey:

"My letter is written to commend and compliment the actions of Captain Douglas Parrott on Flight 245 on December 7, 1974.

"Captain Parrott had three rude, obscene and rowdy passengers deplane in Detroit, rather than continue on the flight to further disrupt and discomfort the remaining passengers in the cabin.

"I find it quite refreshing in knowing that the pilot of my airplane has that kind of concern and consideration for my well being. He certainly deserves a gold star for professionalism!"

Thanks for your good handling of an unfortunate situation -- I am sure your action was also welcomed by other passengers on this flight.

Sincerely,

Donald W. Nyrop

cc: Personnel Dept.

Captain Douglas Parrott
Minneapolis/St. Paul

Letter of Appreciation from Donald Nyrop, CEO

On February 15, 1967, on a scheduled flight from Miami to Chicago with a stop in Atlanta, the one and only Bob Hope boarded in Miami, with the destination of Atlanta. After arriving in Atlanta, I stood by the cockpit door, thanking passengers as they de-planed. Mr. Hope had flown first class and was trying very hard to avoid being noticed, so when I thanked him as he passed by he merely nodded and continued on his way. I later learned that he had purposefully left behind his ticket stub with his name on it in the seat pocket in front of him. The lead flight attendant had found it and kept it as a memory of the famous passenger that she had served.

On clear, sunny days during the flight between Great Falls and Billings I would often cancel IFR after contacting Billings Approach Control, and once on VFR, and I would inform Control that I was diverting east. This would take me over our ranch, and sometimes a few miles further over the Roundup Airport. Both our ranch and some of the neighboring ranches had CB radios on HF frequencies, which we also had on the DC-10. I would call my friends and family and tell them to watch for the "big red tail" that would soon be passing by overhead.

Years later, at a Montana Aviation Conference, I met a gentleman who had learned that I was a retired NWA pilot. He asked me if I had ever flown the DC-10 into Billings, and I told him that I had on several occasions. He was a retired Billings Air Traffic Controller, and he asked if I had ever diverted over Roundup on clear days. I laughed and told him, "Yes, that was me." I then explained about our family ranch, and he went on to tell me that he and the rest of his crew had always wondered why I had done that. We have been good friends ever since, and always looked each other up at conferences subsequent to that one.

To entertain ourselves on redeye flights, we would also use the CB to listen in on truckers driving below us. We would hear their conversations warning each other about, "Smokey" who was parked in the vicinity and to "Beware of Smokey." We figured out that "Smokey" was their code word for the Highway Patrol.

On another occasion, we had a flight attendant enter the cockpit as we were eaves dropping, and she took the radio and started to talk to one of the truckers. We later heard him talking to another trucker about his conversation with a "beautiful babe in the sky".

For the most part, the DC-10 was a great airplane to fly. It had a roomy cockpit, a big windshield for great visibility, comfortable pilot seats, and a well-organized instrument panel. The one thing we sometimes had issues with was the electrical system.

Douglas Aircraft Company had designed the electrical system to work with the modern use of an electrical cable to handle several functions. This saved on weight and it functioned quite well the majority of the time, but there were still many logbook write-ups concerning the system.

On one instance, I was scheduled to pick up a DC-10 flight in Chicago. I arrived to find the airplane parked at the gate, with maintenance personnel checking the log book. There had been some problems with the system, and they tried for hours to correct the issue but couldn't get it to work. The flight was delayed and the airplane was pushed away from the gate and taken to the parking area. There were no electrical plugs in the parking area, so the airplane's batteries were turned off and the electrical units were killed. Later, when they towed the plane back to the gate and plugged it back it, they found that the systems were working normally. So, with a spot of good luck, the maintenance personnel learned that shutting down the airplane's power allowed it to re-program, solving many of the electrical problems.

Continued Legacy of Flying
During the summer, we would always spend a lot of time flying the Citabria out of Roundup. In June, July, and August, I gave my youngest son, Jeff, about twelve hours of dual instruction, and on August 25, 1975, Jeff's sixteenth birthday, Jeff made his first solo flight out of the Roundup Airport. Like his brothers before him, he did a great job, and I now had three sons who had soloed on their sixteenth birthdays. I was, and still am, very proud of their accomplishments.

Continuing the hobby on past their sixteenth birthdays, my son Don passed his private pilot check ride on September 9, 1975—another rated pilot in the Parrott family!

Finally in the Boeing 747

In early May of 1976, I bid for a 747 captain position at the Seattle pilot base to be effective August 1st, 1976. On May 15th, I began my simulator training in the 747 Simulator in Minneapolis. On May 27, after 20 hours of simulator training, I completed my training and received my Type Rating for the 747. This gave me Type Ratings in seven aircraft types: the DC-3, DC-4, DC-10, Boeing 707, Boeing 720, Boeing 727, and the Boeing 747. Before I was able to fly with passengers, however, additional training in the actual aircraft was required. On May 28, I flew NWA Ship number 617, a Boeing 747, from Minneapolis to Salinas, Kansas for the additional flight training. This training consisted of steep turns, approaches to stalls, engine shutdown and restart, and one VFR and ILS approach and landing. We also had to do an IFR takeoff with an engine failure on takeoff, followed by an approach with the engine shut down, and then a missed approach with a circle around the field and a three engine landing. Total flight time for the training was four hours.

I continued to fly the DC-10 through July of 1976, and on August 1, I flew a 747 out of Seattle for a night qualification and landing currency. On August 5, 1976, I flew NWA Flight 901, a freighter, from Seattle to Tokyo. I was accompanied by a safety check pilot, as a pilot that was new to an aircraft was required to log 20 hours with a safety pilot before he could fly solo. I then made several trips across the Orient, to both Hong Kong and Seoul, Korea, all of which required the company of a safety pilot, but it was good to be back in the Orient area.

Northwest Airlines Boeing 747

To continue my streak of first flight incidents, on a takeoff from Seoul, the number one engine failed just as we rotated. I continued with the takeoff as we were past the V1 speed to abort. We went through Paul Soderlind's checklist as we climbed, then the tower cleared us to circle back and land. Everything performed as it was supposed to and I landed the plane without incident.

With just that 25 minutes of flight, I now had my 20 hours of flight time and no longer needed my safety pilot, so both he and the FAA check pilot took the next flight back to Tokyo and left me with the broken airplane.

The next day, another NWA 747 arrived in Seoul with a spare engine mounted on its wing. It looked strange with five engines. Maintenance then removed the good engine from that plane and replaced the bad engine on mine. After they had removed it, they mounted the bad engine back onto the wing of my plane so that I could fly it back for repair. With the extra weight, I could not fly at the usual altitudes, but I can now say that I have flown an airplane with five engines!

On August 22, 1976, I was flying a 747 flight from Tokyo to Hong Kong, and after about 45 minutes at cruise altitude, the lead flight attendant came up to the cockpit and told me that there was a first class passenger who wanted to smoke his pipe on the plane. At that time, all NWA aircraft had designated areas for passengers to smoke cigarettes, but smoking was supposed to be limited to only cigarettes. I told the attendant that I would come back and talk to the passenger.

The first class section on the 747s was large and roomy, and our passenger load on that particular flight was very light. I went downstairs and found the man the attendant had asked about, and to my surprise I recognized the man as our former, long time Montana Senator Mike Mansfield. I sat and spoke with him for a while, learning that he was now the Ambassador to Japan. We visited about Montana, discussing my ranch in Roundup, and he was surprised to find a Montana resident as the pilot of a flight in the Orient.

I told him to go ahead and smoke his pipe and enjoy his flight to Hong Kong. Pipe tobacco smells much better than cigarette smoke anyways. Later, in 1988, Northwest would become the first airline to ban all smoking on domestic flights.

Maule M-5 and the Twin Bonanza

Between all of my flights for Northwest, I would never pass on an opportunity to log some hours in a new airplane make or model. A neighboring rancher friend of ours in Montana, Henry Bedford, had borrowed a Maule M-5 from one of his friends, and I used it to give rides to some family and friends in the area. The Maule M-5 had been introduced only a few years prior in 1974, and I was also giving Henry some dual instruction time in both the M-5 and our Citabria. He wanted to learn to fly so that he could check cattle on his extensive ranch.

On February 7, 1977, we took the M-5 up to a ranch in Alberta, Canada that belonged to a friend of Henry's. It was the Ben Graves ranch near High River, Alberta, and while we were there, I also gave some dual instruction time to the owners of the ranch, Ben and Patty Nelson. Both the flight to Alberta and the return flight were dual instruction time for Henry.

I also got the opportunity to fly a Twin Bonanza when a Dr. Davis, who was also a pilot and an FAA designated medical examiner, moved into Roundup to practice medicine. He had originally asked me if I was interested in going in on a DC-3 with him, but since I was so busy with the ranch and NWA I turned him down, so he purchased a Beechcraft Twin Bonanza instead. He flew it to our ranch on February 20, 1977, where I got on board and after a brief rundown of the plane's instruments, flew it to Bozeman with both Dr. Davis and my son Don. It was a roomy, comfortable aircraft with good takeoff and landing characteristics, but it was not very fast for being a twin engine airplane with that amount of horsepower.

On March 30, 1977, I went to Port Townsend, Washington to test out Captain Marty Fredrickson's Cessna 180. Marty was a retired NWA pilot and he had been a part of the ALPA negotiating committee during our 1968/69 contract negotiations. Marty wanted to sell his Cessna, and I wanted to trade the Citabria for a four place airplane so that I could fly the whole family. We made a deal, and I ended up selling the Citabria to another former NWA pilot, Norm DeShon.

First 747 non-stop flight from Chicago to Tokyo

On June 8, 1977, I was co-captain on Northwest Airlines Inaugural non-stop flight from Chicago to Tokyo. Because the flight time was scheduled for over 12 hours, the rules required a double crew. I flew in the left seat for the takeoff from Chicago, while the other captain was in the crew rest area. We traded off during the flight, and he landed in Tokyo. We switched for the return flight, me in the rest area for takeoff and up front for the landing. With a flight time of twelve hours and forty minutes from Chicago to Tokyo, and eleven hours and forty minutes for the return flight, we held the world record for flight times between Chicago and Tokyo for at least a few days. Subsequent flights surely beat our time, but at least I can claim that I was a record holder for a short while. Later we flew non-stop flights from JFK in New York to Tokyo Japan. The following are some interesting facts about those flights:

Trip Data

Flight Time	13:10 Hours
Fuel Consumed	
Start/Taxi	2,440 pounds
Enroute	297,200 pounds
Alternate	7,200 pounds
10% reserve	21,700 pounds
Intl reserve	9,100 pounds
Total Fuel	337,740 pounds
-or-	48,250 gallons
Total Weight Take off	734,000 pounds
Total Weight Landing	437,200 pounds

Fun 747 Facts

Length 231 feet (on a football field the nose would be on the ten yard line and the tail on the opposite ten yard line. The first two Wright brother's flights could have been flown inside a 747)

Wing span	196 feet
Tail height	96 feet
Cockpit height	32 feet (40 feet in landing attitude)
Nose wheel to main gear	90 feet

Takeoff Thrust	54,000 pounds per engine
Total Thrust	216,000 pounds
Maximum Takeoff Weight	800,000 pounds
Maximum Landing Weight	630,000 pounds

The flight time from New York to Tokyo was only 30 minutes longer than the flight time from Chicago to Tokyo even though a direct flight from New York to Chicago required two hours and twenty minutes. This illustrates the efficiency of the great circle routes.

Emergency Frequency 121.5
During flights, Northwest crews would generally monitor the emergency frequency 121.5 on one of the communications radios. On a few occasions, I would hear a signal and would then try to determine its location and transmit the information to the Air Traffic Control Center.

On Christmas day, 1978, while crossing Alaska at 39,000 feet on NWA flight 3 from Chicago to Tokyo, we picked up a distress call as we passed south of Point Barrow, Alaska. It was a single engine Cessna with only one pilot on board, and when we answered his call he informed us that he had gotten lost north of Umiat, could not receive any navigation aids, and was running low on fuel. We passed the information, along with his aircraft identification number (N34651) on to ZAN Radar Sector. Point Barrow Radar located the airplane and established radio contact. He ran out of fuel 80 miles south of his destination and made an emergency landing, but was uninjured and soon picked up by search and rescue.

Fuel Score
On long, overwater flights, we always kept a fuel score. This was compiled at selected reporting points en-route, and in constructing our flight plan we would compute the fuel that should be remaining at each check point. If we encountered stronger head winds than expected or if we had to fly at lower altitudes for some reason, we would burn more fuel and would record a negative fuel score. If, conversely, we had lighter winds than planned, we would have a positive fuel score.

On one of my non-stop flights from Chicago to Tokyo, the traffic out of Chicago was heavy, resulting in our having to fly below our flight-planned altitude for over an hour. On top of this, we encountered strong headwinds across Canada, resulting in a negative fuel score. Our route took us over Anchorage, so I decided to land at Anchorage for more fuel before crossing over the Pacific (as the old saying goes, there are bold pilots and there are old pilots, but there are no old, bold pilots). However, with the fuel we had on board, we were above the gross landing weight for the 747, and had to dump enough fuel to get down to the required weight.

Anchorage ARTC Center
5400 Davis Highway
Anchorage, Alaska   99506

JAN 18 1979

Mr. Stewart Lee
Director of Flight Operations
Northwest Airlines
Minneapolis-St. Paul International Airport
St. Paul, Minnesota   55111

Dear Mr. Lee:

On Christmas day 1978, your Flight 3 alerted us to a radio transmission
from a lost aircraft in northern Alaska.

The enclosed Flight Assist Report describes the series of events resulting
from the initial information received from NW3.

Please convey our appreciation to the flight crew for monitoring 121.5 while
flying over Alaska.

This is only one of many similar assists from air carriers that has occurred
over the years. In this instance, the fact that the lost pilot's transmis-
sions were heard may have saved his life as he had no winter survival gear
on the aircraft. Without the efforts made following initial alerting of
problem by your flight, the aircraft could have been forced to land in an
unknown area and not have been located for some time.

Sincerely,

DONALD A. ENDERS
Chief, Anchorage ARTC Center

Enclosure

Letter of Appreciation from Chief of ARTC Center

I made a PA announcement that we were stopping for
fuel because of the unexpected headwinds, and as we
descended we began dumping fuel. Safety procedures
required that there was no smoking if fuel had to be dumped,

so I got back on the PA and announced to the passengers that the no smoking sign would be on as we dumped some fuel. As you can imagine, this lead to some confused passengers, announcing that we were dumping fuel shortly after the announcement that we were having to land in Anchorage so that we could get more fuel.

The passengers deplaned for a short time in Anchorage, and while we were waiting, one of the passengers approached me and asked, "If we had to stop for fuel, why did we dump fuel?"

I explained the gross weight requirement to him, and later gave another brief explanation over the PA so that the rest of the passengers would understand our unscheduled landing.

My "Space Shuttle Landing"

During this time period, NASA was frequently in the news with its manned shuttle explorations. I was always impressed with their ability to return from outer space and land in Florida without having any engine power. They would use a very long and precise glide.

Interested in the techniques of such a procedure, I decided to try and see if I could duplicate the astronauts' landings. It was on a New York to Minneapolis 747 freighter flight which stopped in Detroit and Milwaukie. We departed Detroit in the wee hours of the morning, and at that time of day there were very few other flights in the sky. Upon departing Detroit, I climbed to our assigned cruising altitude, which we reached about halfway to Milwaukie. At that point, I requested descent and a straight in, visual approach to runway 25 left. ATC gave us the request, and as we descended I retarded all four engines to idle thrust, and began the descent.

I did not touch the power again throughout the descent, approach, and the landing on Runway 25L. We slowed to 250 knots at 10,000 feet as required, slowed even further to extend flaps and gear for landing, continued on the ILS approach to landing at the proper air speeds, and landed safely. After touchdown, I touched the throttles for the first time since the start of the descent to put the airplane into reverse thrust. We had successfully duplicated the space shuttle's approach and landing without the use of power. It left us with a feeling of accomplishment, and we did it all without violating any rules or procedures.

A Return to Spraying Crops

Deciding we didn't have enough on our plates, we completed the purchase of a two section wheat ranch in Golden Valley County, just west of our ranch. The land laid north and south of U.S. Highway 12, and the crop was planted in alternating strips of summer fallow and wheat crops.

In May of 1978, we purchased a spray unit to install on our Cessna 180. The tank, along with a wind driven pump, was strapped under the fuselage between the main landing gear. The spray booms were hung under the wing struts and a flagger unit was attached to the side of the airplane. The control handle to turn the spray off and on was located on the right side of the cockpit.

I passed the FAA inspection for the aircraft on May 4, and for the first time in 23 years, was back spraying crops. It was different spraying strips rather than the large square fields that I was used to. The flagger unit on the airplane also took some getting used to, but the strips were relatively easy to cover. The powerlines along the highway were high enough to fly under, which made the process go faster.

We farmed that land until 1986 and then put it into the Conservation Reserve Program. I sprayed the wheat crop, as well as some of the neighbor's crops, each year for nine years. We still have the spray unit in the barn.

Doug with Cessna 180 set up for crop spraying

NYC Blizzard of 1978

On January 19, 1978 I flew a 747 freighter flight from Minneapolis into New York's JFK airport. The weather forecast was for a cold front to hit New York at about our estimated arrival time. We arrived at JFK, made our approach and landed without any problem. The storm hit right after our arrival, and closed all of the airports in the New York area. The airports remained closed for three days. We departed on January 22, 1978 in "Blue Bird Weather" for our return flight to Minneapolis. While waiting out the storm here at JFK, I composed a letter to Mike Ferguson, Chairman of the Montana Aeronautic Division.

While flying in and out of the Billings airport, both in my light plane and Northwest Airlines flights, I had noticed on numerous occasions light aircraft taxiing too close behind jet transports. I thought that if this information were published, it might save a light plane from being upset and damaged from jet thrust velocities.

Montana and the Sky Newsletter
Kennedy International Airport, January 20, 1978

Dear Mike:

I'm sitting here in New York in the middle of the "Blizzard of '78". The winds are 35 to 50 knots, the three major New York airports are closed by drifting snow and my 747 flight out is grounded. As I look out the window the thought occurs to me as to what a handful my Cessna 180 would be just trying to taxi around in a wind like that; a good day to leave it in the barn and enjoy the day in front of the fireplace.

Which all brings to mind a common hazard that we light plane pilot's face at some of our Montana airports that have jet air carrier operations. That is, the wind velocities and temperatures coming out of the tailpipes of those turbojet engines. Following are some figures that I would like to share with you and that you might like to pass along to our Montana light plane pilot friends through your monthly Aeronautics Division bulletin.

Each engine of a 727, 737, or DC-9 produces wind velocities and temperatures:

AT IDLE THRUST:

15 feet behind 230 mph	*265 degrees centigrade*
25 feet behind 135 mph	*200 degrees centigrade*
40 feet behind 90 mph	*150 degrees centigrade*
50 feet behind 70 mph	*100 degrees centigrade*

AT TAKEOFF THRUST:

10 feet behind 990 mph	*590 degrees centigrade*
20 feet behind 610 mph	*350 degrees centigrade*
30 feet behind 410 mph	*250 degrees centigrade*
60 feet behind 205 mph	*150 degrees centigrade*

Each engine of a 747, DC-10 or L1011 produces wind velocities and temperatures:

AT IDLE THRUST:

45 feet behind 400 mph	*200 degrees centigrade*
55 feet behind 320 mph	*150 degrees centigrade*

60 feet behind 290 mph	100 degrees centigrade

AT TAKEOFF THRUST:

40 feet behind 990 mph	125 degrees centigrade
45 feet behind 250 mph	110 degrees centigrade
50 feet behind 185 mph	100 degrees centigrade
60 feet behind 125 mph	80 degrees centigrade

From the above you can see that following too closely behind a jet would make New York's "Blizzard of '78" look like a pussy cat. Also, it is interesting to note that the smaller jets with their lower by-pass engines are just as bad at the higher thrust levels as the "Jumbos' high by-pass engines. Taxing a jet is similar to taxiing a prop in that once moving, idle thrust is sufficient to keep moving unless you are extra heavy, in soft asphalt or snow, or taxiing up hill. Like a prop, it takes more than idle thrust to break away and start moving. Most jet takeoffs are computed on a rolling start, thereby requiring thrust to be accelerating as the jet turns onto the runway starting its takeoff roll.

So don't do your run up too close behind a jet that is awaiting takeoff clearance and has not yet lined up on the runway.

I hope that this is of interest to you and it may just be food for thought to keep some of our friends from following too closely behind a jet and possibly spoiling their whole day.

See you around,

/s/ Doug Parrott, Capt. NWA, Roundup, MT

Jeff's Night Instruction

During May of 1978, I gave son Jeff some dual night instruction at the Roundup Airport. The Roundup Airport had runway lights that were controlled by the pilot, and to turn them on the pilot had to tune his radio to the UNICOM frequency 122.8 and press the microphone button three times. The runway lights would then turn on, and stay on for about a half hour.

On that night, we had made a couple of landings in the Cessna, and after one landing, while lining up for another takeoff, the runway lights went out. Jeff said, "I guess we have

168

to put another nickel in." He then hit the microphone three times, the lights came back on, and away we went to complete his private pilot night requirements.

On May 24, Jeff and I flew to Columbus, Montana to meet Gary Wolterman, an FAA Designated Examiner who had agreed to give Jeff his private pilot rating check ride. I explained to Gary the spray unit that was attached to the Cessna, along with all of its components, and he agreed that all was okay. Jeff passed with flying colors, giving us another rated pilot in the Parrott family.

Total Eclipse

On February 26, 1979, on a flight from Tokyo to Chicago, we were lucky enough to witness a total eclipse of the sun from the air. We watched the eclipse develop, the flight attendants providing materials from Tokyo to make sun shades to help the passengers view the event. It was very interesting to watch the moon slowly cover the sun, its shadow sliding across the earth below us. It was forecast to become a total eclipse at around the time we would fly past Portland.

There were other light aircraft departing Portland to view and photograph the event, and we asked center for permission to make a 360 degree turn in order for our passengers to get another good look. It was a very rare occurrence, especially to be viewed from the air. People's excitement for the phenomenon also reached our ranch in Roundup, as many hot air balloons were launched from the nearby airport in Lavina, Montana to view the eclipse. Shirley watched it from the deck of our house, waving to and even carrying a short conversation with one of the balloons as it passed by.

First Flight to Europe

On June 1, 1979, I flew NWA Flight 34, a Boeing 747, from Boston to Prestwick, Scotland. It was my first flight to

Europe and was a 6 hour and 15-minute flight. The Scottish ground crews were our first indication of how friendly the Scottish people are, but they were a bit difficult to understand. After we'd parked, one of the ground crew informed us that, "Yer chokes are in and ya cn' set yer parkbreakes", but his accent was so thick that I was unsure about what he'd said. The second officer double checked and reported back that the chocks were in.

I really enjoyed the layovers in Scotland, our hotel being the Turnberry Arms which was located on the Turnberry Golf Course, which is famous for hosting many British Opens. On one of my layovers I rode a train to Edinburg, observing one golf course after another along the entire route. While in Edinburg, I purchased an authentic, plaid Scottish skirt for Shirley. She really admired the gift and still wears it today.

During another layover, we met up with another NWA crew and four of us took a taxi to a nearby village for a drink. At the tavern, we challenged some of the locals to a game of darts. They were all very experienced and beat all of us except for one captain from the other crew.

The tavern closed at midnight, at which point we learned that the taxis were no longer running. Fortunately, the music group who had been playing at the tavern offered us a ride. They had a small car, however, and with all of their equipment, we were left to sit on each other's laps. This was yet another example of the friendliness exhibited by the Scottish people.

Flying a Glider

In January of 1980, Shirley and I traveled to Phoenix to visit our old neighbors, Lee and Boots Imlay. Lee was very active with a nearby glider club in Estella, Arizona. I joined Lee and we watched the gliders being towed for takeoff behind a Piper Ag plane. I was impressed with how precise their approaches and landings were.

Lee was able to procure one of the club's gliders and

arranged for a tow plane. He then strapped me into the front seat and explained the controls, including the release lever that detached the glider from the plane. Lee rode in the rear seat and away we went.

The takeoff was a thrill, and after the release, Lee headed for a nearby hill which had a good updraft. Once we'd reached a higher altitude, Lee turned control of the glider over to me. It was light on the controls and required coordinated use of ailerons and rudder. To indicate off center or uncoordinated turns, there was a string that hung in the middle of the windshield. After forty-five minutes of flight, we landed, and I now had forty five minutes of glider time in my logbook.

The experience made me want to add a glider rating to my license, so I later returned to Arizona to log another hour. Unfortunately, my dear friend Lee became ill sometime after that and could no longer fly. I have since considered looking for a place that gives glider instruction, and am still interested in the rating.

NWA Ad in Japanese Newspapers

While on layover at Narita, Japan, NWA Chief Dispatcher, Morita, called me at the hotel and asked me if I would pose for a picture to be used in a NWA newspaper ad, featuring its Trans-Pacific service.

That afternoon a Newspaper photographer arrived at the hotel, called my room, and asked me to dress in my NWA Captains uniform. He came to my room and took a lot of pictures.

I never saw the newspapers with the ad but I couldn't have read them anyway. Morita sent me this page that he had copied from one of the newspapers. I don't know what it says, except for the route diagram, and the funny face.

Tokyo Newspaper Advertisement

1980 ALPA Negotiations

The agreement that we had reached for pilot contract in 1972 was set to expire on June 30, 1980. Northwest and ALPA were scheduled to meet regarding the new contract, and I was appointed chairman of the negotiating committee. Our MEC Chairman was Thomas Beedem.

I proposed that we try to start negotiations early, hoping to come to an agreement at a much earlier time than we had in the past. I contacted Terry Erskine, the new Director of Labor Relations for Northwest Airlines, who had recently replaced Homer Kinney. Terry did not agree, so I then contacted the new President of Northwest, Joseph Lapensky.

After we discussed our proposal with Mr. Lapensky, he pondered it for a bit before saying that he would check on it. He then brightened up and said with a smile, "I don't have to check on it, I'm now president!" He had worked under Don Nyrop for so many years that he still carried some of his old habits. He eventually agreed that it was a good idea to start negotiations early, and the next day I got a call from Terry Erskine, setting March 20 as a date to meet and exchange opening letters.

After the first meeting, we scheduled more

negotiations, and each meeting brought more proposals from each side, as well as more progress. The process went much more smoothly than the first time. Mr. Erskine was much more willing to have give-and-take discussions with us than Homer Kinney ever was.

We were almost done with negotiations by our amendable date of June 30. Roger Bruggemeyer, our spokesman for the changes that we wanted to make in pilot retirement plans, addressed some of the provisions that he wanted made at the last meeting. The committee referred Roger to the proposal, showing that they had already made the changes, and with a little "egg on his face", he agreed with the company's proposal as it was exactly what he had asked for.

The agreement was completed and signed on June 28, two days early. This was a first for both Northwest Airlines and its pilots!

More Guests at the Ranch

In August of 1980, Yoshi and Nobuhiro Kubodera visited us in Roundup. They were the sons of one of the Japanese gentlemen that I had met while doing business for the Pacific Basin Trading Company. It was interesting because Mr. Kubodera had three sons, all about the same age as my sons, and his oldest son, Yoshi, was even born on the same day as our oldest son, Joe.

The next month, we also had a guest exchange with Germany. Our guests were Gerhard and Erica Krahm from Peine, West Germany. Erica spoke very good English, but Gerhard spoke none. To communicate, he simply pointed and used non-verbal signs. He was a fireman in Germany, and was very interested in our ranch operations.

I flew most of our guests out over the Musselshell River area in our Cessna, and all of them enjoyed their flights. Later, Shirley and I got the opportunity to visit Gerhard and Erica in West Germany.

747 Freight Flights

I flew 747 Freighters between Minneapolis and New York, with stops at Milwaukie and Detroit, with the same stops on the return flight. On January 4, 1979, I made the first NWA 747 Freighter flight into Detroit. First flights sometimes involve some logistic challenges as described in this letter from NWA Director of Cargo:

NORTHWEST ORIENT Interoffice Communication

To   Captain Doug Parrott - MSP   Date   January 4, 1979

From   Director, Cargo Services   Location   GO

Subject Appreciation - Flight 927/04 January

I don't recall whether we have met or talked previously. I seem to recall the name, but cannot associate a face or circumstance with it. In any case, that is not relevant to this letter. I am writing to thank you for your help and assistance on Flight 927/04 January. Without your cooperation, the flight would have been shutdown in DTW and our new service off to a bad start. I sincerely appreciate the help and hope that we would not have to similarly impose on you for future operations.

At the least, you are entitled to an explanation of some of the causal factors and corrective action. Some of them are beyond the power of individual stations to control; others are actions that can and should be taken by the stations to help themselves.

At JFK there are only two container loaders assigned to the cargo area. We are working to obtain a Cochran 908 to work the lower deck. As you know, one of the two loaders has been out of service with the requirement for extensive repairs by the factory representatives. They are scheduled to be there January 10 and restore the second loader to operation. In addition to the loader situation, our entire container handling at JFK is archaic. We have been and will continue to work with top management to obtain additional racks, carts, and transporters to establish a "1970's" operation. In the meantime, we can and will work with JFK station personnel to improve the caliber of their loading, tie down, and communications.

Today was DTW's first 747F operation. They had sent people to other stations and have been given a considerable amount of training material. As always, there is a world of difference between studying something and actually doing it. A major contributing problem to DTW's handling was malfunction of the main deck loader due to the cold. They were also hampered by JFK's loading. I am confident that DTW will do much better on subsequent operations.

Again, thanks for the help. We will do our best to avoid recurrences.

Sincerely,

D. B. Welton

Letter of appreciation from Director of Freight

Bomb Reported

On February 22, 1981, on NWA Flight 4 from Manila to Narita Airport in Tokyo, we received a radio message from the company that a bomb had been placed on our plane in Manila. The message came through well after we had passed Okinawa and it was too late to return, so we had to proceed on to Tokyo.

Bomb threats were fairly frequent at this time, and NWA did not yet have an exact procedure to follow in the event of a threat. They did suggest descending to a lower altitude and reducing the cabin pressure to avoid a larger cabin breakup in the event that the bomb should explode.

We reported the threat to Japanese Air Traffic Control, and were granted our request to fly at a lower altitude. We descended to 10,000 feet and increased the cabin altitude to 9,000 feet, still below the altitude that deployed the oxygen masks. We informed the lead flight attendant and asked that she discreetly search the cabin and all of the overhead bins. We did not make a PA announcement regarding the situation, as we did not want any panic within the cabin.

Approach Control expedited our approach and our landing once we reached Narita, and after landing the Narita Ground Control directed us to a remote parking area off of the main runway. There was a bomb squad waiting for us there. The passengers de-planed via the stairs. All luggage was taken off of the airplane and placed on the runway, and the passengers were asked to stand next to their bags.

No bomb was found, but after I arrived in Narita, I was told exactly what had happened in Manila. The threat had been received shortly after our takeoff, but it had not been reported right away. Pope John Paul II was scheduled to depart from Manila on his return trip to Rome, and Control had not immediately reported the threat to us for fear that we would return and disrupt the Pope's departure.

I would not have returned to Manila, but rather to the nearby Clark Air Force Base. I was familiar with the base after

175

many 707 MAC trips into the base in the past. I also think that the military personnel would have been much more efficient at searching for an explosive.

I was irritated about the delayed response from dispatch, and I filed a report of the incident to the Head of Flight Dispatch in Minneapolis. They researched the incident and put out a bulletin to all stations, directing them to immediately report any bomb threats to flight crews.

Setting a Cargo Record

In June of 1981, I bid more flights into Europe. I made flights into London, Hamburg, West Germany, Ireland, Scotland, Manchester, Stockholm, Copenhagen, Amsterdam, and the Netherlands. The layovers were usually relatively short, but they did allow for some enjoyable touring of the countries. I was able to visit the American Air Museum in London, see some of the pre-war architecture in Stockholm, and visit some of the ruins left by Allied bombers in Hamburg.

I flew some freighter flights into and out of Amsterdam. Landing in Amsterdam was interesting as the runway actually sat below sea level, and the altimeter would record this after landing (a somewhat disconcerting sight for a pilot). On my first flight into the city, the first officer asked me to check the Swiss Miss chocolate mix that we had in the freighter's kitchen. He bet me that the ground crew would remove them during the night. I checked the next morning, and sure enough they had taken it all! Apparently our American version of the Swiss delicacy was pretty accurate!

On one freighter flight out of Amsterdam, we had a recorded load of 225,000 pounds of freight. With that load, we could not board enough fuel to fly non-stop to New York, and if we made a stop for fuel then we would exceed our duty time. The rest of the crew and I decided that we would rather exceed duty time than unload any cargo. We stopped in Gander, Newfoundland for fuel and then continued on to

New York. We ended up setting the cargo weight record with that flight.

Astronaut John Glenn

On August 12, 1981, I was co-captain on a flight from Chicago to Tokyo, when the gate agent informed me that Ohio Senator, and former astronaut, John Glenn was on board. After reaching our cruising altitude, I went downstairs to visit with John and his wife. We had a pleasant conversation with John telling stories about his 1962 Friendship 7 flight aboard the Mercury Capsule. That flight made John the first man to orbit the earth. He made three orbits in just less than five hours, reaching speeds of 17,000 mph. We discussed how long it might take for the 747 to travel that same distance, and also how many orbits it would take to carry the same number of passengers that we had aboard the 747 in the capsule. It was all just conjecture, but it was very fun to have these discussions with a real astronaut. These talks certainly brought to mind the great strides that the industry had taken since my days at Glenview and my time flying the Stearman. Not even 40 years after training in the open cockpit Stearman, with maximum speeds of around 100 miles per hour, I was sitting in a 747 at a cruising speed of over 500 mph, having a conversation with the famous astronaut who had orbited the earth at speeds around 17,000 mph.

At the end of our conversation, I asked John why he had chosen NWA to fly to the Orient. He replied that he liked the time that was saved by our Great Circle route to Japan, and he also enjoyed the superior cabin service that NWA provided.

Another Unhappy Passenger

As previously mentioned, we would sometimes have to deal with passengers that simply felt the rules didn't apply to them. On another flight from Chicago to Tokyo, we had a passenger who boarded and almost immediately announced to the flight attendants that he was a V.P. for General Electric.

Once we'd reached cruise altitude, the lead flight attendant came to the cockpit to complain about the passenger. He was being disruptive and was possibly drunk, so she asked if I would come back and speak with him.

I found him roaming around the first class cabin, bothering the other passengers. I asked him to return to his seat, and he blurted out that he did not like U.S. airlines because they had "lousy service". Apparently, he had been on board for almost an hour and had not yet been offered a drink. He also accused the flight attendant of being "bra-less". I ordered him to stay in his seat and to behave himself, and then returned to the cockpit.

After a couple of hours had passed, I went to the upstairs lounge to use the restroom, and when I exited I ran into Mr. V.P. himself. I again told him to return to his seat. He complied and, thankfully, passed out for the remainder of the trip.

Once we'd arrived at the terminal in Narita, I ran into him again and thanked him for flying Northwest. I also told him that I was sorry that he was so unsatisfied with U.S. carriers.

A few weeks later, I was called to the Chief Pilot's office to discuss a passenger complaint. Mr. General Electric had written a letter to the company, complaining about his treatment during the flight. I guess you just can't please everyone. He was only the third passenger in my thirty-two-year career with Northwest that had filed a complaint, the first being the shirtless spring-breaker, and the second being the drunk on the DC-10 flight in Detroit. More often than not, passengers were grateful for having the obnoxious passengers removed and would write letters thanking the crew.

Going the Extra Mile
While dealing with self-indulgent drunks was sometimes a part of my job, not all passenger issues were

alcohol related. On May 11, 1982, I was flying NWA Flight 4 from Tokyo to Chicago when a passenger, a retired school teacher from Manila, had an apparent heart attack. After a smooth flight across the Pacific, we were in the vicinity of Lethbridge, Alberta when the lead flight attendant came to the cockpit to inform us of a very sick passenger. There were two doctors on board, one an American and the other from the Philippines; both obstetricians. Each of them observed the passenger and agreed that he may have suffered a myocardial infarction.

I asked the American doctor if the passenger's situation would allow the flight to continue on into Chicago. He stated that if we did, we would be landing with a corpse. With that information, I advised dispatch that we must get the passenger on the ground and to a hospital as soon as possible. We were about an equal descent range to Edmonton, Calgary, Great Falls, or Billings. Dispatch did not want us to land in Canada because of customs and immigration. They chose Billings because they had a tow-bar that could handle a 747.

The Billings NWA station crew was ready at our arrival. They had arranged for our flight to be met by a mobile intensive care unit, which then transported the passenger to the Billings Deaconess Hospital.

The plane was re-fueled and we continued the flight on to Chicago. I commuted back to Billings that same afternoon, and the next morning I went to visit the passenger. His name was Patriotco Fabella. He was 73 years old and had recently retired after 45 years of teaching in Manila. He and his wife were on their way to Chicago to visit their son, Virgilio, who had sponsored his parents for entry into the United States. It had been Patriotco's wish to reside in the U.S. after his retirement.

While at the hospital, I met Mr. Fabella's wife, his son and daughter-in-law, and Sister Michelle of the Billings Holy Rosary Church. They operated on Mr. Fabella, but he never regained consciousness and he passed away on May 22, 1982.

The next day, Sister Michelle called me and asked if I would be a casket bearer at Mr. Fabella's funeral, and wear my airline captain's uniform. I agreed to do anything that might help.

Since the Fabella's were essentially destitute in a strange land, Sister Michelle and her church came to their aid. The hospital wrote off all medical expenses, the funeral home performed the preparation and provided the casket, and the Holy Cross Cemetery provided the grave site, all at no expense to the family. Since Mr. Fabella was a member of the Cursillo Movement in Manila, members of the Billings Cursillo Movement provided the other casket bearers. (The Cursillo Movement is basically an Apostolic movement of the Roman Catholic Church.)

The graveside service was a unique experience for me. At the close of the prayer, the family began crying and wailing, throwing flowers and dirt into the grave. I found the experience to be rather eerie but spiritual.

Northwest provided free transportation for Mr. Fabella's son and daughter-in-law to and from Chicago, and Mr. Fabella's wife continued on to Chicago with her son. The family also received a refund for the unused portion of his ticket. I challenge you to find services like those provided for the Fabella family in today's world.

First Flight into "Red China"

On October 25, 1984, I made my first flight from Tokyo to Shanghai, China. The fall of China to the Communist movement in 1949 led to the US suspension of all diplomatic ties with the People's Republic of China (PRC). After the Cold War years, when America was doing its best to put an end to the Communist movements in the East, the tension between the countries was finally beginning to lift. China had just opened back up to the West and Northwest now had authorization to fly to Shanghai, and Pan Am had authorization to fly to Beijing. These blooming relations would, as we know today, greatly impact the future markets and economy of the United States.

We arrived at night, but there were very few lights on the ground to silhouette the city. The airport was well lit and we had an ILS approach. Upon deplaning, I noticed the armed Chinese Army Guards at the foot of the stairs, and along the route to the terminal building. The terminal was quite nice and modern, and they even had a limousine to take the crew to our layover hotel. On our way through the city, it was interesting to see all of the cars turn off their headlights whenever they were stopped at an intersection. I am still unsure about whether they did this to conserve fuel, or if it was an indication to other drivers that they were stopped and waiting.

The next morning, I got up fairly early and went for a walk from the hotel to the Shanghai Zoo, several blocks away. I noticed that, as I walked down the street, the Chinese pedestrians would all keep their eyes straight ahead as if I weren't even there. I looked back at them after I passed by, and would catch them staring back at me, likely wondering about "that American" in their town.

The zoo was very enjoyable and later that day some of the rest of my crew joined me for a taxi ride tour of the city. The buildings along the waterfront were older, likely 1930s and before, but the inner-city buildings were more modern. Shanghai was definitely catching up with the times. The streets were wide with traffic lights and fairly heavy traffic. For years, the world had been in the dark about what was happening in China under Chairman Mao's rule, as the founder of the PRC. I got an early first-hand look at the reemerging country and its people. It was quite an experience.

We departed that afternoon and returned to Tokyo. I made a few more flights to Shanghai before I retired in January of 1985.

Doug and soldiers during first flight into communist China

Last Flight with NWA

In January of 1985, Northwest Airlines was one of the leading airlines in the world. They had one of the most modern fleets of airplanes, including Boeing 747-100, 747-200, 747F, 767, 727-200, and Douglas DC-10C. None of its planes were mortgaged, making NWA the financially strongest airline in the industry. At the time, they were able to pay cash on delivery for new aircraft, all from internally generated funds.

As illustrated by this narrative, Northwest had domestic routes from coast to coast and border to border. It was the dominant carrier to Alaska, and had many international routes to both Europe and the Orient.

Our "Red Tail" aircraft could be seen all over the world. We had the best safety record in the industry, and our in-flight service was outstanding. On top of that, our employee relations were the best they had been in years. The pilot ranks had increased dramatically since I was hired in March of 1953, and my seniority number had jumped from 452 out of 492, to number 49 on a list of 1,818 pilots.

By contrast, in 1953, the airline had been on the verge of bankruptcy, had a fleet of old DC-3 and DC-4 transports, and ten Boeing Stratocruisers. It also had the poorest safety record in the industry at that time. It was really good to watch the company make such great strides over the years, and to be a part of its remarkable progress.

My last flight with Northwest was a nine day series of flights starting in Seattle on January 18, 1985. We were flying the Boeing 747-200 across the Pacific and through the Orient. It was my last flight with NWA, and it was not without incident.

Captain Parrott during last flight for Northwest Airlines

Our departure on the Seattle to Seoul leg of the trip was delayed because of an Inertial Navigation System (INS) problem with aligning the three units. Maintenance ended up having to replace one of the units.

Once we had actually departed Seattle, we had a smooth flight across the Pacific. But upon entering Korean airspace, we were informed that the Seoul Airport was closed to landing aircraft because of ice and snow on the runway. We contacted a NWA freighter that had just departed, and they confirmed that the breaking action was poor and getting worse.

We diverted to an alternate airport in South Korea — the Gimhae Airport in Busan. Luckily, one of the flight attendants on board was a Korean woman, and she acted as interpreter and helped us to get checked into our hotels once we'd arrived.

The next morning we returned to Seoul and were able to land. We changed planes and took NWA Flight 19 on to Manila. After a few more stops in the Orient, we returned to the U.S. Our destination was JFK airport, which reported as being above the minimum weather requirements, and informed us that instrument approaches would be required. The co-pilot said that, in his time with NWA, he had never had to hold prior to making an approach to JFK. We arrived in their airspace and had to hold over Empire Intersection for about 20 minutes before making the instrument approach. I told the co-pilot that there was a first time for everything.

After this, we again crossed the ocean to Narita Japan. Onboard the flight was the chief pilot of Japan Airlines and his management crew. They had visited the NWA headquarters to compare their operation with ours, and even interviewed me and my crew for an article in their operations magazine (I later mailed the magazine to our exchange student, Chris Shiomi, to have it translated). (APPENDIX 4)

Our return trip to Seattle saw more issues with the weather, but there was a silver lining. Prior to heading for the airplane, after we had done our flight planning, Mr. Shigeaki Morita presented me with a farewell cake to take on board. We shared it with the crew during my last flight.

Shageki Morita with cake for last flight

Alex Hata and Kubodera men celebrating at Narita

Tokyo Dispatch Crew for last flight

Waiting for me in Seattle at a hotel near the airport was a large gathering of my family and friends. Shirley had a cake made with a frosting diorama of a Northwest 747 landed at our ranch. Everyone was there to help me to celebrate the end of my long and colorful career with NWA. Unfortunately, one of the only guests unable to make it to my party was me.

The previously mentioned weather issues in Seattle — a heavy fog that had blanketed the area — prevented us from landing at the Seattle Airport. We were forced to proceed on past Seattle to the airport in Minneapolis. Unsure about what to do, the guests continued on with the party, many standing up to talk about my career with both NWA and ALPA. I hear that it turned out to be quite a roast, so perhaps it was for the best that I was unable to attend...

Cake decorated with 747 landing at Doug and Shirley's Montana ranch

Doug arriving in Seattle one day late for his celebration

On January 27, 1985, I deadheaded back to Seattle where my family and friends still awaited my final arrival. We had a wonderful breakfast at the Red Lion Inn. I had once been told that the last flight is notorious for getting fouled up somewhere along the line, and that you should always call in sick. While that advice was not completely unwarranted (as I learned), I am still glad that I made that last trip. I found messages written on that final flight plan from both the co-pilot and the second officer. The co-pilot simply wrote, "Congratulations and best wishes in your retirement," and the second officer added, "I enjoyed my first trip with you, on your last trip. Thanks for making this trip and this profession the best in the world. Congratulations!" I could not have said it better myself, and the gestures of my crew, my friends and my family, only helped me to realize how wonderful and competent all of the people that I had worked with during my 32-year career really were.

Doug and Shirley at last flight celebration

Summary of logged flight time with Northwest Airlines   (Total: 19,911:35)

Douglas DC-3	2,281:05	Boeing 707 and 720B	6,271:55
Captain	17:05	Captain	4,605:00
Douglas DC-4	1,962:30	Boeing 727	353:35
Captain	958:25	All as Captain	
Douglas DC-6/7	463:15	Douglas DC-10	2,024:30
All as First Officer		All as Captain	
Douglas DC-8C	1,365:20	Boeing 747	4,989:25
All as Second Officer		All as Captain	

Chapter 6: Retired and Still Flying

During my thirty-two-year career with Northwest Airlines, I was very active with general aviation. I owned several light aircraft. Piper Tri-Pacer, Piper PA-18 A, Cessna 180, Cessna 310B, Citabria 7KCAB, another Cessna 180, also with a spray unit. During my time with Northwest Airlines I flew 2,710:45 Single Engine Land, 6:05 Single Engine Sea, and 235:35 Hours in Light Multi-Engine Land. I also flew 705:50 as Flight Instructor. I sprayed our wheat crops for another 49:55 hours of Ag flying. I loved flying, and I would gladly fly for any reason or any occasion. "It truly is **"The Greatest Time to Fly"**!!!

Now Just Flying for Pleasure and Business

My passion for aviation continued well beyond my career with Northwest. I continued to provide dual instruction for many of my friends and family, and I even got the opportunity to provide transport for Richard "Buck" O'Brien while he was campaigning on the Democrat Ticket for Montana Congressman. I flew him on a campaign flight in a Cessna 340, taking both Buck and Georgia Senator Sam Nunn to Great Falls, Montana. It was necessary to have two pilots at the controls when flying a U.S. Senator, so Rick Jansma, of Lynch Flying Service, was the other pilot.

On October 11, 1986 I drove to the Havre, Montana airport to meet Buck for more campaigning in eastern Montana. Buck had arranged for the use of a turbo-charged Beechcraft Baron 58-TC. I had never flown a Baron, so I went early, found the airplane in the hangar, and took it out to practice for an hour and a half, performing stalls, engine out procedures, and ten takeoffs and landings. I was also able to stay after nightfall and re-qualify with three night takeoffs and landings.

The next morning, Buck, his wife Anna Mae, his campaign manager Bill, and Montana Governor Ted Schwinden all arrived at the Havre Airport to set out on the campaign trail. The transport of a governor also required two pilots, so, being a qualified pilot himself, Buck sat in the co-pilot seat.

Our trail took us to Glasgow, Poplar, then to Glendive, Montana where we stayed the night. The next morning we woke to a beautiful, clear day, but seeing that it had frosted that night, I went to the airport to pre-flight the airplane and check for frost on the wing and tail surfaces. Much to my surprise, I found Governor Ted Schwinden already there, wiping the frost from the wings of our airplane. I might be wrong, but I imagine that one would be hard-pressed to find another governor who would do such a menial task as that.

Buck didn't end up winning the election, but it was a fun experience nonetheless, allowing me to add two new aircrafts to my list of makes and models flown, and also the title of "political chauffeur" to my resume.

Korean Air flight 007

Another surprising resume addition made after my retirement was that of "expert witness". On September 1, 1983, two years prior to my retirement, Korean Airlines Flight

007 was shot down over the Kuril Islands, northeast of Japan. The case was ongoing even after my retirement from Northwest, and I was subsequently contacted by Paul Soderlind to see if I would act as an expert witness in New York City. I was recommended because of my extensive experience flying across that North Pacific route in both Boeing 707 and 747 aircraft.

Flight 007 had gone down well north of the route that they should have been on and as a consequence, Russia had located the aircraft, a group of fighter jets was dispatched and the Korean aircraft was shot down. Korean Airlines was blaming their detour on the Inertial Navigation System, and they were using the same, three unit INS system that I had used with NWA. I explained the INS operation to the attorneys on both sides of the case, and I assisted our attorney in cross-examinations in the court room, pointing out any errors in the testimonies regarding the INS system.

I later traveled on a Korean Airlines 747 Freighter from San Francisco to Anchorage as an extra crew member in order to observe their INS operations. At Anchorage I had them set the route and waypoint information into their three INS units. In one unit we purposefully did not enter any en-route information to see if we could enter it later after we were airborne. Another unit we did not turn on until after pushback, causing it to operate erroneously. The third unit we set by the book and turned it on prior to pushback. Once airborne, we proved that we could reinstate the operation of the units that had been disabled on the ground, and load the proper information for the remainder of the flight. I tentatively concluded that Korean Airlines flight 007 had followed departure control vectors, and when directed to proceed direct to Bethel, they did not turn the Auto Pilot Heading mode to off, and turn the INS NAV mode to on, in order to proceed directly to their destination. By leaving the Auto Pilot Heading mode on, the aircraft would have continued on the last heading that was set which, in the case

192

of Korean Airlines flight 007, would have sent them north of Bethel.

Along with the experience of being an expert witness in a high profile case, I also became friends with Marshall Turner, an attorney that I had worked with; he later came to visit us in Roundup during the Great Montana Cattle Drive of '89. I flew groups of friends and relatives over the drive in our Cessna, being careful to not fly too low and spook the cattle.

Not all of my post retirement flying was quite so high profile. I continued to do some instructing and promoting of general aviation. I flew the Cessna 180 to Bozeman to attend the Montana State University Aviation Workshop and to give an airline career presentation. On my return flight to the ranch, I had Doctor Stan Easton, the moderator of the workshop, as a passenger and a guest. I also gave an airline career presentation at the MSU Aerospace and Aviation Workshop in June of 1987, and again in 1988.

Serving the Community

I enjoyed doing community service in my free time, and being a pilot often gave me unique opportunities to do so. On September 11, 1986, my son Jeff and I flew over the Roundup High School football field in our Cessna 180 to drop hardboiled eggs attached to parachutes for kids in a science class experiment. I donated many hours of flight time for community events over the years, including rides for the Musselshell Valley Historical Museum Benefit in 1997 at ten dollars apiece.

Time again to change airplanes

On March 3, 1987, I sold our Cessna 180, and Don and I flew it to Hamilton, Montana to deliver it to Bob Cavill, who purchased it from us. While there, we replaced it with a Cessna 182 that was for sale at the Hamilton airport. After carefully looking over the aircraft, Don and I took it for a test run. We both liked it, so we paid for it and took it back to the ranch.

The next day, I flew the new plane to Helena to attend a State Water Hearing, with passengers Dick Walker, Musselshell County Commissioner; and Tom Hougen and Ken Minnie, both local ranchers. The trip was a worthwhile endeavor, as our input proved to be valuable for the way in which future water rights were administered in the Musselshell River Basin. My passengers were also amazed by the fact that we were able to make the trip in a single day. If we had driven it would have taken two days at least, so the new Cessna was paying off already, or so I told my wife!

I later used the Cessna 182 to fly Judge Nat Allen, along with David Comstock and his wife Barbara over the Bull Mountains and the Musselshell Valley.

In speaking with Mr. Comstock, I learned that he had grown up and gone to school in Roundup. He also detailed that in 1932, at age 17, he built a Pietenpol airplane powered by a Model A Ford engine, and he had done it all from plans he'd found published in an aviation magazine! The Pietenpol Air Camper is a simple homebuilt, parasol wing aircraft. The first prototype (which later became the Air Camper) was built and flown by Bernard H. Pietenpol in 1928. At a much later time I got the opportunity to assist in the restoration of his same Pietenpol for the Musselshell Valley Historical Museum in Roundup.

David Comstock's Pietenpol aircraft after restoration

While I certainly wouldn't consider it community service, I always loved having the opportunity to bring old friends and acquaintances out to the ranch for visits. During hunting season, retired NWA Captain Chuck Michel and Wes Sheirman, a man who spent seven years as a POW in the "Hanoi Hilton" during the Vietnam War, came to Roundup to do some deer and antelope hunting. What a great way to spend my retirement!

Corporate Air

After retirement, I often visited Paul Soderlind at the Billings Airport. He had left Northwest and was now working for Corporate Air as an advisor. Corporate Air had contracts with the U.S. Postal service and Federal Express to haul mail and light freight from its hub in Billings to other destinations in Montana. Corporate Air was flying Cessna Caravan and Rockwell Aero Commanders to forward the freight and the mail, but wanted to add a larger airplane to their fleet. They were considering the Fairchild F-27, but this particular aircraft weighed over 12,500 pounds, and thus required Corporate Air to qualify for a Part 121 Certificate. Paul suggested they hire me to assist them in writing the required pilot manuals for Part 121 operations, and I agreed to do the job on a part-time basis.

They also needed a Chief Pilot for the F-27, but since I was over sixty years of age I was unable to fly the line. I could, however, act as an instructor pilot. In order to do that, I needed to get a Type Rating in the F-27. So, on March 18 through March 23 of 1989, I was in Pittsburg at the USAIR Simulator Division, receiving instruction in its Fairchild F-27 simulator.

On April 12, 1989, I started my F-27 flight training in Greybull, Wyoming, flying an F-27 owned by Hawkins & Powers Aviation, and on April 14, after five hours and fifteen minutes of flight time, plus a one hour and thirty-five minute rating ride, I passed the flight test and received my Type Rating for the F-27.

On a separate note, I was later able to participate in an honorary presentation to Paul for all of his accomplishments. On April 17, 2001, I flew the Citabria to Big Timber to meet Art Daniels, who had located a man who could create a bust sculpture of Paul to be placed in the NWA pilot training facility in Minneapolis. The sculpture was approved by the group of pilots who were voluntarily financing it, and at its presentation there was a large group of pilots present, including former CEO Donald Nyrop, to honor Mr. Soderlind.

Shrine Hospital Flights

Being a member of the Shriners, I would often volunteer my services as a pilot to help the organization. We would make flights to different towns in Montana in order to conduct Shrine Hospital Screening Clinics for children. On May 8, 1992, Shriners Jim Green, Sandy Graham, Bud Rose and I flew my Cessna 182 from Billings to Wolf Point, Montana to do a screening clinic for several children from the Wolf Point area in need of care at the Shriners Hospital for Crippled Children. It was really a humbling experience, and I was pleased that we were able to do the same in Glasgow, Montana in 1994.

On another Shriners flight to Spokane from Billings, we took my grandson Brad along with us, but we encountered bad weather near Mullen Pass, Idaho. I diverted our flight path to Noxon Dam on the Clark Fork River, hoping to follow it to Sand Point, Idaho, then on to Spokane. The weather got worse as we progressed, so we ended up having to turn around and return to Billings. It was disappointing not being able to make the Shriners Hospital, but I was pleased that Brad got some good flight experience during the trip.

Along with the volunteer flights for the Shriners, I would also sometimes do volunteer life flights. On June 26, 1997, I flew the Cessna 182 from our ranch to Glendive,

Montana for a lifeline pickup. I flew the patient and his family from Glendive to Billings, where they were met by an ambulance and then transported to St. Vincent's Hospital. After the patient had completed his necessary examination, I flew them back to Glendive. In 1998, I also did a lifeline flight from Mobridge, South Dakota to pick up two year old patient, Molly March, and her mother. With a fuel stop in Bowman, North Dakota, I took the family on to Bozeman where Molly was to receive treatment. In 1998 I flew patient Kala Amundsen from Billings to Douglas to meet a pilot from Denver, who then picked her up and took her on to the Denver Hospital.

Boeing Stearman N2S Bi-Plane

On June 24, 1995, my son Joe and I drove from his house near Portland to Hood River, Oregon to look at a Stearman with a 300HP Lycoming engine that was advertised for sale. I took it up for a test hop around Hood River, and Joe and I both liked it so I decided to buy it. Joe and I later closed the deal on July 6th and flew it to Troutdale, Oregon. From Troutdale, we flew to Richland, Washington, then to Coeur D'Alene, Idaho, and on to Missoula, Montana. It just so happened that Missoula was hosting an air show the next day, and as we taxied our very colorful bi-plane into the airport, a TV crew took our picture thinking that we were going to be a part of the show. That night we saw our new plane on the local news, but unfortunately we were unable to participate in the air show and had to continue home to our ranch.

I gave both Don and Joe some flight instruction in the Stearman, and we were soon giving many rides to both friends and family. People like the sound of that radial engine, and the feeling of having to wear a helmet and goggles, and a white silk scarf blowing behind you in the wind. It was like stepping back in time, to the days of Lindbergh. I had already had some flight training in a Stearman, piloting the Stearman Primary Trainers at Glenview Naval Air Station, but I now had a different goal. I wanted to carry more than 300 different people as passengers in this Boeing Stearman, an equal passenger load to a Boeing 747. To achieve this would create a connection between my earliest aviation experiences and my career as a commercial airline pilot.

Stearman N2S with cartoon parrot nose art

From July of 1985 through September of 1996, I gave Stearman rides to 92 different people to work toward my ultimate goal of 300.

I gave my son Don more flight instruction, including a biennial flight review, and front and back seat training before his Stearman solo flight on June 17, 1996.

On May 3, 1996, I flew the Stearman to Laurel, Montana to be a display for the Laurel High School Aviation Meet, and on June 1, 1996, I flew it over the Broadview Days parade.

On July 4, 1998, I was asked to do a fly by over the Roundup Fairgrounds for the Roundup Rodeo pre-show. The honoree that year was Merrill Lee, a survivor of the WWII

Baton Death March, and the fair board thought it appropriate to have a WWII aircraft fly over to honor him. Along with my Stearman, a Montana Air National Guard jet fighter also made a fly by.

On July 23, 1998, I flew the Stearman to Billings to meet retired Northwest Captain Ken Morley and five others from the Seattle area who had just flown into Billings in their North American AT-6s. The AT-6 is a single-engine, advanced trainer aircraft which was also used to train pilots during WWII. They were on their way to the EAA fly in, an annual gathering of aviation enthusiasts in Oshkosh, Wisconsin. I invited them to the ranch, but they had just shined up their airplanes and did not want to land on the grass.

Ken Morely's AT-6 squadron in Billings, MT

However, a few days later I was out in our driveway welcoming Ken Ralston, son of the western artist J.K. Ralston, and our former neighbor from Kent, Washington, when we heard a loud buzzing noise building up over the hills. The T-6s came in low from the east in tight formation, giving us a good buzz job before turning and landing on our airstrip. They were apparently no longer worried about grass stains, and Ken was particularly thrilled about their appearance as he had been an Army Air Corp cadet at the end of WWII and had flown the AT-6 in his advanced training. We put all of them up for the night, and it was great to spend more time with some fellow pilots.

On October 9, 1999, I flew the Stearman to the Blain air

strip near Joliet, Montana to participate in a fly-by at Jack Waddell's funeral. Jack was the chief test pilot for the Boeing 747 and lived near Selisa, Montana.

Those familiar with aviation will understand the significance of being the initial, chief test pilot for the Boeing 747. The first 747 was named *City of Everett,* after the home of the factory where it was built, and in 1969 Jack would take it on the first 1 hour and 15 minute test flight, a flight that opened the door for one of the most widely used aircraft in the world still today.

Three other pilots and I flew in a Missing Man formation over the funeral gathering at the cemetery. The Missing Man is a kind of aerial salute, and as we passed over, I dove out of the southbound formation and turned 90 degrees to the right so as to fly west, making me the Missing Man, and a recognition of Jack's spirit flying on ahead (when pilots die they are said to have "gone west"). It was truly an honor.

On March 3, 2000, during the Montana Aviation Conference in Billings, Debbie Alke, the assistant director of the Montana Aeronautics Division, and Moe Bailey, a representative for Air Canada, played hooky from the conference and came with me to the ranch to fly the Stearman. I let Moe fly from the front seat, and took Debbie up for some steep turns and a loop. She was a pilot but had never done a loop before, and I was glad to take her on her first!

Later that year, on September 11, I also took a couple from England, Shaun Marshall and his wife, on a ride in the Stearman. Shaun was an RAF pilot and flight surgeon, but hadn't flown in a while, so after 45 minutes of instruction I handed over the controls, and he did very well. He also loved the open cockpit and the feeling of flying into the past.

On May 9, 2007, during Laurel Aviation Days, I took the Stearman out and parked it on the display line, then later did three passes over the Laurel airport's main runway as a flight demonstration. That evening I flew the Stearman back to our ranch, which was my last logged flight in that aircraft.

Soon after, I sold it to Bruce Garber in Sheridan, Wyoming, where it remains today. Bruce encourages my son Don to take it out from time to time.

During the time that I owned the Stearman, I gave rides to 335 different people (nearly a 747 passenger load), flew the Missing Man formation for Jack Waddell, and had the honor of carrying Al Gillis's ashes to Great Falls. I flew it a total of 323 hours from 1995 when I first bought it, to 2007 when it was sold. It was really a great aircraft and made for a lot of fond memories.

Instructing Rocky Mountain Students in the FRASKA Simulator

During February and March 1995 I gave 36:10 hours of instruction to six Rocky Mountain College aviation students in Rocky Mountain College's FRASKA 142 simulator. The simulator training given to the Rocky flight students consisted of six hours of Crew Resource Management (CRM) and Line Oriented Flight Training (LOFT). It was greatly satisfying to see the Rocky students absorb this training to prepare them for future airline jobs.

Grandson Brad Parrott does his First Solo Flight on his 16th Birthday

August 22, 1995 I gave my grandson, Brad Parrott, Joe's son, his first dual instruction in a Cessna 150 at the Roundup airport. I gave him a total of 7:55 hours in the Cessna 150 at Roundup. I gave him 1:20 hours in Joe's Cessna 172 at the Troutdale, Oregon airport, for a total of 9:15 hours of dual instruction. On November 11, 1995, after waiting several hours for strong gusty winds that were blowing at Troutdale to calm down a bit, Brad and I flew around the airport doing some takeoffs and landings. I was satisfied that Brad was ready to solo and that the wind was no longer a problem. I got out of the airplane, and sent Brad up for his first solo flight.

Boeing Test Pilot Paul Bennett, nickname "Pablo"

June 2, 1996 I flew Paul Bennett, a Boeing test pilot in the 747, to do some aerobatics in the Boeing Stearman. Paul was visiting us at our ranch. Paul, or "Pablo" as he was called by all of his friends, flew the F86 chase plane alongside the new Boeing 747 while Jack Wadell was flight testing it.

**Paul "Pablo" Bennett flying F-86 chase plane
for Boeing 747 test flights**

Pablo also delivered the 747 version of Air Force One to Washington DC when it was completed. He flew it low past Mount Rushmore where the chase plane photographed it. He gave me a copy of that picture, and said don't let anyone see it. That low flight en-route was a no-no! Now you get to see it too.

"Pablo" Bennet flying the new Presidential 747 over Mt Rushmore

1996 RNPA Convention

September 10, 1996 we hosted the Retired Northwest Pilots Association (RNPA) at our ranch air strip. The convention was being held in Billings, Montana, with one day scheduled to be at our ranch.

Retired NWA Captain Norm Midthun suggested that I personally invite Donald Nyrop, retired CEO of Northwest Airlines, to attend the RNPA convention in Billings. Mr. Nyrop is an associate member of RNPA, so I called and he gladly accepted.

Doug, Donald Nyrop, Art Daniel at RNPA Convention

Donald Nyrop, Shirley & Doug at the Parrott Ranch

As head of Northwest Airlines, Mr. Nyrop had been Boeings best customer. He bought many Boeing jet transports and paid cash on delivery for all of them. I thought that with that record with Boeing, Mr. Nyrop would like a ride in an early Boeing built Stearman, however, he declined the offer. There were over 300 RNPA members and wives in attendance at this convention; the very large RNPA Convention. (See APPENDIX 5)

Northwest Airlines Aviation Support in Montana

Through the years since my retirement from Northwest Airlines, I was honored at each Montana Aviation Conference to conduct a drawing for a free ticket for two on Northwest Airlines. Northwest always supported the annual aviation conference and aviation awareness art contest as well. In addition, I would present the "Parrott Family Scholarship" to a Montana High School Graduate, to be used at Rocky Mountain College in Billings, Montana.

Montana Department of Transportation

Aeronautics Division
2630 Airport Road
PO Box 5178
Helena, MT 59604-5178

Phone (406) 444-2506
FAX (406) 444-2519

Marc Racicot, Governor

RECEIVED

JUL 1 5 '96

CUSTOMER RELATIONS

June 27, 1996

John Dasburg, President
Department A1020
Northwest Airlines
5101 Northwest Drive
St. Paul, MN 55111-3034

Dear Mr. Dasburg,

I'd like to take this opportunity to thank you and your great Montana staff of Northwest Airlines for your support of aviation and the youth of Montana.

Over the years the willingness and participation of your staff has been exceptional. I've enclosed copies of our monthly newsletter and photograph showing some of the involvement. Each year representatives of Northwest Airlines attend and support our annual aviation conference and aviation awareness art contest.

Montana is a firm believer in aviation education and having a great partner like Northwest Airlines enables us to continue our programs for young Montanans.

Please recognize Lisa Perry, Chris Saucier, Gordon Brandes (retired) and Doug Parrott (retired) for an excellent job representing Northwest Airlines in Montana. You are very fortunate to have such high quality employees.

Thanks again.

Sincerely,

Michael D. Ferguson
Administrator

An Equal Opportunity Employer

Letter from Montana Aeronautics Administrator

206

John M. Dasburg
President
Chief Executive Officer

August 7, 1996

Mr. Douglas H. Parrott
15596 Highway 12 West
Roundup, MT 59072

Dear Doug:

I would like to share the attached complimentary correspondence from Mr. Michael Ferguson with you. You have undoubtedly made an impact on the youth of Montana and I would like to commend you for your many contributions.

You are making a positive impression for Northwest Airlines in the community. This is a commendable effort on your part, Doug, and I want you to know how appreciative I am.

Best regards.

Sincerely,

enclosure

Letter to Doug from Northwest CEO, Dasburg

More Stearman Flying and Other Flights

May 8, 1997 David Comstock was visiting Roundup. David was the 16-year-old boy who, in 1932, built a Model A Ford powered Peitenpol Air Camper airplane from plans published in an aviation magazine. He was now retired from General Dynamics. He truly enjoyed the Stearman, open cockpit ride; it reminded him of his flying days in his open cockpit Peitenpol.

June 22, 1997 I gave Henry Bedford his recommendation ride for Private Pilot rating.

That same day, Gary Wolterman gave Henry his flight test, in our Cessna 182, for his Private Pilot Rating. He passed with flying colors! We used our Cessna 182 for the rating rides, because it had the radios and instrumentation necessary for the Flight Test. Henry's Citabria had only the basic instruments.

June 26, 1997 Don soloed the Stearman. He made five takeoffs and landings at our ranch airstrip; all very nicely done. He was now a REAL PILOT!

On June 26, 1997 I flew the Cessna 182 from our ranch airstrip to Glendive, Montana for an Air Lifeline pickup. I flew the patient and family from Glendive to Billings, where they were met by an ambulance and transported to the St. Vincent's Hospital. After the patient's medical examination, I flew them back to Glendive from Billings.

On July 4, 1997 I flew the Stearman to the Roundup Airport to give rides for the Musselshell Valley Historical Museum benefit. The riders were charged ten cents per pound. I gave twelve rides that day.

July 26, 1997 I gave Denny Lynch, owner of Lynch Flying Service in Billings and his wife Loiret, Stearman rides over the area from our ranch airstrip. They enjoyed the open cockpit, helmet and goggles.

During the summer and fall of 1998, I gave 18 EAA Young Eagles rides in the Stearman. The kids loved the open cockpit, the white scarf, helmet and goggles, and the sound of that "big round engine". The children ranged in age from eight to seventeen, and the rides were meant to peak their interest in aviation. They received flight certificates, as well as getting their names posted on the EAA web-page. In 2006, Young Eagle Nadine Unterdoefer, a German exchange student who was staying with my son Jeff, came out to the ranch to ride in the Stearman.

Another Air Lifeline Flight on October 4, 1998 from Billings to Sheridan, Wyoming assisted the patient Amelia Messer and her mother destined for Denver, Colorado. I was to meet the Denver pilot in Douglas, Wyoming. The weather at Douglas and south of Sheridan was below VFR minimums, so the Denver pilot filed IFR to Sheridan for the patient exchange. I then flew back to the ranch "Scud Running" in marginal VFR conditions.

On August 15, 1998 Shirley and I flew the Stearman to Powell, Wyoming for their "Wings and Wheels" breakfast fly-in. Beautiful day and a beautiful flight!

Nadine loved flying and did quite a bit during her stay. I even gave her mother, Doris, a ride in the Stearman in 2006 when she visited. After Nadine returned to Germany, she was hired by Lufthansa and sent to Arizona for flight training in order to acquire a commercial and multi-engine pilot rating. As of this writing, Nadine is still awaiting assignment for a pilot position in Lufthansa. I am sure that she will make a fine pilot. I continued to do the Young Eagle flights through August 7 of 2010, providing 162 different teens the chance to experience the wonder of flight.

September 27, 1997 I Flew Jim and Kathy Green to Malta, Montana, and Glendive, Montana for Shriners Hospital Screening Clinics.

April 5, 1998 another Lifeline Flight to Mobridge, South Dakota to pick up a patient, two-year-old Molly March, and her Mom Kamala Webb. I made a fuel stop in Bowman, North Dakota, then on to Bozeman, Montana, where the child was to receive medical treatment. Air Lifeline Flights were entirely voluntary, with no cost to the patient or family.

Billings Gazette
May 5, 1998 I flew Jim Woodcock, a Billings Gazette photographer to take pictures concerning me and my Stearman for an article to be published in the Billings Gazette.

Rancher still loves the cockpit at age 73
Story by Mary Pickett
Photos by James Woodcock

As a boy growing up near Spokane, Doug Parrott would ride his bike out to Felts Field to watch airplanes land, and he would dream about becoming a pilot.

Parrott went far beyond making that dream come true. After serving as a pilot in the U.S. Navy, he joined Northwest Airlines. Eventually he became a 747 captain, making 750 trans-Pacific flights before he retired in 1985.

He sees his long career not only as an accomplishment, but as a whale of a good time. Now a rancher near Roundup, he still loves flying and particularly enjoys piloting an open-cockpit Stearman biplane.

After graduating from high school in 1943, Parrott joined the Navy and became a pilot in a torpedo bomber squadron flying a Grumman TBM, the same plane that former president George Bush flew – and was shot down in – during the war.

Parrott finished training late enough in the war that he didn't see any combat.

"Everybody thinks that the A-bomb ended the war" Parrott jokes. "But actually, when Tojo heard that I was ready for action, he quit".

Released from the service in July 1946, Parrott looked for a job with the airlines. With so many experienced military pilots looking for a limited number of jobs, he was out of luck.

Oregon beginning

He and a friend started a fixed-base operation in LaGrande, Ore. They dusted crops, did fire spotting, dropped supplies to forest firefighters and taught returning servicemen how to fly.

It was in LaGrande that he met his wife, Shirley. They were married in 1951.

When the Korean War drew pilots back into military duty,

airline jobs opened up. Northwest Airlines hired Parrott in 1953.

He spent most of his 32-year airline career based on the West Coast and flew nearly every plane that Northwest had during that time.

His first Northwest route was a milk run hopscotching from Portland to Billings in a DC-3.

"That's when I fell in love with Montana", he says.

He wound up flying as a 747captain for 10 years. A dream to fly, the 747 was reliable, with several backup systems for safety, he says.

Except for some minor glitches, his Northwest flights were mostly routine.

His only real headaches were three bomb threats – all false – on planes he was flying.

Bomb threats

He found out about the first bomb threat when he saw emergency vehicles as he landed in Chicago. The second time, he was told halfway between Portland and Honolulu high over the Pacific that his plane might have a bomb aboard.

"All you could do was to worry all of the rest of the way", he says with a chuckle

The third time he was flying a 747 full of passengers from the Philippines to Tokyo. Because the pope was coming in later that day, the Manila airport was shut down as soon as he took off.

Halfway to Tokyo, he was told that a bomb threat had been called in on is plane. Parrott flew on to Japan, and again no bomb was found.

Later he found out that the threat had been received soon after he took off from Manila, but he had not been told about it because officials didn't want to reopen the airport to allow him to return, which would have complicated the pope's arrival.

Parrott flew into Hong Kong so frequently that he remembers the city's notorious Kai Tak airport without a wince.

To land at Kai Tak, since replaced by a new airport, pilots flew straight toward a rock cliff decorated with a white and red checkerboard. At the last minute, they veered to the right onto the

211

runway. In later years, airline passengers could peer into the windows of high-rise apartment buildings that grew up along the runways.

"It was like barnstorming", Parrott says with relish. "For a pilot, it was a lot of fun".

Over nearly four decades, Parrott flew through rapidly changing aviation technology.

When he started flying a DC-3 in the early 1950's, pilots still followed beacons at night and used low-frequency radios. With no radar, pilots talked to the company on a radio, and the information was forwarded on to air traffic control. Now, pilots talk directly to air traffic control, and radar separates traffic in the air.

Before sophisticated electronic equipment came along for overseas flights, navigators used the stars and a primitive LORAN system to chart their course. LORAN is a Long Range Navigation system that uses land-based antennas. Now airlines use onboard navigational systems and the most up-to-date Global Positioning System, which tracks an aircraft's position with satellites.

Parrott also witnessed a change in passengers' attitudes about flying.

He remembers a time when flying was more relaxed, but at the same time more special.

"People got dressed up to fly", he says.

When he first flew into Billings, friends of passengers could come on board and chat until just before the plane took off.

"Now it's like trying to get into Deer Lodge", he says about tightened security at airports.

During his Northwest career he developed a fondness for Billings.

On one of Parrott's Tokyo-to-Chicago flights, an elderly Filipino man developed heart problems. Two doctors on board determined that the sick man needed immediate medical care. Parrott made an unscheduled stop in Billings, where the man was taken to the hospital and the plane flew on to Chicago.

When the man died a couple of days later, Billings and Northwest rallied to help his family. The funeral home, hospital and doctors donated their services. Parrott returned to Billings to be a pall bearer alongside several Billings men from Cursillo, a spiritual-renewal movement.

Northwest flew the man's son from Chicago to Billings for the funeral and then flew the son and the widow back to Chicago. The airline even refunded to the family the part of the ticket the deceased passenger didn't use.

Parrott liked Montana so much that he and his family bought a ranch west of Roundup in 1973. Until he retired, he commuted from Montanan to his job.

The Parrott family now raises Black Angus-Hereford cross calves on the ranch that stretches 7 miles along the Musselshell River. They also grow hay and corn silage on irrigated land.

Shirley Parrott works on the ranch and has been active in several local groups. She has been a volunteer at the Musselshell Valley Historical Museum for 20 years, was one of the first female supervisors of the Lower Musselshell Soil Conservation District and is a director of the Montana Association of Conservation Districts.

Ranching hasn't nudged out flying for Parrott. The ranch has a grass airstrip that is home to Parrott's Cessna 182 and the 1942 Stearman that he bought three years ago in Hood River, Ore.

The Stearman, a rugged, open cockpit biplane, was built for training U.S. pilots during World War II. Parrott first learned to fly in a Boeing-built Stearman. The last plane he flew for Northwest was a Boeing 747, and now he's back flying a Boeing Stearman.

"That's full circle" he says with a wide grin.

Parrott personalized the red-and-yellow plane with distinctive nose art – a cartoon parrot wearing an airline captain's jacket. Parrott is so proud of the plane that he carries of photo of it in his wallet.

Tan and fit at 73, Parrott still holds a first-class pilot's medical certificate.

The amiable Parrott is well known among his friends for his sense of humor. If he hasn't always flown through life with a steady tail wind, his easy-going manner makes it seem as if he has.

His middle son, Don, remembers going on a week-long Boy Scout backpacking trip into the Cascade Mountains in Washington. Although his father wasn't able to go along, Doug Parrott hinted that he might drop the kids ice cream from a small plane.

Four or five days into the trip, the Scouts saw a plane circling overhead and began eagerly anticipating the ice cream.

They were disappointed when a parachute floated to the ground carrying only a bar of soap. Don, knowing his Dad's propensity to joke around, thought that was it.

"We thought we'd been had," Don says.

The Scouts hadn't realized that Doug Parrott was using the soap to check wind direction.

Soon, the plane came around again, this time dropping ice cream.

Parrott required all three of his sons to solo in an airplane before they got their driver's licenses.

"By learning to fly, they learned safety habits," he says. "They also wouldn't have to show off in a car to their friends."

All three sons have continued to fly. Don helps run the family ranch and is a flight instructor. The oldest son, Joe, is the fire chief in Gresham, Ore., and has a commercial pilot's license. Jeff is a pilot for Airborne Express, lives in Billings and commutes to the company's Wilmington, Ohio headquarters.

"We all got the flying bug from him," Don says about his Dad.

The Parrott's also have five grandsons and a granddaughter.

Three years ago, they established the Parrott Family Scholarship that awards $1,000 to a graduating senior of a Montana high school who plans to enroll in the aviation program at Rocky Mountain College.

"Aviation has given us a fun life and it's a way to give back to aviation," Parrott says. "It's fun to see these kids progress."

Parrott and his family saw much of the world on his Northwest pass, but he doesn't fly on many commercial flights anymore. Parrott is happy to spend most of his time in Montana.

"We're content here," he says. "It's good here."

Young Eagles

During the summer and fall of 1998 I gave 18 EAA Young Eagle rides in the Stearman. The kids really liked that open cockpit, white scarf, helmet and goggles, and the sound of that big "Round Engine". Young Eagles were children ages eight through seventeen who received a ride from an EAA member. The object of the Young Eagle rides was to get youngsters interested in aviation. They received a flight Certificate, and had their names posted on the EAA Internet page.

I started doing Young Eagle Flights on August 12, 1997. I continued Young Eagle Flights through August 7, 2010, flying 162 Young Eagles, 53 of them in the Stearman.

I am still qualified to do Young Eagle Flights, and I plan to do more of them. It is a great way to promote and preserve the future of aviation.

Dear Mr. Doug Parrott,

Thank You
For the wonderful learning time our group
received in the classroom and at the
Roundup Airport.
Flight Camp was a grand success
because of you, your expertise, and the time
you gave to our youth.

Doug - again thanks
for all you did to
make learning fun for
our kids. Carol Wadma.
Flight Camp 2004

Doug telling school children about the Stearman

Last Flight for Al Gillis

I had met Keith Wallace at the Bob Smith Lincoln Mercury Dealership in Billings. Whenever I was in Bob Smith's he would look me up and talk to me about Al Gillis, who was now in his ninety's. Al was a close neighbor to Keith and they became very good friends. Al had told Keith about meeting me at his flight operation at the Billings airport back in the mid-fifties.

Al did not have any immediate family, which made Keith seem like family to him. Al gave Keith his wishes as to what to do with his remains after he died. When Al died he was cremated, and wanted his ashes taken to Great Falls, Montana, where he was born and raised, and be placed in his families Cemetery plot.

Al passed away August 15, 2003, and was cremated. Keith called me and informed me that Al had passed away, and that he had his ashes. I had talked to Keith in the past about my Stearman and its history as a Primary Military Trainer.

Keith asked if I would be interested in flying Al home to Great Falls. I felt honored that he would ask, and agreed to make that last flight with Al. Keith would carry the ashes and take them to Al's family plot.

On August 19, 2003, Keith and his girlfriend drove up to our ranch. I had the Stearman out and gassed and ready to go when he arrived. His girlfriend left to drive to Great Falls. Keith and I got into the Stearman and proceeded to fly to the Great Falls airport. The air was smoky from fires in the area, which made for poor visibility for part of the trip but Great Falls had good visibility when we arrived. As we approached Great Falls, Keith asked over the interphone if we could circle the cemetery and dump some of Al's ashes from the airplane. I told him that was not a good idea, to do from an open cockpit airplane, as most of the ashes would be blown back into the airplane!

We proceeded on to the Great Falls airport, landed, and taxied in to the FBO terminal. Keith was to meet his girlfriend there, and then properly dispose of Al's ashes. He told me later that all went as planned in Great Falls, and that they had a nice drive back home.

After Keith and Al de-planed in Great Falls, I had the Stearman re-fueled, and took off for home. En-route home the visibility got worse; down to less than a mile because of the smoke. I followed the highway through Judith Gap, and on down to the Musselshell River, made a left turn at Slayton, and followed the river to our ranch strip.

Flying with Grandsons

On June 6 of 2001, my grandson Conlin continued our family tradition and soloed for the first time on his sixteenth birthday. Later, Conlin flew his dad's Tri-Pacer to the ranch to get more dual instruction for his private pilot's license, and on August 24, 25, and 26 of 2004 I gave Conlin training in the maneuvers, emergency procedures, radio navigation, and radar directions from Billings Approach Control. On August 26, he took his check ride with FAA Designated Pilot Examiner Gary Wolterman and passed with flying colors! Another official "Flying Parrott".

In early August of 2003 I started giving my Grandson, Lane more dual flight instruction in the Citabria. On his birthday August 15th, Lane made his first solo flight at the Lavina airport, with his Dad Jeff looking on. We now have seven pilots in the Parrott family!

October 26, 2004 my Grandson Teagan and I flew Don's Tri Pacer around the Sheridan, Wyoming airport. Teagan had all of the necessary flight training needed to solo. I could not let him go up solo yet; due to a heart surgery as an infant, the FAA had not yet issued him a Medical Certificate. Teagan flew this entire flight on his own. I did not touch the controls or say anything about his flying.

A short time after that flight Teagan finally received his Medical Certificate. We flew Don's Tri Pacer from the ranch to the Roundup Airport. After we landed at the Roundup

Airport, I got out of the airplane; Teagan then taxied back to the runway and took off for his first real solo flight on December 25, 2004. MERRY CHRISTMAS!! We now have eight pilots in the Parrott family!

Since the origin of my passion for flight to the eighth inaugural Parrott flight on Teagan's sixteenth birthday, I have seen many great leaps and bounds within this industry that I love. From my initial training in the open-cockpit Stearman at Glenview, to the first international flight into the newly opened Red China in a Boeing 747, I am proud to say that I have experienced firsthand the miraculous growth of aviation. And, as illustrated by my continuing pilot instruction and the interest of my students, aviation continues to boom. It has boomed every year since the introduction of the GI Bill at the end of the war, and I believe that it will continue to do so for years to come.

More General Aviation Flights

March 18, 1999 another Shriners Hospital Screening Clinic flight to Glasgow, Montana with Jim Green.

March 28, 1999 another Air Lifeline Flight to Douglas, Wyoming to pick up Kala Amundsen, her little brother Dalton, and her father Douglas for a flight to Billings, Montana. About an hour after departure from Douglas, Wyoming, Dalton really needed a rest stop. So we landed at the Buffalo, Wyoming airport to use its restroom before proceeding on to Billings.

March 30, 1999 Chris, Taku, Shota and Yoshi Shiomi all experienced the thrill of flying in the Stearman. It was one of the highlights of their visit from Japan.

July 24 and 27, 1999 another 13 Stearman passengers added to my goal of 300 Stearman passengers,

July 29 and 30, 1999 I flew to Sheridan, Wyoming to give Don dual flight instruction in a Cessna 337 twin engine, center line thrust aircraft. We completed the training and I signed his logbook with the recommendation for a MEL

Center Line Thrust Rating. On July 31, 1999 Don flew the Cessna 337 to Billings for a rating ride with Gary Wolterman. He passed with flying colors, and now is a multi-engine pilot, restricted to Center Line Thrust.

December 20, 1999 I delivered our Cessna 182 to the Billings Airport, where it was to be picked up and delivered to its new owner in Anchorage, Alaska. In Billings I flew it with Ralph Wyman, the Ferry Pilot, who was to fly it to Alaska. He was satisfied with the airplane, its log books, and maintenance records, paid me for the airplane, and departed Billings for his flight to Alaska. We had all enjoyed the 182 and hated to see it go. Many fond memories went with it.

January 25, 2000 we purchased a Citabria 7KCAB in Watertown, South Dakota. I flew it home to the ranch with stops on Mobridge, and Miles City. It was a 5:50 hour flight in "Blue Bird Weather.

Once back home at the ranch it was kept really busy giving rides and checking Jeff out in a 7KCAB. It brought back memories of our other 7KCAB that we had when we purchased the ranch in 1973.

On April 8, 2000 I completed the Tail Wheel endorsement for Amy Woody in our Citabria. Amy was enrolled in the Rocky Mountain College Aviation Program. Amy was the first recipient of "The Parrott Family Scholarship" to be used at Rocky Mountain College for flight lessons and courses needed to qualify for a degree in Aviation Science.

July 1, 2000 the nearby town of Lavina held its All School Reunion party. I flew the Stearman to the Lavina airport to give airplane rides. But, first I flew over the parade in Lavina. I then took up eight different people for their school reunion airplane rides.

September 11, 2000 I took two passengers from England, Shaun Marshal and his wife Sadie, for rides in the Stearman. Shaun was an RAF pilot and Flight Surgeon. He hadn't flown recently, so I gave him forty-five minutes of

219

instruction. He then did really well flying the Stearman, and truly enjoyed the flight. We communicated via mail for several years after that flight.

On December 31, 1999, Tony Schaff and I went up for an hour in the Citabria for the last flight of the Millennium, and the Twentieth Century. There was a lot of concern expressed about what would happen at midnight of the new millennium. GPS navigation aids, radar, etc. could go berserk at the stroke of midnight. I asked midnight where? Greenwich time, Eastern time, our Mountain time or what?

On January 1, 2000, Tony and I again went up for an hour and twenty minutes in the Citabria, for a flight down river to Melstone, Montana and back, for the first flight of the millennium, and the Twenty First Century. All was normal, the radios, GPS, clocks, and everything else all worked as normal. So much for all of the scare rhetoric coming from Washington, D.C.

Shirley and my Fiftieth Wedding Anniversary was January 9, 2001. Joe came out to join the family in the celebration of that event.

While he was here we went up in the Citabria. I gave him the necessary instruction to re-qualify in the Citabria, he then took his wife Elaine for a flight around the area.

On April 17, 2001, I flew the Citabria to Big Timber, Montana to meet Art Daniels. Art had located a man near Big Timber who could create a bust sculpture of Paul Soderland to be placed in the NWA pilot training facility in Minneapolis.

It was later approved by the pilot group that was voluntarily financing the sculpture. At its presentation in Minneapolis there was a large group of pilots in attendance, as well as Donald Nyrop, past President and CEO of NWA.

The Oshkosh EAA Fly In
On July 28, 2003, I decided to make a trip to the EAA Fly In in Wisconsin. I flew the Citabria to the Padlock Ranch in Wyoming to meet Don, who was flying to Oshkosh in his Tri-

Pacer. My grandson Conlin rode with me, giving me a chance to give him some dual cross country instruction. Don had his son Teagan, Chad Siroky, and Charlie Linhart as passengers, plus all of the camping gear and the suitcases.

From the Padlock in Sheridan, we flew to Spearfish, South Dakota; to Huron, South Dakota; to La Crosse, Wisconsin where we spent the night. The next morning, we flew into Oshkosh following the special NOTAM arrival procedure.

Arrival into Oshkosh during the Airventure show was very exciting. During the week of Airventure, the Oshkosh Wittman Field is the world's busiest airport. So dense is the traffic that pilots are not allowed to respond verbally to the controller's instructions. Rather, the pilot will rock the wings of his aircraft to acknowledge the instructions. To accommodate the high volume of traffic, pilots are directed to land on large colored dots located on the runway end, center, and midway from center to the end. In this way, several aircraft could land at the same time on the same runway.

The Airventure fly-in was a really great experience for all of us, with flying events, aviation displays, restaurants, and more. There were aircraft ranging from ex-military, to current military, to antique, to home built, and each day was an air show with some truly amazing aerobatics. It was almost like a Sturgis Rally for pilots.

We stayed for three days, and on the return trip home I had Charlie as my passenger. I could see that he had been bitten by the "flying bug", so I gave him some cross country instruction. He said that he intended to buy an airplane and become a pilot, and he did both almost immediately after his return.

We have been back to Oshkosh several times since that first trip, and I am planning to return this summer. It is always a great bonding experience for both pilots and family.

Cessna 310B

After we sold the Stearman, on December 18th, 2007, I purchased a twin Cessna 310B from the Denny Lynch family. I traded two wings for two engines just as the price of gas doubled; really letting my "pilot economics" shine. It was the same year and model as the Cessna 310B that we had owned back in the 1960s, only it was red and black instead of yellow and brown.

1958 Cessna 310 Joe, Don, and Jeff on the wing with Doug (the same pose as early 1960's photo)

Denny had kept the 310B after selling Lynch Flying Service at the Billings airport, where it had been used as a multi-engine trainer for many years. He completely restored the airplane to its original 1958 appearance, giving it a new paint job and even using the same color scheme that was used on the '58 model. He also restored the cabin interior to its original style. It is really a handsome airplane.

Chairman of the Airport Board
On July 1, 2008, the Musselshell County Commissioners appointed me to serve on the Roundup Airport Board. The Airport Board consisted of four aircraft owners and pilots and a County Commissioner. I was honored when, at my first

meeting with the board, the other members elected me as their Chairman.

My first item of business was the zoning of the airport. This was necessary because of a new housing development plan that would surround the airport. The zoning included placement and height of structures, and any residential lights that could interfere with aircraft night operations. Our zoning plan was approved, and is the first and only zoning in Musselshell County.

At the time of my appointment to the Board, the fixed base operator at the airport was mainly focused on agricultural operations. He had a combination fuel/chemical truck that he used to fuel local and transient airplanes, but when he was away on agriculture operations there was no fuel available at the airport. The board decided to apply for funds from the FAA Airport Improvement Plan and the Montana State Board of Aeronautics to finance and build a self-service fuel facility in order to negate this issue. We accomplished this with both a 100 octane aviation gasoline facility, and later with a jet fuel facility. This attracted itinerant traffic into the Roundup Airport, as well as improved fuel service for local aircraft.

Our next project was acquiring an airport courtesy car. The Montana State Board of Aeronautics paid half of the cost for a courtesy car, and the local airport agreed to pay the remainder of the balance. I made a deal with Paul Funk, the owner of Musselshell Valley Equipment Co. , our local Buick Dealership, to purchase a used Buick sedan. Paul donated the airport's half interest in the car, and thus we acquired a courtesy car at no cost to the airport. I also donated signs to be installed on the side of the car, stating that it was "The Roundup Airport Courtesy Car", and was donated by the "Montana State Board of Aeronautics and Musselshell Valley Equipment Co." I also donated an open carport, complete with a "Courtesy Car" sign and a key box.

The Roundup Airport Board decided that a GPS

Instrument Approach would be valuable to the Roundup community, providing all weather service for the medical flights coming in from the Billings hospitals to transport Roundup patients back to Billings. It would also make the Roundup Airport and alternate airport for any IFR flight planning purposes.

Our previously established airport zoning provided part of the IFR requirements, but additional clear zone requirements had to be met. Some of the airport's wild game fence had to be moved away from the runway ends, and land on both approach ends of the instrument runway had to be deeded to the airport and kept clear of obstructions to the instrument approach path. Also, a small hilltop in the approach zone had to be lowered by removing the top portion of the hill and hauling it away.

After all of this was finished and the required flight tests completed, the FAA approved a GPS Instrument Approach for the Roundup Airport. I personally tested the new GPS Approach in my Cessna 310. It is a good approach, and easy to fly, and I like to brag to my fellow Roundup pilots that we actually had to "move mountains" to make the approach possible.

The Roundup Airport Board has continually applied for FAA AIP funds to maintain and improve the airport. The airport now has a "Super AWAS" (an Automated Broadcast System) that gives pilots the current wind and altimeter setting on the UNICOM frequency. A new and up-to-date runway high intensity lighting system, with a Precision Approach Path Indicator (PAPI) has also been added on both ends, and we have partly completed a parallel taxiway along the main runway.

Currently, the Roundup Airport does not have a fixed base operator. When I became Chairman of the Board there were two operators on the airport: one strictly an agriculture operation, the other an agriculture operation with some student instruction, aircraft maintenance, and charter flying.

They have both either ceased air operations or have left the area. Today the airport is often used by out of town agriculture operators who do work for local farms and ranches.

As Chairman, I appointed Kelly Gebhardt to be Airport Manager. Kelly is a local saw-mill operator, has three airplanes and two hangars on the airport, is a licensed A&P mechanic, does aircraft maintenance and annual inspections on a part time basis. He is also a former Montana State Legislator and State Senator, so he is accomplished at getting things done with the government. I appointed Kelly as airport manager in exchange for free lease space for his two hangars, and the use of the airport's main hangar and maintenance shop—a very good deal for the airport! Kelly has been a terrific teammate in operating and improving the Roundup Airport.

The Wright Brothers "Master Pilot" Award

While attending the 2005 Montana Aeronautics Conference, I was presented with the Wright Brothers "Master Pilot" Award, dated February 6, 2005. The award is given in honor of over fifty years of dedication as a pilot. Flight Safety Director Office representative, Steve Jones, made the presentation to me and to four other Montana pilots. My son Jeff and grandson Lane were present, and it felt great to stand in recognition of a lifetime dedicated to aviation.

FAA Master Pilot Award

Northwest and Delta Merger

On April 15, 2008, Delta Air Lines and Northwest Airlines announced a merger agreement. The merger of the two carriers formed what was then the largest commercial airline in the world, with 786 aircraft. Although it was announced as a merger Delta treated it more as a takeover and repainted all of the NWA fleet to fit the Delta color scheme, thus eliminating the famous NWA Big Red Tail. All the flight crew uniforms and the NWA pilot wings, which were the original "US Air Mail Gold Wings", were replaced by Delta. It was sad to see the company that I had worked for essentially disappear but, I will always have fond memories of the Big Red Tails.

Prairie Dog Hunting at our Ranch

Our Ranch and some of the surrounding ranches have some pretty extensive prairie dog towns. Prairie dogs are a real challenge to hunt. They will often come out of their holes and stand on their mounds. They are very quick to dive back into their hole if they see someone nearby. Thus you have to stay a good distance from their town and wait for them to pop up, and be immediately ready to shoot. Some of the hunters come out in their pickup trucks equipped with rifle rests, and scopes in the back. They use rifles with high speed bullets and powerful scopes to quickly shoot a prairie dog when it pops up out of its hole.

Two retired NWA Captains, Eric Linden and Harry Upham, came out several summers to hunt prairie dogs and to visit us here at the ranch. Eric Linden worked with Paul Soderlind at Northwest. Eric ferried four-engine 707 and 747 aircraft that had failed engines to the Minneapolis maintenance shop for an engine change. This was less expensive than flying a crew of mechanics and an engine to the airplane. Eric became famous for his record number of flights in three-engine 707's and 747's.

Harry Upham learned to fly just before WWII broke out. Because the U.S. did not enter the war right away, Harry went to Canada and joined the Royal Canadian Air Force. When he completed his training and received his RCAF wings, he was sent to England to fly the Hawker Hurricane fighter to protect London from the German Luftwaffe bombing raids. At the completion of his duty with RCAF, and the end of WWII he hired on as a co-pilot with NWA on May 9, 1945. Harry was also based in Spokane at the same time that I was based there. Harry did not live too far from us in Spokane and always celebrated "Boxing Day", the day after Christmas. When he came to our house, we would join him on his Boxing Day rounds to friends and neighbors, exchanging gifts and libations, and then they would join us and continue the rounds. We often ended up with quite a crowd of friends.

South Central Montana EAA Hangar
The Experimental Aircraft Association (EAA) has a very active Hangar at the Billings airport. They meet at least once a month, for dinner and aeronautical presentations. This is the Hangar that sponsored the re-building of the Pietenpol that is now on display at the Musselshell Valley Historical Museum in Roundup.

One of our Hangar members is Astronaut Frank

Borman; the Apollo 8 commander. Apollo 8 was the first spacecraft to orbit the Moon. Frank later became CEO of Eastern Airlines. After he completed his career with Eastern Airlines he bought some property near Billings and bought a hangar on the Billings Airport. Frank owns several airplanes, and has restored and modified several of them. He recently restored a Cessna L-5 Korean War era observation aircraft. He replaced the piston powered engine with a turbo-prop engine.

Frank flew it to the Roundup Airport's Pancake Breakfast on June 26th and drew quite a crowd of pilot admirers. Prior to his departure, I asked him to demonstrate its short takeoff and climb performance. He did so, it rolled about 150 feet before liftoff, and then climbed steeply as he turned over the crowd of on lookers.

Doug and Apollo Astronaut Frank Borman

More General Aviation and Other Flying
While in Minneapolis presenting the Paul Soderlind Bust, I had the opportunity to fly the 747-400 simulator. It was my first flight in a "Glass Cockpit" simulator. It was quite an

experience relating the Glass Cockpit configuration to my life time experience with "round gages". Captain Tim Olsen was the Instructor Pilot. He had me seated in the left seat, the Captains Seat, and located the Simulator over Boston. I made a couple of ILS approaches into Boston.

I was amazed at the accuracy of the visual depiction of the landscape and Boston Harbor as we approached the Boston Airport. It was exactly as I recalled, having flown into Boston many times in the past. It was quite an improvement over the early DC-10 visual simulator.

July 21, 2001 I flew the Stearman to the Air Show in Bozeman, Montana. I put the Stearman on display that afternoon and the next morning, then flew it back home to the ranch.

Spotting Lightning Caused Forest Fires

August 4, 2001 I took several of our neighbors on flights in the Citabria, over the Bull Mountain area south of the Musselshell River, for fire spotting and directing practice. We were all members of the Dean Creek Volunteer Fire Department.

I flew many flights on the mornings after any prior evening and night thunderstorms looking for smoke from fires that lightning strikes may have caused.

If I spotted a fire or smoke I could direct the ground fire fighters to the location, via two way radio communications. This way they could extinguish the fire before it produced enough smoke to be seen from the ground; at which time it would have been a much larger fire and much more difficult to extinguish or control.

New Training Aircraft for Rocky Mountain College

April 23, 2002 I traveled to the Laurel Airport to join other Rocky Flight Advisory Committee members to fly and recommend a new aircraft to be used in the Rocky Mountain College aviation flight training program. The aircraft being demonstrated were a Piper Worrier PA-28, a Diamond DA 20 two place, and a Diamond DA 40 four place. Both Diamonds were fully aerobatic, so I had to try a few aerobatic maneuvers. They each handled very nicely and performed very well. The bottom of the windshield was very low, which put the instrument panel even lower, thus making the space between the bottom of the windshield and the instrument panel too narrow to be obscured by an IFR hood while the pilot was sitting upright. That would make it difficult to instruct simulated instrument flight.

We all concluded the Piper PA-28 to be the best trainer for the Rocky program. Rocky purchased six PA-28 aircraft. They are still using the PA-28 today, even though some of the earlier ones have since been traded in for newer ones.

This made three new airplanes to add to my list of different aircraft makes and models that I have flown.

Musselshell River Survey Flights

May 24, 2002 Bob Leonard, an engineer for the DNRC, requested that I fly him down the Musselshell River to its mouth at Mosby, Montana, for an aerial survey of the river. On the way back from Mosby, we both needed a potty stop. I picked a spot on a county road that was suitable to land on, with no nearby houses that could observe our stop.

June 13, 2002 Teri Hice, Water Manager for the Musselshell River below Deadmans Basin, requested a similar flight up stream to the Bair Reservoir, and back to the ranch. The next day on June 14, 2002 we flew downstream on the Musselshell River to the Fort Peck reservoir, and back to the ranch.

More Fun Flights

June 26, 2002 Shirley and I flew over our local area of the Bull Mountains looking for any signs of a fire after the thunderstorm the evening before. We spotted a fire, reported it to the Dean Creek Volunteer Fire Department, and told them how to get to it. They found it okay and brought it under control.

On July 20, 2002 I flew to Billings to pick up Brock Hindman, a Rocky Flight Instructor as he needed a backseat check-out to instruct from the backseat in a tandem seated aircraft. We flew from Billings to Lavina and did air work along the way to Lavina. We performed eleven takeoffs and landings at Lavina, and flew back to Billings, with more air work on the return trip.

August 3, 2002 Jeff and I flew the Stearman to the Montana Antique Aircraft Association fly in at Three Forks, Montana. I exhibited the Stearman, and did a few flybys. It was a great show of older airplanes.

The Retired Northwest Pilots Association (RNPA) had its convention in Nashville, Tennessee. While at the convention the group went out to one of our pilot's airstrip near Nashville for a picnic and air show. One of the air show airplanes was a Pitts S2B. The pilot, Steve Johnson, put me in the front cockpit, and took me up. He let me fly it in the air. I did a loop and a couple of rolls. The roll rate of the Pitts was phenomenal. I laid the stick over to the left and in nothing flat we had completed the roll. He then let me take it in and land it. The Pitts sits very low to the ground. On landing I thought that I would never touch down. I finally did, but thought that I could put my hand over the side and touch the grass on the runway.

December 14, 2002 my young friend Tanner Woodcock needed a Tail Wheel checkout and endorsement for the Flight Instructor Rating he was pursuing. He came to the ranch and we rolled out the Citabria and began to train him for the Tail Wheel and Spin Endorsement. After three hours of training at Lavina and our ranch, which included many three point landings, slips, spins, wheel landings, and air work, including steep turns, and spirals. I endorsed his logbook for tail wheel qualification and spin training.

Later that month my son Joe was visiting us for the

Christmas holiday. While he was here I gave him a BFR and some spin training in the Citabria.

Nothing gives me more pride, however, than to see my passion for flight being handed down from generation to generation. I think back to that young boy, watching the contrails of the B-17s cutting over the horizon, and I can hardly express the gratitude that I feel for having been a part of such an amazing industry. Being able to witness firsthand the Golden Age of Aviation, and the tremendous advancements that have taken place since my first flight with my father out of Felts Field, I can truly say that I am excited for what lies ahead for aviators such as my sons and grandsons. Even today, whenever I watch the ground fall away and feel that invigorating freedom of the heavens that Lindbergh once so eloquently alluded to, I can't help but think that this is still the greatest time to fly.

Ode to a Wonderful Aviation Career
I marvel at the changes I've seen down through the years.
From the Boeing Stearman open cockpit Bi-Plane,
To the Douglas DC-3 and Boeing Jumbo Jets.
From mountain Airway Beacons and Low Frequency Radio Range
To VOR, DME, GPS, and Radar Separation.
From over water Navigators,
To LORAN, Doppler and INS Navigation.

Although I'm now a "has been" and the game has passed me by,
When all is said and done I've no regrets.
I've never flown around the world, I've never won a race,
I've never tried to reach the speed of sound,
No epic flight, no daring deeds, nor have I thrilled,
The crowd with trick and fancy flying near the ground.

My name is not emblazoned in the books of flying lore,
Nor the Aviation Hall of Fame,
But when my logs are tallied up the pages will reveal,

I've done a lot of flying just the same.

No one can slow the March of Time, nor stay the hand of Fate,
And certain things we have to understand,
No flight can cruise forever - soon we all must throttle back,
Drop the wheels and bring her in to land.
And me? Flying now is all fun and pleasure,
Flying my pretty 310 is now time that I Treasure!
And while the years pass swiftly by,
I'll dream and reminisce,
And watch the jets lay contrails in the sky.

Epilogue: More Notable Moments

2003 A Wonderful Year of Flying

January 15, 2003, Brock Hindman came up to the ranch to get some instruction in landing and taking off in snow as we had about five inches of snow on the ground. Once again I rolled out the Citabria. We did not have skis for the airplane, so we had to be careful that we didn't have too much snow or that there were any really deep drifts across the runway. I showed him how to taxi in snow by keeping the tail down and taxiing slowly. I taught him to be prepared to use more throttle if necessary, or to stop if forward progress could not be made. We didn't want to chance putting it on its nose in a snow drift.

When taking off we used for full power, keeping the stick back enough to hold the tail down and not cause excess drag by getting the tail wheel too deep into the snow. Let the airplane lift off as soon as it can, then build up speed by leveling off until climb speed is reached, then a normal climb out. On landing, approach as slow as reasonable and then hold it off and let it settle in. Once down add enough power to keep it moving ahead and decelerate smoothly, also be prepared to add throttle if the tail starts to raise up. To "go around" use the same procedure as for takeoff.

Don Buys a Piper Tri-Pacer

Don had been looking to buy an airplane for some time. I had suggested a Piper Tri-Pacer, a nice flying four place high wing airplane that was not too expensive to buy and maintain. It has good performance, and a reasonable cruise speed.

Don found one advertised in Salem, Oregon. His brother, Joe, lives in Salem, so he telephoned Joe and asked him to look at it. Don had confidence in Joe, after Joe had first looked at my future Stearman and recommended it. Joe was satisfied that it was a good Tri-Pacer, which had low time since the engine had been overhauled, and had recently been re-covered with new fabric and a fresh paint job. High lift droop wing tips had also been installed.

I traveled to Salem, looked at the airplane and agreed with Joe that it was a good plane, and a good buy. We bought it for Don, and I agreed to fly it home for him. On August 20, 2002, I took off from Salem, flew to Richland, Washington, and then on to Coeur d'Alene, Idaho, where I stayed overnight. The next morning, I flew on top an overcast sky to Helena, Montana, and then on to the ranch. It took just under eight hours of flying time.

I gave rides in Don's new Tri-Pacer to Shirley, Jeri Burnett, and Tony Schaff. They all liked it and thought that Don would be happy with his new airplane.

On August 24, 2002 Don came home to the ranch to get his new airplane. I flew with him from our ranch airstrip to the paved Roundup Airport, to properly check him out in his new Tri-Pacer. He loved the airplane and flew it back to Sheridan, Wyoming where he now lives. He flies it regularly, and uses it a lot to come to the ranch, an easy one hour flight; much faster than the nearly three-hour drive from Sheridan to the ranch.

Don's 1956 Piper Tri-Pacer

More Fun and Instructing

September 9, 2003, I flew with Don in the Padlock Ranch Cessna 337, giving him a BFR and some partial panel instruction.

September 27 and 28, 2003 I gave Trace Lear flight instruction toward a tail wheel endorsement. He did very well, and I endorsed his logbook, making him an official tail dragger pilot.

On September 30, 2003 I went to Laurel, Montana with our Lavina neighbor, Craig Jenson, to pick up, and ferry back to Lavina, the Citabria 7GCBC which he had just purchased.

Craig has a private Pilot License, which he earned while attending Montana State University in Bozeman. All of his training was in tricycle gear airplanes. His Citabria is a conventional gear or tail dragger. Thus he needed some training for a tail wheel endorsement. It had been a long time since Craig had done any flying, so it took some extra time to build up his confidence. After 14:00 hours of dual instruction with lots of air work, including slips, stalls, and spins and

236

many landings and take offs at Lavina, our ranch strip, and the Roundup airport for pavement practice, I soloed him and endorsed his logbook for tail wheel aircraft, and a BFR.

In December 2003, Henry Bedford purchased a Cessna 337 Sky Master, twin engine centerline thrust airplane. Don picked the airplane up and flew it to Roundup. I then flew him back to Sheridan, and brought the airplane back to Roundup.

On December 18, 2003 I gave Henry his first lesson in the Cessna 337 at the Roundup Airport. Henry had a hangar there that he had used for his Citabria. Now that his Citabria was at his ranch, the Roundup airport hangar was available for the C-337. His Roundup hangar did not have any pavement from the taxiway to the hangar door, so when it was wet we had to push the heavy C-337 into the hangar. After a couple of snows, thaws, ice, and mud, it wasn't long before Henry had a concrete pad poured in front of the hangar.

May 30, 2003 I flew Dons Tri Pacer from the Padlock Ranch in Wyoming to our ranch airstrip. Passengers were Shirley and our pet, a Pug dog, named "Mack".

June 12, 2003 I started giving grandson Lane dual flight instruction in the Citabria.

2004 Another Wonderful Year
From December 18, 2003 through March 16, 2004, I gave Henry 24:00 hours of dual instruction in his C 337. On March 16, 2004 Henry passed his check ride with Gary Wolterman in Billings. Henry now had a Multi Engine Center Line Thrust Rating.

My granddaughter, Cheryl, her husband Rob and their son, Kanyon, came from Portland, Oregon to visit us at the ranch. While they were there I gave them airplane rides. On March 22, 2004, I gave Rob and Kanyon a ride around the area in the Citabria. I then took Cheryl for a ride in the Stearman. While we were up I motioned to her in the mirror that we could do a loop. She nodded yes, so around we went. You wouldn't believe the BIG GRIN that she had when we leveled off after the loop.

Grandson Lane, came up to the ranch on March 27, 2004 to do some flying in the Citabria. We flew to Lavina, and on the way did some low maneuvers, S-Turns, and Rectangular Course. He then did a couple of takeoffs and landings at Lavina, before returning to the ranch.

Tail Wheel Training for a Top Gun

On April 5, 2004 I started giving retired Navy Captain John Nash some training for a tail wheel endorsement. During the Viet Nam war John led a "Top Gun" squadron. His Navy nick name was "Smash Nash" as he had 930 traps (Carrier Landings). A lot more than my 23 traps! John was building a Kit Fox at the EAA Hangar in Billings. The Kit Fox has a conventional gear landing gear making it a "tail dragger". John's Navy flight training was all done in tri-cycle geared airplanes, so he needed a tail wheel indorsement before flying his Kit Fox

I gave John 3:50 hours of dual before signing him off. It was hard for him to break some of his old Navy flying habits. It took several sessions just to teach him a standard traffic pattern and final approach path. We finally got it done and I signed his Logbook with a Tail Wheel Endorsement. Some months later on May 25th I gave him a BFR.

John finished his Kit Fox and flew it a few times. On a flight from Billings over the Comanche Flats, west northwest of Billings, his engine failed and he had to make a forced landing in a field that was covered with sage brush. The sage brush caught up on the landing gear and forced the airplane to roll upside down. That ruined the Kit Fox, so he scrapped it out.

More Instructing and Fun

Jamie Foy flew his Piper PA-18 Super Cub up to the

ranch. Jamie was working toward a Flight Instructor Rating, and needed some spin training. We did some stalls, spins, and crossed controlled spin entries and recoveries in my Citabria. We then went up in the Stearman for a little air work. After that we went up in his PA-18 and did more spin training. That was the airplane that he would use to take his Flight Instructor Rating ride. I then endorsed his logbook for the completion of the required spin training.

On June 27, 2004 Pete Whiting, a retired Navy Pilot, flew his home built Piper PA-11 with a 150 horse Power engine from Billing to our ranch strip. He let me take it up for a flight. I put Conlin in the backseat and away we went. It is a great performing airplane.

On July 24, 2004 I met two Roundup school teachers and their nine students at Roundup Airport. I gave them all rides over Roundup in the Stearman. Nine more Young Eagles!

Casey Holst, a Parrott Family Scholarship winner, stopped by the ranch, on August 4, 2004. I gave him a ride in the Stearman. He loved the Stearman, and wished that Rocky Mountain College had one to fly in their aviation program.

Later that year we had our Japanese Exchange Student, Chris Shiomi, now a school teacher in Japan, and some of his family and school students as guests. On August 6, 2004, I brought the Stearman out of the hangar and gave Young Eagle rides to the Japanese students, Genchi Yoshimi, Akane Shiomi, Karumi Momotsu, Mina Shiomi, Ryo Ogino, and Ryunosuke Sakamoto. A great experience for those Japanese students; it could not be done in Japan.

On September 22, 2004 I flew with Craig Jensen in his Citabria 7GCBC out of the Lavina airport. Craig wanted some more training. We did stalls, spins, cross control spins, spiral to landing, takeoffs and landings with flaps and no flaps, slips, wheel landings, and low work, S-turns, and turns around a point. A 1:20 hour workout for Craig.

And Now For 2005

February 25, 2005 I started giving our neighbor, Mark Hamill some dual instruction in our Citabria. Mark has a Private Pilot Rating. He is building a low wing, tail dragger, single place airplane from a kit. He had not flown for quite a while. We continued flying together through the spring of 2005. On May 28, 2005, after 10:25 hours of dual instruction, I entered a tail wheel endorsement in his logbook, and a BFR.

Conlin hadn't flown the Citabria in quite a while, and wanted some dual instruction to get the feel of a tail wheel airplane again. He had only been flying his Dads Tri Pacer for the last year or so. We took off from the ranch strip on April 16, 2005, and flew to Lavina. We did a few landings and take offs there, and then we climbed up to 5,000 feet to do some air work. We did stalls, spins, cross control spins, snap rolls, loops, and then a spiral to a landing back at the ranch. He was thrilled to get the aerobatic training. He practiced on many of his flights after that.

On July 26, 2005 I took Al Herem, a WW II USAF glider pilot. He flew Stearman PT-13 as a Cadet in the Army Air Corp in 1942, before training in gliders. Getting back into a Stearman again was a big thrill for him. I gave him the controls for a while. He hadn't lost his touch.

McCollum Aviation was an ag operation based at the old Lemmon hangar at the Roundup airport. They had an Aviat Husky two-place high performance airplane that they used for checking fields before they sprayed them. The owner's son, Cade McCollum had checked out in it, but needed some more dual instruction in 3 point landings. It didn't take him long to figure them out and to do a good job of setting the airplane down. Another airplane make and model to add to my list of airplanes flown.

During 2005 I flew more Young Eagles, gave a lot of Stearman rides, and did a lot of flight instructing.

And Now For 2006

On June 29, 2006 the Peitenpol Girls were in Roundup, to view the new hangar at the Museum, where the Pietenpol airplane that they had restored, is to be displayed. I invited them out to the ranch for rides in the Stearman. Kalin Stone, Sabrina Brawley, Krystune Berg, Kimberly Randal, Austin Williams, all became Young Eagles. Mrs. Jean Randal was escorting them and also had a ride in the Stearman.

August 27, 2006 Bruce Garber and his wife, Sonya, were visiting Don here at the ranch. I took them both up for rides in the Stearman. I also gave Don a front seat check out in the Stearman.

August 27, 2006 Pete Whiting and his grandson, C. J. Wilkinson, flew into the ranch strip in Pete's homebuilt 150 HP PA-11. I gave them both rides in the Stearman. They plan on coming back for more.

September 9, 2006 Bruce Garber came back for more instruction in the Stearman. He came again on October 28, 2006 for more Stearman flight instruction. We flew to Lavina for a couple of landings, then to Roundup to land and takeoff on pavement, then back to the ranch. I got out and he flew his first solo in the Stearman on that date. He did a good job too!

Pilots for Kids

Before Christmas every year, a group of pilots organized, as "Pilots for Kids", give Christmas gifts to children who are hospitalized. There were a group of pilots in the Billings area that joined in on the Hospital visits to present the gifts. I was among them for many years.

Pilots for Kids handing out Christmas toys to young hospital patients

Here Comes the Next "Wonderful Year of Flight" 2007

April 28, 2007, Bruce Garber was here again, so we flew the Stearman to Lavina and Roundup and back, and did ten more take off and landings.

May 9, 2007 was again "Laurel Aviation Days". I flew the Stearman to Laurel and parked it on the display line.

The next day, May 10, 2007, I flew three passes over the Laurel airport main runway as a flight demonstration. People were gathered at the airport to look at the airplanes, and listen to presentations given by local aviators.

That evening I flew the Stearman back to the ranch. That turned out to be my last logged flight in our Stearman.

During the time that I owned the Stearman, I gave rides to 335 different people, and Al Gillis' ashes; nearly a 747 passenger load, but only one at a time. I flew my Stearman 323 hours during the period of time that I owned it, 1995 through 2007.

Soon after that last flight in my Stearman, Bruce Garber bought my Stearman and flew it to Sheridan, Wyoming.

Bruce and Don are good friends and Bruce generously lets Don fly his Stearman on occasion.

2008 another Wonderful Year

January started out with Don and Jeff having fun flying our new Cessna 310B. Also Shirley, Tony, Mack (our pug), and I flew the 310B to Sheridan to have lunch with Don and Sue. A one hour and fifty five minute round trip. The time driving one way, is over three hours. A bit faster, and safer via 310B!

Later that month, I gave Jim Page a little over five hours flight instruction in our Citabria, and signed him off for Tail Wheel and Spin endorsements.

On March 10, 2008 I gave John Nash another BFR in our Citabria.

On March 20, 2008, grandson Lane drove up to do some flying. I gave him an hour and a half of dual instruction. We did eight landings and takeoffs at Lavina. He then soloed for fifteen minutes at Lavina making several more takeoffs and landings. Lane had purchased a pickup, and had a special Montana license plate with the number 87009, the Citabria's "N" number.

May 16th Don and I flew David and Jonathan Kawulok to Pullman, Washington. Jonathon was considering attending the University of Idaho, in Moscow, Idaho. They toured the campus of the University of Idaho, checked with the Registrar, etc. and he did attend the University of Idaho that fall.

Son Joe, his wife Elaine and son Brad came to the ranch for a visit in May 2008. We made several trips around the area in the 310B. I also gave Joe a BFR in our Citabria. Joe doesn't do very much flying between visits to the ranch, so this way he is current at least once a year.

July 14, 2008 I flew Craig Jensen to Kalispell, Montana in our 310B. I flew back home alone direct from Kalispell to over fly Great Falls, Montana. That track took me over the Bob Marshall Wilderness Area near Glacier National Park.

One outstanding geological feature in the wilderness is the China Wall. It is a beautiful and very steep ridge that runs for miles within the wilderness area. The visibility and light was perfect for me to have a good view of the entire wall as I passed over it on my way to Great Falls. What a treat! From Great Falls, I flew direct to Roundup.

We made many more flights in the Citabria and the 310B that summer and fall. Some flights were made to look at the electricity producing wind generator farm in Judith Gap, and several others to follow the progress of the new rail line being built from Broadview, Montana to the Bull Mountain coal mines.

And Now 2009

I gave Bob Miller, a neighbor east of us on Highway 12, dual in the Citabria. He hadn't flown tail wheel airplanes in quite a while. We did lots of take offs and landings on grass, strips and paved runways at the Roundup airport. I even gave him a back seat check out. We flew just over eight hours in all.

July 27, 2009, Jeff, Conlin, Teagan, and I took off from Roundup headed for Oshkosh. Don flew his Tri Pacer to join us in Oshkosh. We all gathered there, camped out by our airplanes, and enjoyed another great fly in, air shows, displays, etc. We returned home on July 31, 2009. All of us planned on Oshkosh again next year.

August 30, 2009, I conducted another BFR for Conlin in the Citabria. We also did stalls, spins, spirals to a landing, slow work, and lots of take offs and landings. Good job Conlin!

September 5, 2009, Jeff and I flew the 310B to Madras, Oregon, and on into Billy Chinook Airstrip, near Joe's lake cabin. That was the wrong airstrip! Joe drove over to greet us and tell us that we were lost. Joe and I then got back in the 310B and flew to Three Rivers Airstrip which was just a few miles away, a twenty minute flight. Jeff rode to Three Rivers in the car with Elaine. It was Joe's 55th birthday and a great party was had by Joe, his neighbors, and us. Jeff and I flew back to Roundup on September 7th.

Jeff, Teagan, Don, and I took the 310B up for an emergency flight review. One thing that we wanted to actually do was manually extend the landing gear. We followed the book, and it worked perfectly.

Shirley and I went up in the Citabria on June 28, 2010 to check along the river after some flooding. **On that flight I logged my 26,000th hour!**

My friend Ken Morley flew into our ranch in his Navion; he had sold his beautiful T-6 for this equally beautiful Navion. He was accompanied by Jesse Lofquist, flying his Riley 55 twin engine Navion. On July 14, 2010 I gave Jesse some dual in his airplane, and then did a BFR check ride. He did well, except he was used to flying closer to a sea level altitude. Our higher altitude and a warm day affected his airplane's performance, most notably while doing engine out maneuvers. He felt that the experience was very valuable for his future flying.

Shirley and I drove out to Oregon to visit friends and relatives. While visiting my cousin Lorraine Gabel, Hank Troh's daughter, at her home on the Independence Airport, I gave her a BFR in her Piper PA-28. Another fun flight!

July 24, 2010 we took off headed for Oshkosh, in the 310, with Don, Teagan, and Bruce Garber. We returned on July 28th after another "Great Time at Oshkosh".

I flew another group of Young Eagles from the Roundup airport in my 310, on August 7, 2010. I made two flights with three Young Eagles on each flight.

Don, Jeff, Conlin, and I, loaded up the 310 on September 18, 2010 for a flight to the Reno Air Races. While in Reno we stayed at the same motel that Joe and Elaine were staying at. Needless to say a good time was had by all. The Air Races were exciting and well done. There were a lot of good displays, racing airplanes, and famous aviators to meet.

Jeff was out for a few days, and while he was here we saddled up the 310 and flew to Sheridan to have lunch with Don and his family.

On October 6, 2010, I met Henry Bedford at the Roundup airport. He was due for a BFR. We first went up in his Citabria for an hour and completed his BFR in that airplane. He also wanted a BFR in his twin engine Cessna 337. So we went up for an hour in the 337, and completed a BFR in his twin engine airplane. Two BFR's in one day, quite a day for Henry.

A few more fun 310 flights at year's end 2010, a BFR for Don, a night flight with Jeff and Kelly Gebhardt, to check the new runway lights at the Roundup airport, and Jeff gave me a BFR.

Now 2011 a Great Year Coming

During April and May of 2011 we had an excess of rainfall, which caused lots of flooding along the Musselshell River. Roundup was isolated for a short time because of flooded roads and highways. We could not drive to Roundup from our ranch. Shirley had a Museum meeting to attend in Roundup, so we flew the Citabria from our ranch airstrip to the Roundup Airport, and then used the airport courtesy car to drive into town.

Shirley attended her meeting, drove the courtesy car back to the Roundup Airport, and we flew the Citabria back to the ranch. We were one of the few in our area that could get into town - thanks to an airplane.

Our Lavina neighbor, Craig Jensen, had his Citabria at the Roundup Airport for an annual inspection. When the inspection was finished he could not drive to Roundup to pick up his airplane. He drove to our ranch, where we then cranked up my Citabria and flew to the Roundup Airport. He then flew his Citabria back to the Lavina Airport.

The Citabria was kept busy flying folks over the flood, and later surveying the floods damage. I flew another neighbor in our Citabria to look for a missing horse. We found it after about a half an hour of searching. An airplane can surely be very handy during times of floods or other emergencies.

During Mid-May of 2011, the Roundup VFW was having its Annual State Convention in Anaconda, Montana. Our Post Commander, our Post Quartermaster, and I were to attend the Convention. We flew the 310 from Roundup to Anaconda in one hour and forty minutes - it would normally be close to a six hour drive by car - we flew back in an hour and fifteen minutes. Needless to say they were impressed, and said that, "Air is the only way to travel". I wholeheartedly agree!

July 24, 2011 Don, Teagan, and I flew the 310 to La Crosse, Wisconsin and met Jeff who arrived by airline. We then flew the 310 into Oshkosh for the big Airventure show.

I entered the 310 in the EAA Contemporary Category of airplanes to be judged. My 310 won the EAA Contemporary Outstanding Cessna 310 of the year 2011. I felt that it was a tribute to the memory of Denny Lynch who had done the restoration.

EAA Award for 1958Cessna 310B

July 28th Don, Jeff, Teagan and I all flew back to Roundup. Another great time was had by all at Oshkosh.

To top off another great year of flying, Jeff gave me a BFR in the 310. 2011 provided me with fifty-five hours of enjoyable flying!

Now 2012

Don and I started the New Year right with a flight in the 310 on New Year's Day, 2012. We flew to Harlowton, Montana and back, using Don's I Pad for navigation. It worked great. Hand held devices are proving to be very useful tools.

On my birthday, January 29, 2012, Don came up from Sheridan to give me a flight in the 310 as a Happy Birthday present. Every flight is a happy flight, birthday or not, but what a great thought on Don's part!

In March, 2012 Jeff and I flew to Columbus, Montana to visit some friends at the airport there. As we approached to land we spotted flocks of geese on the runway and flying over the river north of the airport. We had no desire to be another Hudson River accident because of hitting geese in flight.

During April, 2012 Shirley and I were visiting friends and relatives in the Salem, Oregon area. While visiting Lorraine Gabel at her home on the Independence, Oregon Airport, I gave her another BFR in her Piper PA-28. I wonder if I'll be back next year to give her another BFR. Two years in a row now.

In late June of 2012 there was a lightning strike that created a fire across the river and a little east of our ranch. The wind was blowing at over fifty miles an hour, so the fire spread very rapidly. In just a couple of hours it had spread east across Highway 87, south of Roundup. Shirley and I flew the Citabria over the fire area the next day. You could see just how fast it had traveled by looking at the way that it had just burned the tops of the trees as it streaked along. The Citabria and the 310 were kept busy for a while, flying folks to look over the fire area.

On July 2, 2012 Don, Jeff, and I flew the 310 to Rawlins, Wyoming to visit its museum, which had a display featuring "Big Nose George Parrott". We can't trace any relationship to him, but he was a very notorious criminal during the early Western Days.

In September, 2012 Don, Jeff, Teagan, and I flew the 310 to Reno, Nevada to again watch the "Reno Air Races" and again we met up with Joe and Elaine there. During the flights down to Reno and back home there was very dense smoke in the air. Even though we were VFR we still used the instruments to properly fly the airplane, since there was no distinguishable horizon to fly by.

On October 31, 2012 I gave Don a BFR in the 310 and he did another great job. After the BFR we flew the newly completed GPS approaches to the Roundup Airport. They worked out real well, right down to their minimums. They start at a higher altitude, so the approach legs seemed like a cross country flight.

Joe and Elaine were visiting us at the ranch over Christmas. While they were here I gave Joe a BFR in the Citabria. He did a good job, even though he doesn't do a lot of flying throughout the year.

Don gave me a BFR on December 28, 2012. It was a really smooth day for flying! It was a really nice way to finish another "Wonderful Year" of flying.

2013 was another Greatest Time to Fly

Don and I started out the year, 2013, by flying the 310 over the new Hardin, Montana airport. It was not yet open for flying but we could see really nice runway, taxi ways, and parking areas. It will be a huge improvement over their current airport down near the railroad freight yard.

The year started out with lots of local pleasure flights and flight instruction in the 310 and the Citabria.

On June 20, 2013 I flew the Citabria upstream along the Musselshell River to Deadman's Basin and return. My passenger was Ken Brenner, a professional photographer, who had been hired to get some aerial photographs of a couple homes along the river. It was a fun flight and he got lots of good pictures. When we returned to the ranch, we circled and he snapped a few pictures of our ranch and the airstrip.

Cessna Owners Convention

June 27, 2013, Don, Jeff, and I flew to Wichita, Kansas for The Twin Cessna Flyer Annual Convention. It lasted several days, and had some very good training sessions. We met a lot of interesting people who own twin Cessna's and our 1958, fully restored Cessna 310B, was an attraction.

This was one of the few years' that we missed the Oshkosh EAA fly in but we went to the Wichita Cessna Flyers convention instead. I still missed going to Oshkosh.

September 7, 2013, John Davis, and I flew to Sheridan, Wyoming for its annual fly in. It was a good time again, and lots of fun. However, when we were ready to leave Sheridan, the 310's batteries were dead, and we had to jump start the airplane.

On September 12th I installed new batteries in the 310. It cranked up and started a lot easier that it had in quite a while.

I again checked Conlin out in the Citabria. He hadn't flown it in quite some time but he did really well.

September 28th I flew John Davis and his brother, Bill, over the local area. John is really starting to catch the flying bug!

Don and I finished the year flying the 310, with three landings and take offs, all at the Roundup Airport.

2014 Another "Wonderful Year of Flight".

In April, 2014, I flew Don, and Jeff, and Jeff's wife

Brigitte over the area in the 310. It was a beautiful day for flying.

July 20, 2014 Don, Jeff, and I loaded up the 310 and headed for Oshkosh. Our first stop this year was at Dickinson, North Dakota to pick up Teagan as he was working in the Bakken Oilfields as a surveyor. We flew on to La Crosse, Wisconsin to meet Conlin and his lady friend Janna Smith as they had flown the Citabria from Sheridan, Wyoming to La Crosse. The next morning, Don joined Conlin in the Citabria to fly into and land at Oshkosh. Jeff, Teagan, Janna, and I flew the 310 into Oshkosh. Upon our arrival at Oshkosh, the tower advised us that the airport was closed because of an aircraft accident on the field. We diverted to the Fond Du Lac County Airport, landed there and waited for Oshkosh to reopen.

We had another great time in Oshkosh. There was a beautiful night air show and fireworks on the last night there.

On the way home we landed at Dickinson to let Teagan off, and for all to unload and go into Dickinson for lunch. Jeff was flying the leg to Dickinson, and I was in the right seat. The weather just east of Dickinson had low ceilings and poor visibility, but was forecast to improve. As we crossed the hills east of Dickinson, the ceiling lowered, but the visibility stayed pretty good. We decided to continue VFR into Dickinson.

I told Jeff to fly the airplane clear of the clouds and stay VFR if he could, and I would watch out of the windshield and side window to make sure that we were clearing the terrain, and that it was not rising to block us. Just like the old days in the DC-3's flying across Montana. We made it on into Dickinson with no problem. The weather at the airport was now VFR. I flew the route from Dickinson to Roundup. The weather was now Ceiling And Visibility Unlimited (CAVU).

When Conlin and Janna arrived back in Sheridan, the Citabria tail wheel tire went flat just as they were parking. We all counted it lucky that it happened there, instead of at some smaller field that they had stopped at along the way which had no maintenance facility.

October 11th was another BFR for Don in the 310 - another job well done.

November 6th Don and I flew the 310. The main paved runway at the Roundup Airport was closed for the installation of a new runway lighting system so this was a great opportunity to check Don out in the 310 for takeoffs and landings on a grass strip. He didn't have any trouble doing it in the 310, just lift it off at the single engine speed, and approach at just ten miles per hour above stall speed, and hold it off until it practically stalls at touch down. No problem for Don.

During 2014 I did a little less flying, but with its adventures and variety it was still another "**Wonderful Year of Flight".**

General Aviation Still Booming

As you can see from all of my different students and their occupations, general aviation is still very active. General aviation has boomed ever since the end of WW II when the GI Bill paid for veterans flight training, and many new makes and models of general aircraft were being designed and produced.

Aircraft Makes and Models that I Have Logged Time in:
Aero Commander 500B
Aeronca 7AC Champion
Aeronca Chief
Aeronca Sedan
AG-1 (CAA & Texas A & M Ag Plane)
Aviat Husky S1
Beechcraft Bananza (several models)
Beechcraft Baron B55
Beechcraft Baron 58
Beechcraft Baron 58TC
Beechcraft Twin Bananza

Beechcraft C23 Sundowner
Beechcraft Stagger Wing
Bellanca Cruisair
Bird 1932 Biplane
Boeing N2S Stearman 220 HP
Boeing N2S Stearman 300 HP
Boeing N2S Stearman 450 HP
Boeing 707 320B
Boeing 707 320C
Boeing 720B
Boeing 727 100
Boeing 747 100
Boeing 747 200
Boeing 747F
Callair Ag Plane
Cessna 120
Cessna 140
Cessna 150
Cessna 152
Cessna 170
Cessna 172
Cessna 172 XP 210 HP
Cessna 180
Cessna 180 Ag Plane
Cessna 182
Cessna 190
Cessna 195
Cessna 208 Caravan
Cessna 210
Cessna 237 Skymaster
Cessna 337 Skymaster
Cessna 310
Cessna 340
Cessna 414
Cessna UC-78
Citabria 7KCAB

Citabria 7GCBC
Citabria Decathalon
Diamond DA20
Diamond DA40
Douglas DC-3
Douglas DC-4
Douglas DC-6B
Douglas DC-7C
Douglas DC-8
Douglas DC-10
Ercoupe
Fairchild PT-19
Fairchild PT-23
Fairchild PT-26
Fairchild 24
Fairchild F-27
Funk
Globe Swift
Gruman TBM Avenger
Gruman F6F Hellcat
Hiller 360 Helicopter
Interstate Cadet
Luscombe 8A
Luscombe Sedan
Maule M-5
Navion
Navion Riley 55Twin Navion
Nelson Homebuilt
North American SNJ
Piper J-3
Piper J-4
Piper J-5
Piper PA-11
Piper Twin Cubs (Wagner J-3 + PA-11)
Piper PA-12
Piper PA-18

Piper PA-18A Ag Plane
Piper PA-28
Piper Twin Super Cub (Wagner)
Piper Clipper
Piper Pacer
Piper Tri-Pacer
Piper Twin Tri-Pacer (Wagner)
Piper Vagabond
Piper Tri-Vagabond
Piper Colt
Piper Comanche
Piper Cherokee
Piper Twin Comanche
Piper Apache
Piper Aztec
Piper PA-25 Warrior
Piper PA-11 (Whiting home built 150 HP)
Pitts S2B
Republic Seabee
Schweitzer 233 Glider
Stinson Voyager
Stinson Station Wagon
Taylorcraft 40 HP
Taylorcraft BC-12D
Taylorcraft BC-12D on floats
Taylorcraft L-2
Taylorcraft 4 Place
Vultee BT-13
Waco UPF-7

A Total of 112 different Makes and Models of aircraft

Hours in different categories of flight
Agriculture flying 800:30
Flight Instructor 2,403:20
Northwest Airlines 19,911:35

Other 3,059:00 **Total Logged Pilot Time 26,173:15**

Flight Simulator time 420:10 hours
<u>FAA Airman Certificates currently held</u>

Airline Transport Pilot #626760
Airplane Multi-Engine Land
Type Ratings: B-707, B-720, B-727, B-747, DC-3, DC-4, DC-10, F-27
Commercial Privileges
Airplane Single Engine Land & Sea

Flight Instructor #626760CFI
Airplane Single and Multi-Engine: Instrument Airplane

Flight Engineer #1496717
Turbo Powered, Reciprocating Engine Powered

My Flying Era:
First Solo Jan. 20, 1945
Latest BFR Jan. 30, 2016, day after my 90th Birthday

It truly was
The Greatest Time to Fly

Works Cited

"NavSource Online: Aircraft Carrier Photo Archive." *Aircraft Carrier Photo Index: USS TICONDEROGA (CV-14)*. N.p., n.d. Web. 20 July 2016.
http://www.navsource.org/archives/02/14.htm.
"Dangerous Heat in the Central U.S. This Week." *History of the National Weather Service*. N.p., n.d. Web. 20 July 2016.
http://www.weather.gov/timeline.
"Education and Training." *History and Timeline -*. N.p., n.d. Web. 20 July 2016.
http://www.benefits.va.gov/gibill/history.asp.
"The History of Airline Industry." *Travel Tips*. N.p., n.d. Web. 20 July 2016. http://traveltips.usatoday.com/history-airline-industry-100074.html.
"Northwest Airlines -- a Look Back at Its Long History." *Minnesota Public Radio News*. N.p., n.d. Web. 20 July 2016.
http://www.mprnews.org/story/2008/01/09/nwa_history.
"The Air War in Vietnam." *The American Legion*. N.p., n.d. Web. 20 July 2016.
http://www.legion.org/magazine/214340/air-war-vietnam.
http://www2.glenview.il.us/about/gnashistory.shtml
http://airandspace.si.edu/collections/artifact.cfm?object=nasm_A19610123000

APPENDIX 1
My Orient Report
Joe Parrott
February 1966

We arrived at the Tokyo International Airport. We went through customs. The first thing I noticed were the cars. The steering wheel was on the right side. They drive on the left side of the road. The billboards are all lit up in neon lights. They are very colorful. We went to bed very tired.

The next morning, we got up and got dressed. We went down and had breakfast. Then we took a taxi to the fish market. The fish market is a very busy place. There are fish of all sizes, shapes, and colors. There are squid, octopus, crabs, clams, and oysters. It is the largest fish market in the world.

Then we went to the fruit and vegetable market. There are lots and lots of vegetables there. I noticed some carrots that were fat and small and some that were long and skinny. We were there during a sale. They talk very fast. It's very interesting. We walked back and saw all the shops.

The next day we went to Kamakura. We saw the Great Buddha. It was created in 1252, which is 240 years before Columbus discovered America. It was once inside a building. The building was washed away by a tidal wave in 1497. It has been exposed to the weather since then. The statue is made of bronze. It is 44 feet high and weighs 121 tons. We saw the ancient shrine at Kamakura.

From Kamakura we went to Lake Hakone. It's a beautiful mountain lake, with a beautiful view of Mount Fuji on a clear day. The Japanese waterski on this lake. They have big tour ferry boats on the lake. We also saw a boat on the lake that was like the one they used in the show Mutiny on the

A

Bounty.

From there we drove along the hot spring resort of Atami. From there we drove along the beautiful pacific coast of Japan to Yokohama. At Yokohama we visited the Japanese home of our friend Mr. Hata. We had a Japanese dinner called sushi. It consists of raw fish wrapped in rice and seaweed.

The next day we went to Nikka. It has many, many temples and shrines. We saw one shrine that was called Toshogu Shrine. It had many beautiful carvings on it. Then we went by bus up a steep mountain. It had 48 hairpin turns. It was a real thrill. At the top we saw a big waterfall. It is called Kegon Falls. It is 316 feet high. It had big icicles along the side. We also saw a road that was lined with 300-year-old cedars.

The next day we went to Nagoya by special express train. It is a very fast train. It goes 210 kilometers which is 120 miles per hour. It is the fastest train in the world. When we arrived at Nagoya we got a Japanese hotel room.

From there we went to the Hodaka motorcycle factory. We went to the motor plant first. Then we went to the assembly plant where they put a motorcycle together for us. They start with a frame and go along putting other parts on it. They put it together by hand. It's very interesting. It takes about 30 minutes.

We also saw an old farm house. It is three stories high. It had a rice straw roof. The roof was very steep. It's called a Gashu Zukuri, which means praying hands. The old houses didn't have chimneys. The smoke from the hibachis went through the straw roof. The family lived on the first floor. The second floor was their workshop. On the third floor they store their straw.

For dinner we had a sort of chicken sukiyaki served in the traditional Japanese way. You eat at a low table. You sit on the floor on cushions. The men sit cross legged or "Indian style". The women kneel. Sukiyaki is boiling vegetables and meat in front of you on a hibachi.

We went to the Matsusaka Beef Ranch, which was only one large barn. The large barn held 40 finished feeding cows. The stalls were very clean like show barns. They only use heifers for the sukiyaki meat. We had sukiyaki meat for lunch. It is very delicious. They feed their cows beer.

Then we went to a pearl dealer's house. He showed us his finest pearls. They were very beautiful. Then we went to a shrine in Ise Shima National Park. It had beautiful grounds and gardens. We had a tempura dinner that night. This I liked very well. It is made out of deep fried fish, shrimp, and seaweed.

The next day we went to Kyoto. It was the home of the shogun while he ruled. There were five other buildings beside it. They were where the shogun stayed. The shogun had taken other countries by force so there were lots of people who wanted to assassinate him. That's where the nightingale floors come in. The nightingale floors were designed to squeak when walked upon thus giving warning to the shogun. The shogun was the actual ruler at that time. The emperor was the head of the religion. In 1868 the shogun returned control of Japan to the emperor at which time the capital was moved to Tokyo. We also saw the Golden Pavilion. The Golden Pavilion is covered with gold leaf, which is reflected into a pond.

The next day we went to Nara. We went to see the

biggest Buddha of them all. It is 54 feet high. It is the biggest bronze statue in the world. In the park we fed the deer. It was much fun. There are hundreds of these running loose in the city. They consider them sacred. We also saw a temple that had 3,000 lanterns by it. Some of them dated as far back as the year 1,000.

We went to Osaka also. We went to the top of a big castle. It had a beautiful view of the city. It's used as a museum now. Osaka is the second largest city in Japan. It's the major industrial center also. We took the special express train back to Tokyo.

The next day we went up Tokyo tower. It's taller than the Space Needle. It is 1,000 feet high. It has all the major television stations in it. It has a wonderful view from the top. We also saw a big department store. It is as modern and well stocked as ours.

The next day we went to Taipei Taiwan. The cities are very sooty but the countryside is very green and clean. The money is different. You get 40 Taiwan dollars for one U.S. dollar. It's like Monopoly money. The newspaper cost $1.70. If it cost $2.00 it would be like an American nickel. A glass of orange juice cost $10.00

We took a car trip and saw the countryside. We saw a fishing village that was about the size of Kent that had 500,000 people in it, about the population of Seattle. We saw some rice fields that were terraced against the mountain. Their other industries are coal, sulfur, bricks, handicraft, and manufacturing.

We visited a Confucius temple. We had some Chinese food in China that was really good. We also had a Mongolian Bar-b-q that was tasty. Taiwan is about the same latitude as

D

Hawaii. Taiwan also raises pineapple and other tropical fruits.

The next day we arrived at Hong Kong International Airport. The runway extends 8,000 feet into Hong Kong Bay. The limousine boarded a ferry and took us to Hong Kong Island. The city is modern. The people are friendly. They speak good English. The city is a colony of Britain. It has 3 ½ million people in it.

We took a cable car up Victoria Peak. It was built in 1888. It has operated without a single accident. At the top it has a marvelous view of the city and bay. We climbed to the top of the peak and there we saw Red China. During our climb we saw caves that the Japanese stayed in during World War 2.

We took a ferry to Kowloon and back. Kowloon is on the mainland. We saw many, many boats on the harbor. There was everything from Chinese junks to great big ocean liners on an area about the size of Lake Washington. When we returned we took a rickshaw ride to the hotel.

While I was in Tokyo I went to see a movie. It was in English. Japanese writing was on the side for their people. The theater was as modern as ours. The movie was James Bond in Thunderball.

APPENDIX 2

NATIONAL MEDIATION BOARD
WASHINGTON, D. C. 20572

OFFICE OF THE CHAIRMAN

June 24, 1969

Mr. D. K. Parrott
Northwest Airlines Master Executive
   Chairman, NEC Committee
Air Line Pilots Association, International
24442 156th Street, SE
Kent, Washington 98031

Dear Doug:

Please excuse a little delay in writing this letter
since I didn't return directly to Washington after our little
around-the-clock session in Minneapolis.

The purpose of this letter is to thank you and all
the members of the Committee for the high degree of cooperation
you gave the Mediation Board during your long, difficult negotiations with Northwest Airlines. At any time that I personally
or Mr. Hampton requested, you were always present, on time and
stayed with us just as long as we wanted to make you work. Furthermore, you came a long distance and remained on call for whenever you might be needed. All members of the Committee conducted
themselves in the best spirit of negotiators representing a great
and highly respected organization.

Without this hard work and spirit of cooperation upon
the part of yourself, of Dick Barton and of every other member
of your Committee, this settlement would probably have not been
accomplished. It seems to me the settlement you received was
very fair, both ways, and I think it is an agreement that the
Pilots and the Company may both be very proud of accomplishing.

With best regards, which I hope you will also convey to
your group,

Sincerely,

Leverett Edwards

a

AIR LINE PILOTS ASSOCIATION
SEATTLE JOINT COUNCIL OFFICE
18601 PACIFIC HIGHWAY SOUTH
SEATTLE, WASHINGTON 98188
(206) 243-7172

AFFILIATED WITH A.F.L.-C.I.O.

INT'L — — — — — — — — — — — — — — — — —

July 23, 1969

Mr. Leverett Edwards
Chairman - National Mediation Board
Washington, D.C. 20572

Dear Lev:

Thank you for your kind letter of June 24, 1969. I would like to take this opportunity in behalf of the Negotiating Committee and myself to express our sincere appreciation for your talented efforts which assisted us in making an Agreement with Northwest Airlines, which as you have stated, is a fair settlement both ways.

I was truly amazed by the effectiveness of your methods of mediation. ("Red Book"). I was also very appreciative of your willingness to work and your keeping the parties together and working. I feel that nothing worthwhile has ever been gained without some good and honest effort having been put forth first.

I am leaving office as Chairman of the NWA-MEC on July 31, 1969. My time spent in that position gained me a valuable education in human relationship which could not have been acquired in any other manner. I want to thank you for your part in that education.

I am taking the liberty of sending a copy of your letter to all of the Northwest Pilots in order to convey your regards to the entire group.

Sincerely,

Doug Parrott
Chairman, NWA-MEC

DP:cp

cc: MEC Members
     Negotiating Committee
     C. Ruby, President, ALPA
     R. Bruggemeyer - MSP   (P.S. appeared on original only)

P.S. Luke Koch and myself were extremely interested in the small Sony stereo tape
     outfit that you had in Fort Worth. I am again flying to Japan and am interested
     in picking up a couple over there for Luke and myself, but I have lost the model
     name and numbers which you had previously furnished to me in Fort Worth. I
     would appreciate   "SCHEDULE WITH SAFETY" it if you would send me that
                                        information again. Thanks. Doug

APPENDIX 3

D. H. Parrott......MEC Chairman
Stan Baumwald ...MEC Vice Chrm.
R. C. Blad ....MEC Member
J. M. Freeburg ...   "   "
W. S. Plue........   "   "

REPORT FROM THE MEC CHAIRMAN

This will be my last report to you as your MEC Chairman. The next report will come from Captain Roger Bruggemeyer - MSP, who will succeed me as MEC Chairman on August 1, 1969.

In leaving office I'll not recount the tasks accomplished since October 1, 1967. Instead, I will make a few comments and observations concerning our organization's present position and its future prospects.

"Both management and the pilots have built a solid foundation upon which they may continue to build a better understanding and an improved relationship. We have a new agreement, one of the best in the industry, our grievance machinery and System Board are now functioning in the manner for which they were intended, that is to allow for an orderly settlement of any dispute which may arise between the company and a pilot or pilots, all of the old disputes and issues have been disposed of (except the Rall-Lee case which has become a lawyer's battle), we have shown the company that we intend to be professional in our duties and conduct, the company is growing at a remarkable rate thus providing job security and advancement for all of us, top management has expressed a desire to improve company-pilot relationships for our mutual advantage and last, but not the least by far, is the fact that ALPA has regained the support of its members and the respect of management.

The foundation which we have built is not the result of any one man's effort or even that of several men's efforts. It is the result of the combined efforts of all the pilots who have served so well as your officers and committee members, and particularly the silent members of our organization, many of whom I do not even know personally, who have given their complete support to their organization whenever and by whatever means was required.

I am especially heartened to see our younger members participating so actively in all phases of our organization. It is my firm belief that the added ideas and participation of our younger members coupled with the experienced guidance of our older members will allow our organization to remain dynamic, effective and representative of the entire pilot group."

It has been my privilege to serve as your MEC Chairman for the past twenty-one months. I would like to sincerely thank all of the dedicated and responsible officers, committee members and pilots who have provided me with direction and guidance during some of the more trying times. I would like to publicly thank my family, particularly my wife, Shirley, for their patience and silent endurance.

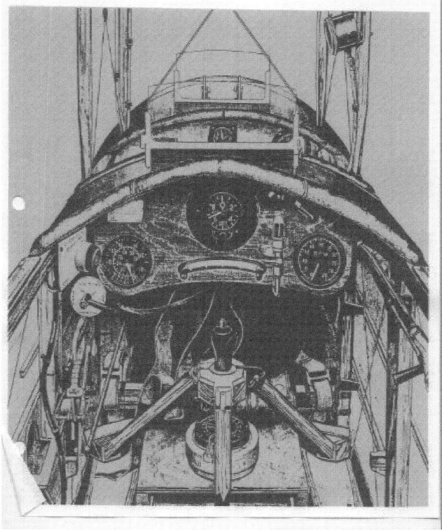

Code 0   Smooth
1   Occasionally Light Turbulence
2   Light Turbulence
3   Light to Moderate Turbulence
4   Moderate Turbulence
5   Moderate to Severe Turbulence
6   Severe Turbulence
7   Extreme

このフライトにとって最も重要なメッセージは、HNL Radio を通し、NEEVA の1時間程手前で送られてきた。

「NEEVA to RJAA ALT HND 103.0

ETE4：15，H/O 79.0，ALT 73；

10％ RSV 7.0，RSV 9.1：NRT Dispatch…」
つまり NEEVA から NRT までの Minimum Required Fuel は 103,000 lbs、ALTN の HND へは 7,300 lbs、10％ RSV は 7,600 lbs，-- Reserve（holding fuel）は 9,100 lbs であった。高度については、フライトプラン上、NEEVA より FL410 に昇ることになっているので、FL410 のデータとのことであった。

103,000−79,000＝24,000 lbs

つまり、これが NRT での Fuel Remaining の Minimum となるわけである。NEEVA では、フライトプランより Fuel は若干浮いているので、103,000 lbs 以上残っているし、VOLMET では NRT も HND もお天気がよいので、NW 017 便は NRT への進行となったのである。

また、Re-Release Message を受ける前、機上からは特別なレポートは何も行なっていなかった。NEEVA から

さて、このあたりで、この日のコックピットクルーにても触れておこう。

マルチ編成の場合、JAL と同じようにパイロットは を3等分してデューティーと、レストをとる。S/O は2等でデューティーに就いている。そして、その時在席にいるフテンがその程度 PIC となり、SIC の考えは無いようる。この日は Capt. Parrott の定年前のラストフライト点のことで、テイクオフ、ランディング両方をデューチするとのことであった。

▲ Capt. PBYY2222 氏のラストフライト 隣は S/O その時の時のひとこま

今回の往らのパターンは1月18日に SEA を発て、郭 MHL、SEL、NRT、JFK、NRT と、到着地に1） るだけで毎日フライトをし、NRT 発 SEA 行、NW 0 で1月26日に SEA に帰り、Capt. Parrott は定年 えるのである。（Capt. Wooden と S/O Kawail は NW AL MSP であり NRT − JFK − NRT のスー線に移

2

■経費効率のよさで着実に歩む
ノースウェスト航空の運航方式

B747 運航乗員部欧州第4乗務室　機長　小松 利夫〔ロ-〕

ある4月23日、パンナムがユナイテッドに太平洋路線の全運航権を売却することになったというショッキングなニュースをきいてから、あと1日が長い。幻年乗り見慣れた世界のパンナム機の姿もが何故に遠方から見えるのかと違うと、一抹の寂しさを感じるが、月間に連近のアメリカの航空業界再編成の波がその Airline Deregulation Act（いわゆる規制緩和法）の下に本格的に押し寄せてきているなという思いを新たにして待った。

1978年にデレグが発足してからというもの、必要以上の運賃競争による売売り合戦が繰返され、市場は混乱し、そのなかでいくつかのエアラインが倒産したり経営の危機に見舞われてきた。

このような状況下の航空業界でノースウエスト航空は、経費を低くおさえながらもサービス等で向上をはかり、営業収益ではアメリカの主要航空会社の中でも上位にランクされているという点で、注目に値する。

そこで、同じ太平洋ルートを飛んでいる各航空会社の中でも、特に経営的にも着実に歩みの深い、ノースウエスト航空が、一体どのような運航方式になっているのかについて、ニューヨーク一東京間に的を絞り、運航の実態をオブザーブしてみることとした。

―――――・―――――

ケネディー国際空港（JFK）にあるノースウェスト・オリエント航空の Flight Operation は、倉庫の中の一室といった感じの飾り気のない小さな運室だった。

NW01便、JFK発NRT行のフライトをオブザーブするためのショウアップ時間を確認したところ、出発の1時間前との事であった。半信半疑で待っていると、1時間前にクルーが同着し、各自荷物のチェックインを済ませる。その後シップへ、乗務証を見せ厳しいゲイト・ツーガート

▲ JFKのノースウエスト・フライト・オペレーション・ルーム

ショップへ、S/Oとキャビンクルーはそのまま後方に各自の座席にかかっている。オペレーションにはデータ類を入れたり準備したりする女性が1人いるだけで、ディスパッチャーは配置されていない。

ノースウェスト の本社のあるミネアポリス（MSP）のディスパッチャーより、その日のNW01便に送られてきたデータは、JFKからNERVA経由ANC行のフライトプランとその必要資料、およびJFKからNRTへの直行フライトプランで、これには Burn-Off Fuel と NRT および Reserve Fuel のみ表示されている。さらに出発時、KGL上、目的地、という具合に順序よく整理された気象および予報天気、NOTAM といったものであった。JFKで得られたものは航路上の実気象だけで、これはJALの場合とはほぼ同じ内容である。また、この日はノースウェスト のあるタービュランスに関する情報は特に無かった。

ショウアップしたコックピットクルーは、Capt. Parrott, Capt. Wander, F/O Tosch, S/O Kowall, Female の5名で、マルチ編成（或るはAUGMENTと呼ぶ）です

3

Flight Crew News 7 (1985 Vol 14) pp. 6 – 13
by Toshio Komatsu, a captain in the department of No.4
route to U.S.A. pilot division.

On April 22 last year (1984), it was just recent that I heard the news of Pam American's Pacific routes being sold to the United Airlines. I feel a bit lonely to think that world famous Pam American airplanes which I had seen for about 30 years would disappear, and at the same time I realized that the movement of reorganization of American airlines was coming under Airline Deregulation Act.

Since deregulation was introduced in 1978, a cheap ticket war had been heated, the market became in chaos, and in the situation some airlines had been bankrupted and were suffering from crisis.

In this situation, North West Airline has been reducing the costs, raising the service standard, and it places at the higher position in the American major airline companies, which is worth paying attention.

Therefore, among the other companies which cover the Pacific routes, I tried to observe how North West Airlines, historically familiar company, does the service focused on the New York – Tokyo route.

The flight operations of North West Airlines at Kennedy International Airport were done in a simple room in the back of the ticket counter at their terminal.

When I checked the show up time to observe the NW017 which left JFK for NRT, it was one hour before the departure. When I waited half in doubt, the crew appeared one hour before the departure time, and went into their operation room after checking in their baggage. The second officer and cabin crew proceeded to the airplane and started preparing for the departure. In the operation room, there is only one lady who organized and prepared the data and there was no dispatcher.

From the dispatcher in the head office in Minneapolis (MSP), the data sent to NW017 was about the flight plan from JFK to NRT, the fuel, and the direct flight plan from JFK to NRT which had only Burn-Off Fuel and Reserve Fuel at Narita. Furthermore, the situations, weather forecast and NOTAM (notice to an airman) at the departing place, on route, and the destination were methodically written. This is the same as JAL. On this day, there was no information which North West Airlines was very good at.

The consisted of five members, Captain Parrott, Captain Wooden, F/O Tosch, S/O Kowall, S/O Hensley, they were in the multi crew members (they call it AUGMENTED CREW), and the previously mentioned two S/O' s were preparing for the flight in the plane. The captains were checking the data sent to them, filling the briefing sheet for the cabin crew with the crew's names, ETE, the weather report on the route and at the destination, and filling the route map for the passengers with today's route, the altitude, the speed. The F/O attached the teletyped flight plan sent from MSP on the position report paper and filled in the necessary items. When the captain signed the sheet, the whole job at the operation finished.

Because we were watching, they seemed to have taken longer than usual, but they finished it in 25 minutes and left for the ship (airplane).

As you can tell by now, different from JAL, the briefing and discussion to the crew by dispatcher, the briefing to the cabin crew by the captain, the discussion on the emergency duty were not done.

The flight plan was signed by the captain who was in the senior position according to the year he joined the company. There was no sign in the dispatcher. In the ship, they gave the briefing sheet and route map that they made to give to the cabin crew (lead fright attendant), and after a brief meeting they went into the cockpit.

5

It was only twenty minutes before the departure when the captains and F/O sat. The set up before the departure and the check list time was about the same as JAL. At the right time, F/O received the ATC clearance. They soon a "Ready" call, the push back began. There was no five-minute-go call.

At the right time (11 a.m. at NYC time), they started the engine during the push back, blocking off, this was the same procedure. The captain talked to the ground by the intercom, the F/O operated the ignition switch. The S/O checked only the monitors which he was in charge of. On the Pilot Center Instrument Panel, from the left, EPR, N1, N2, EGT, F / F, Vertical Scale instruments were placed, so the engine start procedure was different from the one in JAL. After finishing the push back and the engine start, they received the clearance and began the taxi.

The F/O was very busy during the taxi. Through the radio, the information about the passenger number, Cargo WT, Zero Fuel WT, Fuel at Take off, Takeoff WT, CG and other data was sent to from a lady in operation. Based on that information, they prepared the take off data.

Before the block out, there was no Weight and Balance sign nor the passenger number report form the cabin crew like JAL. Take off briefing was to check the SID. This did not include the routine work. Other procedures were the same as JAL, took off from RWY22R, based on the route of flight plan by the radar vector. While going up, there was hardly any shake movement and went into the FL310.

(The interview of Mr. Lee is omitted here.)

6

In the North West Airlines, they collect the information of the position report, especially wind and temperature not only of their company but also the other airline companies that are on the same route. This data is then included in the weather map for the flights area. The accuracy of the weather and turbulence forecast was greatly enhanced in this way. Accordingly, this information, particularly mountain waves, was incorporated into navigation charts by the Jeppeson Company to avoid turbulence depending on prevailing winds. These new enroute charts had position points depicted with the names of dispatchers showing the location of the mountain waves.

When reports were made to ATC pilots normally used longitude and latitude to depict their position. However, when they used dispatchers names to depict locations, they were demonstrating how closely dispatchers, weather briefers, and aircrew members were working together. We can tell that Mr. Sowa and Mr. Impagliazzo took great pride in their flight plans.

The flight continued as planned through Alaskan airspace and out over the Bering Sea. Until this point the route was over land and the contact with ATC was the same as JAL with contact made every hour. They made reports to the company on ARINC and Canadian FSS. During the company report they used a dispatchers name to describe their position. These reports are relayed to Flight Watch MSP to forecast turbulence information. At the end of the position report of NWA they would designate code

0 Smooth
1 Occasionally Light Turbulence
2 Light Turbulence
3 Light to Moderate Turbulence
4 Moderate Turbulence
5 Moderate to Server Turbulence
6 Severe Turbulence
7 Extreme

The most important message on this flight was one hour before NEEVA through HNL radio NEEVA to RJAA ALT HND 103, ETE 15, B/O 79.0, ALT 7.3, 10% RSV 7.6, RSV 9.1, NRT Dispatch. The minimum required fuel from NEEVA to Narita is 103,000 pounds with another 7,300 pounds for the alternate at HND. The reserve and holding fuel was 9,100 pounds. According to the flight plan from NEEVA we would climb to FL 410 which would leave remaining fuel on board upon arrival at Narita 103,000 – 7,900 = 24,000 pounds. Therefore by NEEVA less fuel had been consumed than was flight planned – more than 103,000 pounds remained. As VOLMET were adequate the crew decided to continue to Narita as the weather was good. Before the crew received a clearance to land, they made no special report. From NEEVA to Narita by Red 20 was the same route used by JAL.

Now a word about the crew. In the case of multi crew flights NWA is the same as JAL. The pilots divide duty time between crew members depending on ETE. The pilots duty time was divided into three parts. The second officers duty time is divided by two. At this time the Captain in the left seat becomes the PIC and the Captain in the right seat becomes SIC. Normally the Captain who has the take off will sit as copilot or SIC for the landing at the end of the flight. However on this flight, because it was Captain Parrott's last flight he was PIC for both the take of and landing portions of the flight.

The schedule this trip is to leave SEA on January 18, 1985, proceed to SEL and then land at MNL. The next day MNL to SEL, then SEL to Narita the following day. Then from Narita to JFK for and overnight layover, and then return to Narita. At each destination you stay only one night and fly everyday. The last leg of the schedule was from Narita to SEA where Captain Parrot was to retire from his airline career with NWA. Captain Wooden and Second Officer Kowall were based in MSP and were on only the legs from JFK to Narita and now from Narita to SEA. Captain Parrott was a good natured gentleman with thick gray hair and a very reliable Captain. I want to draw attention to S/O Kowall also as he was nearly 61 years old and until last year was a NWA 747 Captain but returned after retirement as a SO. Allowing Captains who had reached the mandatory retirement age of 60 to return as S/O's, was new to the industry last year. Though SO Kowall was senior in age, the crew worked perfectly together.

The long flight was nearly concluded and similar to JAL radar vectors were given to the approach for runway 34. After the landing at Narita ground control directed us to the south wing which we were not familiar with. After stopping the fuel remaining was 42,300 pounds. The flight time was almost as planned. I recalled the face of Mr. Impagliazzo at dispatch in MSP. We thanked the cockpit crew and cabin crew for their kindness and cooperation for this observation trip. The biggest impression I got from this visit was NWA's commitment to reducing the operating costs of the flight. During the flight the crew did not conduct any three pack operations. After landing reversers were engaged to 70% N1 until the aircraft slowed to 100 K and used auto braking as much as possible after that. The crew received very good information about turbulence from the company's detailed analysis. These all contributed to accumulated cost savings for the company. In a country as advanced in aviation as America not only the crew but the all ground support personnel must be dedicated to containing costs to beat the competition. I came to appreciate the value of Americas contribution to aviation but fear it as a competitor. In conclusion, I want to thank the many people at the MSP office as well as Mr. Lee, Captain Parrott, and all members of the crew for their warm, generous, insightful information.

APPENDIX 5

RNPA

RETIRED NORTHWEST AIRLINES PILOTS ASSOCIATION

RNPA NEWSLETTER #120   NOVEMBER 1996

✈ **1996 RNPA CONVENTION AT BILLINGS**

✈ **SPECIAL FEATURES**

✈ **SOCIAL EVENTS**

ROUNDUP, MONTANA FLY-IN AT DOUG PARROTT'S ◊-P RANCH

1

RNPA ROUNDUP AT THE ◇-P RANCH

The Weather Gods were once again kind to RNPA during their 1996 Montana Convention Reunion. What a beautiful day we had September 10th. Mid September weather can be anything in Montana from Snow to Winds to Storms to Blue Bird Days. Just call us lucky!

The Schladers, Staffords, Rockwells and all the rest of the crew that organized and put together the 1996 Convention in Billings really put on a "Reunion" that will be long remembered.

We also had a great crew here at the Diamond-Bar-P ◇-P preparing and spiffying up the place for your visit. (We sometimes need an occasion such as this just to inspire us to catch up on our ranch housekeeping). Shirley is our organizer and spark plug. Son Don & his wife, Sue took care of the many details. Tony, our hired hand, saw to it that the place was neat and the machinery clean and put away. RNPA members, Ken & Linda Morley, Dave & Judy Napier and Lee Bradshaw all arrived earlier in the week, and stayed with us to assist in watering down the ramp area, fetching the tables and chairs and straw bales, etc., in preparation for the big day. My part was getting the Biffies, Dance Band, Cook and Crew, Beer, Pretzels, Wine, Pop, Ice, Airplanes, Cars, Horses and Wagons all to arrive on time for the Sept. 10th Blowout! Shirley, Sue and Julie Michel prepared the snacks and Rocky Mountain Oysters.

Of the 15 Airplanes that participated, 6 were furnished by RNPA members:
Ken Morley, North American T-6 (SNJ).
Lee Bradshaw, Great Lakes. Lee put on a great aerobatics show for us.
Art Daniel, Cessna 180.
Bonnie Daniel, Piper J-3 Cub.
Hal Balin, V Tail Bonanza
Doug Parrot, Stearman (N2S)
The other 9 planes were all from nearby in Montana.
Davis Carte, Delta Airlines 747 Capt, Fairchild 24.
Mike Ferguson, Director, Montana Aeronautics Division, the States B-36 Bonanza.
Larry Larson, Pipeline Patrol, (Little Bumpy Airlines) Piper PA-12 Supercruiser.
Leroy Monson, Billings Rancher, PA-11 Piper Cub Special.
Jack Marmon, Roundup Dentist, Cessna 140.
Tim Blattie, Columbus, MT, Piper PA-18 Supercub 150HP
Allen Rickman, Columbus, MT , Piper PA-18 Supercub 90 HP. This is the Coast to Coast Non-
    stop, no radio, record setting airplane, the "Stillwater Express" flown by the late UAL
    Capt. Jim Damron. Allen had just flown from the Mexican Border to the Canadian
    Border, Non-Stop, the day before, setting another record, and was on his way home to
    Columbus, when he stopped in to visit our RNPA get together.
Mike Strong, Capt. Delta, Retired, son of NWA Capt. Lyle Strong, displayed his Straight Wing
    Waco. This airplane was once owned by Nick Mamer, who established the air route from
    BIL to SEA which NWA bought. Nick was killed in a Lockheed 14H near BZN while
    flying for NWA. Mike flew the straight wing back to Laurel, MT, and returned with his
    Taper Wing Waco to put on a great aerobatic show for us. Some of you left on the early
    bus and missed some good air show acts.   -continued-

2

Doug Parrott - continued -

As well as the airplanes, we had some other aviation celebrities as guests: Jack Waddell, Chief Engineering Test Pilot for the Boeing 747, Mike Ferguson, Director of the Montana Aeronautics Division, Joe Burris, retired BIL Tower Chief and, of course, our own Donald Nyrop, Past President and CEO of NWA.

The classic cars were brought in by the Roundup Classic Car Club. The horses and wagons were furnished by our friends and neighbors. Monty Sealey and Frank Skidmore furnished, for free, the music for the Hangar Dance. The Biffies were furnished by George Smith at no charge.

In recognition of the community contributions to our affair, RNPA contributed $500.00 to be given to community projects. $100.00 was given to each of the following; Roundup EMT and Ambulance Volunteers, Golden Valley Quick Response Unit, Roundup Schools Associated Student Activity Fund, Musselshell Valley Historical Museum and the Roundup Progressive Community Club, for Main Street flowers and shrubs.

We want to thank the folks that smoke for being so considerate of our dry conditions and fire hazard.

Doug & Shirley Parrott

We also want to thank the Governors' office for sending out the Montana Travel Packets and the Montana Aeronautics Division for sending out Aviation Packets to the prospective RNPA flyins. I'm sure that they contributed to the great turnout. The many nice cards and letters that we have received from you since the Convention are greatly appreciated and make it all worthwhile.

We were sort of busy that day and did not have a lot of time to visit with all of you. If you are driving through Montana in the future, swing up on Highway 12 to Mile Post 156, or if your are flying by, stop in and visit. The Coffee Pot is always on.

Doug (Calhoun), Shirley,
Don and Susan Parrott"

DAY AT PARROTT'S RANCH

Welcome to the C-P Ranch

Neil & Lorraine Potts, Ray Severson

Jan Loveridge, Shirley & Doug, Bob Loveridge
Note the "Parrott Ranch" T-shirts

Eric Linden, Jimmie & Ken Brinnon
Bill Halverson in Back

John & Barb Hastings in Doug's Ford
John's in the rumble seat

Bev & Max Kroll take a buggy ride

Crank'er up, Lem - Herm's steering

Horse & Farm Cart - a ride on the hay

Page 19

4

FLY-IN AT PARROTT'S RANCH

Doug Parrott & Grandson Conlin
Stearman N2S

Dee & Ray Dolny
note Parrott Ranch Logo on Doug's Stearman

Straight Wing Waco & Fairchild 24

Art Daniel in his Cessna 180

Fairchild 24
Ken & Helen Marsh

Piper J3 Cub

Super Cub, Cessna 140
Straight Wing Waco

Page 21

Mike Strong, Bob Jondahl, Ken Marsh, Dick Happ
Mike's Straight Wing Waco

5

Ken Morley and his North American T-6(SNI)
Cowboy Don Tomlin and his horse

Harman P. Muto (Editor)
434 Southwest 174th
Seattle, WA 98166

BULK MAIL
U.S. POSTAGE
PAID
SEATTLE, WA
PERMIT NO. 669

Made in the USA
San Bernardino, CA
19 May 2019